Contemporary Scenography

Performance + Design is a series of monographs and essay collections that explore understandings of performance design and scenography, examining the potential of the visual, spatial, material and environmental to shape performative encounters and to offer sites for imaginative exchange. This series focuses on design both for and as performance in a variety of contexts including theatre, art installations, museum displays, mega-events, site-specific and community-based performance, street theatre, design of public space, festivals, protests and state-sanctioned spectacle.

Performance + Design takes as its starting point the growth of scenography and the expansion from theatre or stage design to a wider notion of scenography as a spatial practice. As such, it recognizes the recent accompanying interest from a number of converging scholarly disciplines (theatre, performance, art, architecture, design) and examines twenty-first-century practices of performance design in the context of debates about postdramatic theatre, aesthetic representation, visual and material culture, spectatorship, participation and co-authorship.

Series Editors
Stephen Di Benedetto
Joslin McKinney
Scott Palmer

Consuming Scenography: The Shopping Mall as a Theatrical Experience
Nebojša Tabački
978-1-3501-1089-2

The History and Theory of Environmental Scenography: Second Edition
Arnold Aronson
978-1-4742-8396-0

Immersion and Participation in Punchdrunk's Theatre
Carina E. I. Westling
978-1-3501-0195-1

The Model as Performance: Staging Space in Theatre and Architecture
Thea Brejzek and Lawrence Wallen
978-1-3500-9590-8

Scenography Expanded: An Introduction to Contemporary Performance Design
Edited by Joslin McKinney and Scott Palmer
978-1-4742-4439-8

Sound Effect: The Theatre We Hear
Ross Brown
978-1-3500-4590-3

Forthcoming titles

Digital Scenography: 30 Years of Experimentation and Innovation in Performance and Interactive Media
Neill O'Dwyer
978-1-3501-0731-1

Sites of Transformation: Applied and Socially Engaged Scenography in Rural Landscapes
Louise Ann Wilson
978-1-3501-0444-0

Contemporary Scenography

Practices and Aesthetics in German Theatre, Arts and Design

Edited by
Birgit E. Wiens

methuen | drama
LONDON • NEW YORK • OXFORD • NEW DELHI • SYDNEY

METHUEN DRAMA
Bloomsbury Publishing Plc
50 Bedford Square, London, WC1B 3DP, UK
1385 Broadway, New York, NY 10018, USA

BLOOMSBURY, METHUEN DRAMA and the Methuen Drama logo are trademarks of
Bloomsbury Publishing Plc

First published in Great Britain 2019
Paperback edition published 2021

Copyright © Birgit E. Wiens and contributors, 2019, 2021

Birgit E. Wiens and contributors have asserted their right under the Copyright, Designs
and Patents Act, 1988, to be identified as the authors of this work.

The research work for this book was funded by the DFG - Deutsche
Forschungsgemeinschaft (German Research Foundation), WI 1833/6-1 and WI 1833/7-1.

For legal purposes the Acknowledgements on p. xx–xxi constitute an extension
of this copyright page.

Cover design: Louise Dugdale
Cover image © Thomas Aurin

All rights reserved. No part of this publication may be reproduced or transmitted
in any form or by any means, electronic or mechanical, including photocopying,
recording, or any information storage or retrieval system, without prior permission
in writing from the publishers.

Bloomsbury Publishing Plc does not have any control over, or responsibility for, any
third-party websites referred to or in this book. All internet addresses given in this
book were correct at the time of going to press. The author and publisher regret any
inconvenience caused if addresses have changed or sites have ceased to exist, but
can accept no responsibility for any such changes.

A catalogue record for this book is available from the British Library.

Library of Congress Control Number: 2019938989

ISBN: HB: 978-1-350-06447-8
PB: 978-1-350-19486-1
ePDF: 978-1-350-06449-2
eBook: 978-1-350-06448-5

Series: Performance and Design

Typeset by Deanta Global Publishing Services, Chennai, India

To find out more about our authors and books visit www.bloomsbury.com
and sign up for our newsletters.

Contents

List of illustrations ix
List of contributors xi
Foreword   *Christopher Balme* xv
Acknowledgements xx

Contemporary scenography: Practices and aesthetics in German theatre, arts and design – an introduction   *Birgit E. Wiens* 1

PART ONE Scenography in and beyond the theatre: Aesthetics and epistemes 31

1 'I am trying to add more layers to the story': From the model to the stage: Scenographic thinking and artistic practices in Aleksandar Denić's theatre works with Frank Castorf and others   *A conversation between Aleksandar Denić and Birgit E. Wiens* 33

2 Notes on Bert Neumann's stage and costume designs: Scenography as a co-player and counterpart in theatre performances and rehearsals   *A conversation between Sophie Rois and Birgit E. Wiens* 46

3 Scenographic materiality: Agency and intra-action in Katrin Brack's designs   *Joslin McKinney* 57

4 Composing scenography: Reflections on Klaus Grünberg's collaborations with Heiner Goebbels and others   *David Roesner and Klaus Grünberg* 73

5 Spatial reorganizations and moving dynamics of the active spectator   *Thomas Irmer* 93

PART TWO Circulation of scenographic knowledge and cultural transfer 103

6 Notation: On the aesthetic potentials and epistemic functions of scenographic scores *Kirsten Maar* 105

7 One cannot not stage: Scenography – beyond theatre: Scenographic practices in museums, exhibitions and corporate design *Uwe R. Brückner and Linda Greci* 119

8 The art of thinking and designing space: Notes from the studio *Annett Zinsmeister* 139

9 Don't be afraid of the art of *parCITYpation*: Scenographic intervention as social design *Benjamin Foerster-Baldenius* 153

PART THREE Rethinking scenography 167

10 The ungovernableness of the scene *Dieter Mersch* 169

11 Scenography and actor–network theory: Analytical approaches *Wolf-Dieter Ernst* 183

12 Scenography: Research, education and training in the German-speaking countries – some observations *Thea Hoffmann-Axthelm and Robert Kraatz* 198

Staging the unknown: Scenography and its future potentials – preliminary résumé *Birgit E. Wiens and Serge von Arx* 213

References 227
Index 243

List of illustrations

Figure 0.1   Google Ngram Viewer: search results for the term 'scenography' in its English, French and German variants xvi

Figure 0.2   Volksbühne Tempelhof by Francis Kéré (Summer 2017, preliminary version) xviii

Figure I.1   Façade of the Volksbühne am Rosa-Luxemburg-Platz, Berlin, 2014/15 season; banner, flags and posters by Bert Neumann 8

Figure I.2   Rimini Protokoll, *Remote X*, Houston edition: *Remote Houston* (2016) 21

Figure 1.1   Aleksandar Denić, *Reise ans Ende der Nacht* (Journey to the End of the Night), directed by Frank Castorf, Munich, Residenztheater, 2013 37

Figure 1.2   Aleksandar Denić, computer-generated 'white model' for Frank Castorf's staging of *Faust*, Volksbühne Berlin, 2017 42

Figure 1.3   Scenic design for Castorf's staging of *Faust* by Aleksandar Denić (2017), physical scale model 43

Figure 2.1   René Pollesch, *Ein Chor irrt sich gewaltig* (A Choir Is Totally Wrong), stage and costume design: Bert Neumann, Volksbühne Berlin, Prater, 2009 52

Figure 2.2   René Pollesch, *Bühne frei für Mick Levčik!* (Clear the Stage for Mick Levčik!), stage design: Bert Neumann, Schauspielhaus Zurich 54

Figure 3.1   Stage Design by Katrin Brack for Dimiter Gotscheff's staging of *Kampf des Negers und der Hunde* (Black Battles with Dogs), Volksbühne Berlin 2003 62

Figure 3.2   Katrin Brack, sketch for *Iwanov*, Volksbühne Berlin 2005 70

Figure 4.1   Klaus Grünberg, *De Materie*, directed by Heiner Goebbels, Ruhrtriennale 2014 78

LIST OF ILLUSTRATIONS

Figure 4.2 Klaus Grünberg, *Europeras 1*, directed by Heiner Goebbels, Ruhrtriennale 2012 83

Figure 4.3 *Stifters Dinge* (Stifter's Things), Théâtre Vidy, Lausanne 2007 85

Figure 5.1 Bert Neumann, black scenography / interior of the Berlin Volksbühne 2015–17 95

Figure 5.2 Sven Sören Beyer, *Neither*, directed by phase 7 performing.arts, Radialsystem V Berlin, 2012 97

Figure 5.3 Vegard Vinge/Ida Müller, *Nationaltheater Reinickendorf, Container 1–9*, Berlin 2017 100

Figure 6.1 William Forsythe, *City of Abstracts,* Museum for Modern Art (MMK), Frankfurt, 2015 106

Figure 6.2 William Forsythe, *Instructions 2015*, braille print on paper 108

Figure 7.1 Uwe R. Brückner: Diamond of Suspense, EuroVision – Museums Exhibiting Europe, 2013 125

Figure 7.2 Atelier Brückner: Notation for State Grid Pavilion, Expo Shanghai 2010 130

Figure 7.3 Atelier Brückner: *That's Opera*, Exhibition Project, Brussels 2008/09 137

Figure 8.1 Annett Zinsmeister, *virtual interior* (2007/15), commissioned installation, MOMA New York 146

Figure 8.2 Annett Zinsmeister, *virtual interior* (2007/15) 147

Figure 9.1 raumlaborberlin, *Eichbaumboxer*, Mülheim an der Ruhr 2008–11 157

Figure 9.2 raumlaborberlin, *Hotel Shabby Shabby*, Mannheim 2014 159

Figure 9.3 raumaborberlin, *Rush Hour Rest Stop*, Durban, South Africa 2014 161

Figure 9.4 raumlaborberlin, *Théâtre des Négociations*, Nanterre, France 2015 162

Figure 9.5 raumlaborberlin, *Forms of Turmoil*, Milan, Italy 2017 164

Figure 11.1 Dominic Huber/Blendwerk, *Situation Rooms*, a project by Rimini Protokoll, Ruhrtriennale 2013 185

Figure 11.2 Rimini Protokoll, *Situation Rooms*, Ruhrtriennale 2013 193

List of contributors

Serge von Arx is an architect, scenographer, professor of scenography and the artistic director of the Scenography Department of the Norwegian Theatre Academy (at Østfold University College). Since 1998 he has collaborated with Robert Wilson on a regular basis; since 2003 he has been a mentor and consultant at the Watermill Center on Long Island, NY. His practice and research focus on the amalgamation of theatre and architecture. He is a member of the curatorial board for the Prague Quadrennial in 2015 and 2019.

Christopher Balme holds the chair in Theatre Studies at the University of Munich (LMU). He currently edits the journal *Forum Modernes Theater*. Recent publications include *The Cambridge Introduction to Theatre Studies* (2008) and *The Theatrical Public Sphere* (2014).

Uwe R. Brückner is architect, stage designer, scenographer and curator, founder and creative director of the internationally operating Atelier Brückner, Stuttgart (www.atelier-brueckner.com) and Professor of Scenography and Exhibition Design at the University of Applied Sciences and Arts Northwestern Switzerland, Basel. With more than forty publications, his most recent books include the monograph *Scenography 2: Staging the Space*, ed. by Atelier Brückner (2019).

Aleksandar Denić is stage designer and scenic designer for theatre and film and Professor of Film, TV and Set Design at the Megatrend University of Belgrade, Serbia. Since 2012, he has been continually collaborating with the German theatre director Frank Castorf. He has received many awards for his theatre, film and architectural work; for more details, see his website, www.aleksandardenic.com.

Wolf-Dieter Ernst is Professor of Theatre at the University of Bayreuth. His research topics include postdramatic theatre, media art and the history and theory of acting. Recent publications include *Psyche-Technik-Darstellung. Schauspieltheorie als Wissensgeschichte* (Psyche-Technology-Performance. Reading Acting Theory as a History of Science), edited with Anja Klöck and Meike Wagner (Munich 2015).

LIST OF CONTRIBUTORS

Benjamin Foerster-Baldenius is an architect from Berlin. He is co-founder and member of raumlaborberlin, a working group for experimental architecture and artistic projects in public space (http://raumlabor.net/). Currently, he is co-organizing the raumlaborberlin initiative *floating university berlin*, an offshore campus for cities in transformationm, and is teaching at University Witten/Herdecke, Design Academy Eindhoven and at the Royal Academy of Art (KABK), The Hague, the Netherlands.

Linda Greci is a cultural studies scholar working at Atelier Brückner, Stuttgart, in the field of concept, content and interpretation. From 2012 to 2016 she was project leader for the European research project *EMEE – EuroVision – Museums Exhibiting Europe*. As an assistant to Uwe R. Brückner and co-author, she has been responsible for numerous joint publications about exhibition design, design philosophy and scenography/scenographic thinking.

Klaus Grünberg is a stage designer and lighting designer based in Hamburg. He has worked with the directors Tatjana Gürbaca, Sebastian Baumgarten, Roger Vontobel and Barrie Kosky at theatres and opera houses across Europe, as well as in Kuwait and Buenos Aires. Also, he collaborates with the composer and director Heiner Goebbels on a regular basis; www.klausgruenberg.de

Thea Hoffmann-Axthelm is a stage and costume designer who works in public theatres in the German-speaking countries (Düsseldorf, Munich, Frankfurt/Main, the Burgtheater in Vienna, among others) as well as in European countries like Greece and Latvia. She is also member of the German theatre-collective Prinzip Gonzo. With her colleague Robert Kraatz, she co-authors and co-edits an internet blog on stage design, www.ueberbuehne.de

Thomas Irmer is a scholar and theatre critic regularly contributing to the cultural magazines *Theater Heute* and *Theater der Zeit*, and author of TV documentaries, both German and international. He also works as a lecturer in theatre history and the theory of the theatre. Recent publications include a monograph on the theatre director Frank Castorf (2016), as well as numerous articles and book chapters on practices and aesthetics in contemporary European theatre.

Robert Kraatz is a freelance stage and costume designer, producer and author, who works in public theatres as well as in fringe groups or as an individual, furthering his artistic endeavours in narration, urban space and installation. In 2017 and 2018, he worked with Robert Wilson as production manager (for the piece *The Sandman*). Together with Thea Hoffmann-Axthelm, he is author and editor of the blog on stage design, www.ueberbuehne.de

Joslin McKinney is an associate professor in scenography at the University of Leeds, UK. She is the lead author of the *Cambridge Introduction to Scenography* (2009) and co-editor of *Scenography Expanded: An Introduction to Contemporary Performance Design* (2017). Publications include articles and chapters on scenographic research methods, scenographic spectacle and embodied spectatorship, phenomenology, kinaesthetic empathy and material agency.

Kirsten Maar is Junior Professor of Theatre and Dance Studies at Freie Universität Berlin. She was a member of the DFG-Collaborative Research Centre 'Aesthetic Experience and the Dissolution of Artistic Limits'. Her research fields are the intersections between visual arts, architecture and choreography, scoring practices and composition. She is co-editor of *Assign and Arrange: Methodologies of Presentation in Art & Dance* (2014).

Dieter Mersch is Professor of Philosophical Aesthetics and director of the Institute for Critical Theory at Zurich University of the Arts, Switzerland. His main publications include *Was sich zeigt. Materialität, Präsenz, Ereignis* (What is Shown. Materiality, Presence, Happening; 2002), *Ereignis und Aura* (Event and Aura; 2002), *Medientheorien zur Einführung* (Theories of Media. An Introduction; 2006), *Posthermeneutik* (Posthermeneutics; 2010) and *Epistemologies of Aesthetics* (2015).

David Roesner is Professor of Theatre and Music-Theatre at the LMU Munich and works on contemporary performance on the boundaries between theatre, opera, music and dance. His publications include *Composed Theatre* (co-ed. with Matthias Rebstock, 2013), *Musicality of Theatre. Music as Model, Method and Metaphor in Theatre-Making* (2014) and more recently he edited a special issue of *Studies in Musical Theatre* on 'New Music Theatre – Work in/and Progress' (11/2, 2017).

Sophie Rois is an actress in theatre, television and film, who has received numerous awards for her works in these various fields (most recently the prestigious 'Gertrud-Eysoldt-Ring' theatre prize). From 1993 to 2017 she was an ensemble member and a leading actress at the Berlin Volksbühne at Rosa-Luxemburg-Platz. In 2018, she joined the ensemble of the Deutsches Theater, Berlin.

Birgit E. Wiens is a researcher, senior lecturer (PD) and DFG-Heisenberg-Fellow at the Ludwig-Maximilians-University Munich. She has published widely on acting and performance theory, dramaturgy and scenography, including the book projects *Theater ohne Fluchtpunkt / Theatre without Vanishing Points. The Legacy of Adolphe Appia: Scenography and Choreography in Contemporary Theatre*, ed. with G. Brandstetter (2010) and *Intermediale Szenographie* (Intermedial Scenography; 2014).

Annett Zinsmeister is a freelance artist based in Berlin and Professor of Art, Experimental Design and Theory at Frankfurt University of Applied Sciences, Frankfurt/Main. Her work is represented in international exhibitions and collections such as MoMA New York, USA. She is author and editor of several transdisciplinary books, including *Kunst / Design?* (Art / Design?; 2013). A monograph on her artistic work, *Annett Zinsmeister – Searching for Identity*, was published in 2012.

Foreword

Christopher Balme

The subject of this book – scenography – is extremely timely because it is a subject that not only pertains to theatre and performance studies – my own field – but to art history, architecture and design. The conference from which most of the chapters in this volume are drawn took place in Munich in November 2016 and was organized by the editor, Birgit E. Wiens. The response to the call was remarkable. The topic evidently struck a chord well beyond the field of stage design within theatre studies and academies of fine arts.

This meeting was of some historical significance because it was the first conference on scenography in Munich in forty years, since the International Federation for Theatre Research (IFTR) devoted its world congress to the topic of theatrical space in 1977 (Arnott 1977). Although the term 'scenography' does not feature in the title of the published proceedings, a glance at the contents reveals that a multifaceted understanding of theatrical space was under discussion, of which scenography in the sense of stage design was only one aspect.

Research priorities fluctuate, and scenography has been somewhat off the radar but now it is back. We can verify this by drawing on empirical evidence. The Google Books Ngram Viewer is an online search engine that uses data mining to chart frequencies of words in the text corpus of Google books, currently amounting to about 5.2 million items. This resource has led, in turn, to a form of computational cultural analysis known as culturomics.[1]

A search for the term 'scenography' in its English, French and German variants in Google's Ngram Viewer reveals that, despite its ancient provenance from the Greek *skénographia*, the word did not really catch on until the 1960s.

To understand this data more precisely, we must distinguish between 'emics' and 'etics' – a differentiation used by cultural anthropologists. The words or viewpoints that the natives themselves use are called 'emic', and the terms and explanations anthropologists/scientists use to study the natives are designated 'etic'. They are both different and complementary ways of looking at and speaking about the same phenomenon. Scenography is an example

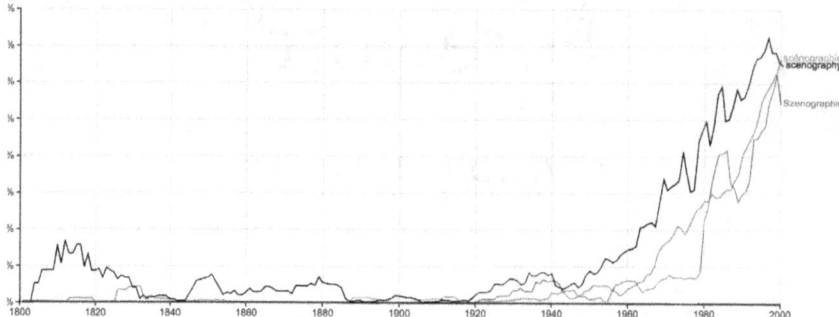

FIGURE 0.1 *Google Ngram Viewer: search results for the term 'scenography' in its English, French and German variants.*

of etics – a term used more in academic discourse than by the natives themselves: the artists and practitioners. For them, the old terms are still current: set design, *Bühnenbild*, *décor*, decoration and so on.

The rediscovery or reinvention of scenography is closely tied to the rise of theatre studies as a discipline and especially its theoretical turn in the 1980s. The publication of Patrice Pavis's *Dictionnaire du théâtre* in 1980 is a key orientation point in this process. In his dictionary, which introduced semiotic concepts to the field of theatre studies, Pavis defines scenography as *'l'écriture dans l'espace'* (writing in space; Pavis 2005 [1996]: 314). We see the textual metaphor so beloved by semiologists at work here but, beyond the metaphoricity, a more complex understanding of the term also is visible.

Pavis's definition is influenced by two main developments: first, the modernist revolution of the early twentieth century, associated mainly with Adolphe Appia and Edward Gordon Craig, whose contributions to theatre reform were primarily scenographic: Appia's concept of mise-en-scène, emphasis on light and space, is essentially a theory and practice of scenography. The most influential of Craig's writings on theatre – leaving aside his infamous essay 'The actor and the Über-marionette' – are those devoted to scenographic questions, most notably his screens.

Second, Pavis points to the influence of the designer–director teams of our own time: Richard Peduzzi and Patrice Chéreau, Yannis Kokkos and Antoine Vitez, Wilfried Minks and Peter Zadek, Karl-Ernst Herrmann and Peter Stein. So-called director's theatre (*Regietheater*) is invariably designer's theatre too. The visual impact is often the signature moment of such directorial teams.

Another move has also been central: an expanded understanding of scenography to encompass more than just the set design. If scenography is writing in space, then it must include all those elements that define the spatial dimension of theatre, most notably costume and light design. The natives, that is, professional practitioners, do of course distinguish between set, costume and light design, mainly because they usually reference different people and areas of responsible. However, on a theoretical etic level, they can and should be seen as one dimension.

Despite Google Ngrams and terminological redefinitions, scenography has remained at the margins of the discipline of theatre studies. This is puzzling in the light of recent 'turns' in the humanities, notably the spatial and pictorial turns, both of which privilege the visual and spatial. In theatre and performance studies, these turns have been sidelined by the corporeal and performative turns, which privilege a highly performer-centric understanding of the discipline. We can almost speak of a fixation on the body, which in turn results from a move towards media specificity on the part of theatre and performance studies. This approach argues that each artistic medium needs to concentrate on those materials unique to it, which in this case is the live body in performance. The visual and spatial aspects are tangential or at best supportive of this corporeal core. One consequence of this approach is the recognition that the visual aspects of theatre can be outsourced to neighbouring disciplines: the text to literature, music to musicology, and scenography to art studies.

However, as we have seen, this marginalization seems to be changing, especially in the new millennium. There are perhaps two main factors to account for the rediscovery and, above all, revalorization of scenography as a field of study. The first has to do with a definition of scenography's function within a performance context. If we look at the current mission statement of the IFTR Scenography Working Group, we can see that it focuses upon the history, theory, aesthetics and practice of scenography – design for and as performance. The formulation design as (rather than just for) performance marks an important shift in how scenography is understood. The second factor is linked to recent research into intermediality, a relatively new field of study that understands different art forms in terms of their medial differences and interrelationships. Birgit E. Wiens's own recent book, *Intermediale Szenographie* (2014),[2] encapsulates and demonstrates a new and expanded understanding of scenography by including crossovers with installations, and especially the use of video technology, perhaps the greatest challenge to set design in the traditional sense.

Also crucial is the relationship to theatre architecture, which itself has undergone an expansion and dissolution of established boundaries within academic discourse. The borders between scenography and architecture often blur and mix. In her study, Wiens deals extensively with the work of Bert Neumann at the Berlin Volksbühne. She calls his designs, especially for the installations outside the confines of the Volksbühne, 'provisional architecture' (*Architektur auf Zeit*). She even includes his work as a graphic designer, associated with the firm logos, within her concept of scenography.

A news report that was published during the Munich conference fits into this tradition. It reported that Francis Kéré (the architect associated with Christoph Schlingensief's *Operndorf* in Burkina Faso) had planned to build a provisional theatre for the Berlin Volksbühne at Tempelhof airport. The scenographic implications are clear: the provisionality that has always been inherent in stage design is now being extended to architecture, once synonymous with permanence.[3]

At least Bert Neumann can be identified as being a scenographer or set designer. But what are we to make of Rimini Protokoll's projects, especially the audiowalks such as *Call Cutta* or *Cargo Sofia*, both of which have been performed at various locations in different countries. Can these also be subsumed under the term 'scenography' as Birgit E. Wiens argues? Is this scenographic performance or do these performances have a dimension that we can isolate as scenographic and study it?

If scenography is writing in space and we understand writing as something we do with our senses too, then such performances are just that they enable participants to perceive space differently and, in fact, impose their own scripts and stories on the spaces that are encountered. In such performances, we overcome the apparent dichotomy between body and space, spatiality and corporeality.

FIGURE 0.2 *Volksbühne Tempelhof by Francis Kéré (Summer 2017, preliminary version). Photo © Andrea Maretto for Kéré Architecture.*

This volume gathers together natives and anthropologists, practitioners and scholars. These many and varied contributions both identify and overcome such dichotomies and thereby improve not only scenography's digital footprint but its place in both academic study across disciplines and its teaching and practice. Although the focus here is on developments in the German-speaking countries, which represent an interconnected theatrical system, the implications are much wider, even global, as scenography represents the dimension of theatre that most easily transcends cultural and linguistic borders.

Notes

1 This method is discussed in Michel et al. (2011: 176–82).
2 Wiens (2014a).
3 See Dege (2016), www.dw.com/en/architect-francis-kéré-to-build-huge-mobile-theater-at-berlins-tempelhof-airport-ramp/a-36415167 (accessed 1 May 2018). The mobile stage designed to seat 1,000 spectators is located in a hangar and can be moved in and out as determined by the needs of the performance. Owing to a combination of economic and political factors linked to the controversy surrounding the appointment of Chris Dercon as artistic director of the Volksbühne (Dercon announced his resignation in April 2018), the performance space at Tempelhof was never completed.

Acknowledgements

This book results from an ongoing research project that is based at the Institute for Theatre Studies at the LMU University of Munich. The editor Birgit E. Wiens would like to take this opportunity to acknowledge the work of the contributing authors, scholars and all the contributing artists who allowed insights into their ateliers, creative work processes and scenographic thoughts. This interdisciplinary and practically focused volume builds on contributions made to the international conference on *The Art of Scenography: Epistemes and Aesthetics* that took place in Munich in November 2016. The conference welcomed numerous participants, both from abroad as well as from all parts of Germany. Since then, the articles in this book have been redrafted, edited and amended to include ongoing discussions, workshop talks with the artists and designers and additional scientific contributions. This research work and the conference were funded by the Deutsche Forschungsgemeinschaft (German Research Foundation). Preparing this book has been exciting: it occurred through intensive mutual exchanges and an ongoing dialogue with the parties involved.

In the course of undertaking this project – above and beyond the participating authors and artists – there were several people, as well as institutions, who supported it in various ways. My special thanks go to Joslin McKinney, who suggested that we include this book with the focus on 'Contemporary German Scenography' in the *Performance+Design* series. Given our focus on cultural specifics especially, it was important for us that our discourse took place in close connection with international networks and colleagues. Heartfelt thanks go out to Arnold Aronson (New York), Joslin McKinney again (Leeds), Thea Brejzek (Sydney), Laura Groendahl (Helsinki), Michael Simon (Zurich), Pamela Scorzin (Dortmund), Katrin Brack (Munich/Vienna) and Patrice Pavis (Paris) for their input, their criticism – coming from the most varied of perspectives – and inspiring discussions. In Munich, the support provided by Christopher Balme, colleagues and students at the Institute for Theatre Studies at LMU Munich that accompanied the various project stages is greatly appreciated. Miriam Althammer, as project assistant, took on the work of transcribing the recorded discussions and interviews. Marc Heinitz, as language editor and proofreader, was an invaluable help for the realization of the project. Furthermore, I would like to thank all the artists, photographers and the German Theatre Museum in Munich for providing the photo material within the book with a very special mention for Thomas Aurin who provided the photo of Bert Neumann's scenography for René Pollesch's *Der perfekte Tag* (The Perfect Day), Mülheim 2010 (see cover of this book). At Methuen Drama, I wish to thank Lara Bateman and her colleagues for all of their professional help, kindness and patience.

Contemporary scenography

Practices and aesthetics in German theatre, arts and design – an introduction

Birgit E. Wiens

What are we talking about today when we speak of scenography? This question cannot be easily answered; there is no simple or even generally accepted answer at hand. The artistic approaches, designs and forms of spatial productions that can be found in contemporary theatre and, in addition to this, in other artistic and cultural fields, are too manifold, too diverse and too heterogeneous: the spectrum ranges from theatre scenography, stage sets and performance environments through museum and exhibition scenography, film and media scenography to temporary architecture and 'urban scenography', as well as spatial design and the scenography of commercially oriented events. Historically and etymologically, the concept of scenography is closely connected to the theatre; originally, within the antique Greek theatre world, the term was used to describe the painting of or the design of a *skene* (i.e. the stage backdrop) within the spatial constellation of the theatre as a whole (*theatron*). Nowadays, though, 'scenography' has become a generic concept or a search term that is hard to grasp as it, in itself, encompasses numerous different strands of definition and characterization. This has been the case ever since scenography has operated as a spatial art and design practice both in and beyond the theatre. Scenographic practices have – so to speak – 'migrated' from the theatre into neighbouring genres and creative disciplines, so they can be observed in various contexts and in very different cultural fields.

Scenography is everywhere? Contemporary scenography and its contexts

Scenography, as can be seen in the late twentieth and early twenty-first centuries, has become a remarkably multifaceted design and art practice; these developments also became reflected in recent research that seeks to examine these emerging fields by observing and analysing the ongoing hybridization, as well as the cross-disciplinary dynamics of what has been identified as 'scenographic practice'. Often these publications – for example Pamela Howard's book *What is Scenography?* (2002) and, even more recently, *The Routledge Companion to Scenography*, edited by Arnold Aronson (2018) – find it necessary to, first of all, offer a discussion of the available definitions of 'scenography' and of the artistic phenomena and designs that the term encompasses. Moreover, some of the studies – when focusing on contemporary scenography's broad spectrum – have suggested tentative concepts such as 'extended' scenography (Brejzek, Greisenegger and Wallen 2009) and 'expanded scenography' (Lotker and Gough 2013; McKinney and Palmer 2017), as well as alternative terms such as 'performance design' (Hannah and Harsløf 2008). Also, a 'scenographic turn' has been propagated, combined with fears that the whole concept of scenography might collapse due to the difficulties of grasping the emerging diversity of contemporary practices through a sufficiently precise terminology (McKinney and Palmer 2017: 3); consequently, there is – in addition to available approaches – an ongoing need for theoretical discourse and for new research approaches towards the field.

This book wants to join this discussion by focusing on the scenographic practices and discourse within the German-speaking countries (with a particular focus on Germany, and a few glimpses into Austria and Switzerland). The starting idea here with regard to analysis and methodology is to bring in a more cultural context-oriented perspective and, in turn, to assess such an approach. One of the initial questions was to what extent – above and beyond the art and design discourse and discussion of aesthetics – further conditions, for example institutional, political or economic ones, come to bear (part of this is the state-funded support system through which in Germany the arts as well as theatre are subsidized). The question is how these have supported (or even propelled) the emergent differentiation of the artistic and the design forms of scenography here in recent decades and which factors have led – above and beyond the art world – to an extension of scenographic practices into very different urban, media-related and even commercial areas. Another initial observation was that the discourse on scenography – as it was conducted in the German-speaking countries – and especially the use of the term 'scenography' (in German: *Szenographie*) is quite different compared with the term's usage and the discourse in the Anglo-American world. The contributions to this book are, in parts, based on papers presented at the international conference *The Art of Scenography: Epistemes and Aesthetics* (Munich 2016), which were later developed further and supplemented by additional articles. At the conference, renowned German or German-based artists and designers who specialize in various fields (theatre, environmental scenography, exhibition, temporary architecture and public urban space) and work in different contexts (both nationally as well as internationally) presented their work and artistic thoughts in a dialogue with academic scholars (from the disciplines of theatre studies, art history, architecture, design theory and philosophical aesthetics). During the conference we asked ourselves the question, among many others, in how far contemporary scenography nowadays is a 'globalized art form' (McKenzie 2008) or if there are actually still any culturally specific traditions at work. Another question was to what extent there is a repertoire of 'scenographic knowledge' being created or already at hand and how this is dealt with in the various fields of artistic practice and research. In addition, one should also include the fields of research and teaching at universities and art schools and the need to have a closer look at this transfer of knowledge. Based on this, our project once again poses the question: What do we actually mean when we talk about scenography?

The discussion in the German-speaking countries as it has taken place to date has been largely separated by types and genres. At the same time, the ongoing diversification and inter/transdisciplinary 'expansion' of scenographic practices, which McKinney and Palmer describe as being a general development within contemporary scenography, can be observed here at a significant level. Yet one can say that the term 'scenography' has only partially become accepted in the German context and very slowly for various reasons. In the theatre and in theatre studies up to now – even when describing experimental spatial designs within the theatrical context – the term '*Bühnenbild*' (stage design) is still a lot more common, even though the term 'scenography' has, from the very beginning, been closely linked to theatre history. According to a basic theatre studies definition formulated by Christopher Balme under the entry 'Scenography' in the *Metzler Lexikon Theatertheorie* (2014 [2005]), the term encompasses 'all visual and sculptural elements (including the stage design, light and costume design) that portray the scene of the action in the theatre in a realistic, abstract or symbolic manner' (Fischer-Lichte, Kolesch and Warstat 2014: 347). Its first usage is documented in the well-known *Poetics* by Aristotle (around 335 BCE) as a term used to describe the painting of the stage house front that visually marked the performance area and helped to situate the play (Fischer-Lichte, Kolesch and Warstat 2014). Later on, at the start of the modern age, first in Italy around 1600, closed theatre buildings were built (at the time the invention of spatial pictorial presentation occurred; that is, the cultural technique of the perspective) and *Scenographia* was equated with the 'perspective presentation' (Haß 2005: 188–95). The proscenium stage, constructed for perspective, remained dominant within the world of (European) theatre for a very long time. From this point on, histories on scenography usually take a very big leap and go straight to the scenography discourse of the modern era, which started at the turn of the twentieth century with a number of iconoclasms. The criticism and disposal of the proscenium stage and its scenery apparatus in favour of the spatial stage, the introduction of practicable stage elements, equipping the sets with modern technology (including electric light), artistic experiments with theatre technology and various stage formats (as for example the revolving stage), as well as introducing other media (e.g. film), became the most important developments. Scenography, traditionally a visual art, became a spatial art. This turn in scenography history is well documented[1] and, as we know, the impulses that came from artists such as Adolphe Appia, Edward G. Craig, Oskar Schlemmer and the Bauhaus school, as well as Friedrich Kiesler, Erwin Piscator and Bertolt Brecht, together with his 'stage builders' Caspar Neher, Teo Otto and Karl von Appen, just to mention a few of the more important names, still resonate today. With their criticism of the illusionary stage and with their experiments, they all contributed to reorganizing the scenic space and to allowing for new forms of scenographic expressions. According to Balme, the terms 'set design' and 'scenography' (this latter term being understood as the experimentally defined spatial art of the theatre) have come to be separated definition-wise. Consequently, he suggests a differentiation between a 'transhistoric' (i.e. general) and a 'historic' (i.e. especially related to the twentieth and twenty-first centuries) scenography definition (2014 [2005]: 347–8).

The field of research has thereby been defined, at least timewise. Still, in theatre studies and the related art sciences (once again the focus being on the German-speaking countries), stage design and scenography are research fields that, even today, have – compared with other elements of theatre and performance production, that is, acting and dramaturgy – not been paid much attention. For a long time, the reason for this seemed to be that they fall into the grey area between the various disciplines. A further reason may lie in the academic discussion as well as method development: An analysis under the auspices of theatre studies, related to performance, usually focuses primarily on the actors, singers, dancers and performers involved, as well as on what has been termed the 'autopoietic feedback loop' between them and the audience (Fischer-Lichte 2008 [2004]). Scenographic design remained out of focus most of the time, even though it contains within it manifold forms and a lively artistic practice. Nevertheless, a certain shift in perspective was induced by what Hans-This Lehmann, in his study of the same name, has identified as 'postdramatic theatre' (2006 [1999]). One aspect of these theatre and performance practices that have emerged during the late twentieth century in the Western world (celebrated examples were Robert Wilson's works, as well as Christopher Marthaler and Anna Viebrock's stagings, Frank Castorf's Berlin Volksbühne, and many more) is the detachment of theatre scenography from the predominance of literature and the dehierarchization of the theatre elements. In the German-speaking countries, artists such as Heiner Goebbels, who, together with his stage designer Klaus Grünberg, put forward the idea that scenography, the space, its media and the objects should not be seen as fittings or even only as backdrop or décor but instead as equal 'actors', 'co-players' or 'counterplayers': 'The stage is not just an illustrative décor, but in itself a work of art; the actor has to accept the fact that he has to share the presence with the involved elements that belong to the reality of the stage' (Goebbels 2015: 12). Due to this changed perspective, 'doing scenography' does not mean to 'build and prepare a set design' any more, but rather denotes artistic processes of 'composition' and 'orchestration' (McKinney and Butterworth 2009) of spatial constellations and performance. According to this, scenography has to be understood as a sort of autonomous actor as well as co-player in the performative process.

Parallel to this shift happening in theatre scenography, one could observe that artistic approaches and design parameters of scenography and stage design had been taken up and 'translated' into the field of museums and exhibition spaces (Eberhard Siepmann, the former director of the Werkbund-Archives in Berlin, called this the 'performative turn in museums', Siepmann 2001). Ever since the World Exhibition EXPO 2000 in Hannover, exhibition scenographies in museums, as well as in the festival and trade fair sectors, are on the rise and have turned into an expanding field, separate from the theatre, that can also avail of manifold platforms (annual symposia, publication series, specialized journals).[2] In the field of architecture, scenography became a theme as temporary architecture, participatory design and artistic intervention into public urban spaces (Wolfrum and Brandis 2015).

Briefly outlined, this has been the genre-related discourse so far, and it may be the impression that in the German-speaking countries, scenography strongly clings to the demarcated boundaries that have been drawn over the years. Moreover, in recent decades, the discourse and the practice concerning these various fields have developed quite differently, but nevertheless, the definitions of scenography continue to be discussed. As is well known, it has its origin in the theatre (which might still have a pivotal role to play in this field); however, its extension and expansion into art and design practice, within the German context, can hardly be overlooked. In fact, also here, as McKinney and Palmer pointed out for the international context (2017: 4), the formation of modern and contemporary scenography occurred in three waves, fuelled (1) by the multiple artistic movements of the historical avant-garde and (2) by 'postdramatic theatre' in the early and the late twentieth century, (3) up to the proliferation of new spatial forms in and beyond theatre and performance since the millennium that is termed 'expanded scenography'. Yet approaches that try to understand scenography in an inter- or transdisciplinary manner have so far met with little response in German-speaking countries and have mainly been proposed by design theorists. Christian Barthelmes, for instance, has come up with the formula that it is 'a discipline dedicated explicitly to space and its staging'. Its uniqueness is the fact that it demands various forms of competency and that it, today, operates on numerous fields: 'Compared to the arts, namely architecture, the fine arts, the dramatic arts, music and literature, scenography is at once a sub-discipline and a discipline that integrates' (in Atelier Brückner 2016 [2011]: 12). Similarly, Ralf Bohn and Heiner Wilharm redefine scenography very openly as a 'practice field at the intersection of event and presentation, exhibition and performance culture' (2009: 7). Thus, the assumption was made that the distinction between scenographic phenomena according to artistic categories, or even between art versus not art (applied art, design) has become almost, if not entirely, obsolete: 'In emphasising process, event and construction, previously distinct creative genres – from design through architecture, theatre, exhibition, exposition and museum to *mise-en-scène* – are combined into gestures of spatiality' (Brejzek, Mueller von der Haegen and Wallen 2009: 371). Here, the concept and category of scenography have been indeed much 'expanded'; at the same time, this holds the danger of the category expanding so far that it might become almost inoperable and, thus, useless.

In the discussion presented in this book, the genre and classification-related view is not given up *a priori*. What we are aiming at is rather to grasp the various concepts of scenography related to their respective genres and, at the same time, to inspire a new way of examining the multifaceted, rapidly changing fields of this cross-disciplinary art and design practice. Based on the case studies, analyses and practice-related discussions with renowned artists and designers assembled in this book, we have differentiated between two approaches that are interlinked with each other: on the one hand, a mainly artistic research *into* scenography (in the sense of research in the arts) and, on the other hand, a mainly academic and scientific development of theory and research *on* scenography. The main focus is on the question how contemporary scenography actually operates within its very diverse fields. Different from what numerous other publications have undertaken, the approach here is not primarily focused on analysing the semiotic, performative and atmospheric aspects of the perception of scenographed constellations. The interest lies much more in the observation of scenography *in* and *as* performance and targets the production side of the spatial arts, that is, art and design practices, artistic processes, production modes, epistemology and what is termed here as 'scenographic knowledge'. Following Patrice Pavis, who decidedly described it as 'art' as well as the 'science of the organization of the stage and the performance space' (Pavis 2007: 969), we are suggesting here that one needs to understand scenography as an 'apparatus' (*dispositif*) in the Foucauldian sense (Wiens 2016). Its main characteristic and function comprise – so the theory is – the creation of spaces that are a contrast to everyday environments because of their *heterotopic* and temporal character. So both human as well as non-human actors and spectators are brought into more or less open constellations that each follow set rules (the course of the performance, the play, the interaction, the participation). Foucault's definition stands for a concept for the observation and description of conjunctions ('networks') of discourses, people, institutions and practices.[3] Analysing scenography as a *dispositif* means to question how it actually occurs within the context of institutions (be it theatre, museum or public space and urban environments), given architecture, administration, the conditions of production, virulent discourses, established aesthetics, implicit knowledge and habitual practices. With this approach, we are calling for the analysis of scenographic art and design practices – above and beyond their artistic features and aesthetics – in a decidedly context-related manner (i.e. with a view to the respective cultural as well as social conditions and the conditions of their production and reception).

Reflections on contemporary German scenography: Investigating cultures of scenographic art and design

Starting from these premises, this book places its main focus on contemporary scenographic practice and discourse within Germany after 1989. Facing the end of the political divide, as well as the mediatization of communication (digital turn) and the challenges of globalization, German-based stage designers and scenographers have reacted since then to a cultural landscape that has been, and still is, in transition – politically, socially, economically. After the reunification of East and West Germany, and particularly after the fall of the Berlin Wall after more than four decades of its dividing a city, one could observe the clash of different cultures, art practices and audience expectations all within an ongoing process of convergence, conflict and negotiation – even though those involved shared certain traditions (some of them 'rooted' in German history, for example Appia's legacy, that of the Bauhaus school, the stage sets by Teo Otto, Karl von Appen and Caspar Neher); however, these were remembered and reinterpreted in different ways. Similar transformations, negotiations and rejections took place all across Europe.

FIGURE I.1 *Façade of the Volksbühne am Rosa-Luxemburg-Platz, Berlin, 2014/15 season; banner, flags and posters by Bert Neumann. Photo © Stefan Bock. www.blog.theaternachtgedanken.de, 2014.*

But due to the somewhat loaded political legacy, post-1989 Germany – and especially Berlin – was particularly exciting with regard to these social, political and cultural upheavals; here one could observe the processes as if 'through a lens'. This – in many aspects momentous – turning point (also much discussed in the so-called 'spatial turn' debate: Crang and Thrift 2000; Bachmann-Medick 2009) manifested itself in culture and the arts, there where scenography takes place. Scenographic work – either conceived and produced at (publicly subsidized) theatres, museums and exhibition spaces or realized elsewhere (either as independent productions or subsidized as well, or undertaken on a commercial basis) – have become a remarkable driving force, often referring to scenographic traditions of the past but also reacting to current issues such as internationalization, globalization and migration. If one, for example, looks at the art scene in Berlin, one can see a huge melting pot, attracting artists, designers and visitors from everywhere in the world. In addition, productions travel and go on tour within Europe or worldwide, becoming part of a dynamic and complex cultural intercourse.

It may seem almost impossible to provide a 'mapping' of this rich and dynamic field but it might be feasible to identify and sketch out some major developments. As Matt Cornish wrote in *The Routledge Companion to Scenography*, in his chapter entitled 'Worlds of German Design in the Twenty-First Century', there is 'no one scenographic movement, particular school or style that dominates the stages of Germany today' (Cornish 2018: 475). This holds true. Even so, there are artists, designers, collaborative groups and institutions that have shaped the discourse and, through their work, have become particularly influential in recent years. As he also observed, many of the works, especially within the world of theatre, stand '*sui generis* or even *ex nihilo*' (Cornish 2018: 465) in a historical relationship and rapport (one example of this would be the ongoing confrontation with the legacy of Brecht). Moreover, much of what can be seen today would not be conceivable without certain inputs that date back to the second half of the twentieth century but prepared the path for today's artistic variety. One prominent example here is the works of the late stage designer Wilfried Minks who, since the 1960s, brought pop art, the cinema and even comics – in other words, the present – onto the stage, often using striking or even provocative symbols. His collaborations with directors such as Peter Zadek, Klaus Michael Grüber and Peter Palitzsch often started with an empty, whitewashed basic space.[4] Other famous examples are the works by Robert Wilson and Achim Freyer that became described as *Bildertheater* ('visual theatre'), and Freyer stating the aim 'to find a new visual language for the theatre', beyond words (Simhandl 1993: 136 and 144). Also, with regard to the more recent developments, it is again inevitable that certain names must be named – these artists often shaped, via their artistic positions, the art world and their productions became particularly formative, receiving a lot of attention. This (non-exhaustive) list of scenographers and stage designer may include Anna Viebrock, Bert Neumann, Aleksandar Denić, Katrin Brack, Olaf Altmann, Klaus Grünberg, Michael Simon, Penelope Wehrli, Johannes Schütz, Stefan Hageneier, Harald B. Thor, Martin Zehetgruber, Muriel Gerstner, Barbara Ehnes, Katrin Nottrodt, Janina Audick, Annette Kurz, Jan Pappelbaum, Herbert Fritsch, Ulrich Rasche, Mona el Gammal, Vinge / Müller, Lena Newton, Rimini Protokoll, Dominic Huber/Blendwerk, raumlaborberlin and numerous others (as well as the many emerging young designers and artists in the field) who have not been mentioned here. In addition, the designers and design studios that work in the fields of museum and exhibition design, corporate scenography and staged commercial events need to be included; their list would also be a long one. Just to name a few, as representative of the creative players within this large scene: Atelier Brückner, ART+COM, Tamschick Media+Space and TRIAD Berlin. Therefore, contributions in this book will not cover all currently observable phenomena of contemporary German scenography, nor are they meant as an attempt to capture what is happening in theatre, museums and the public sphere as a whole. There is no claim for completeness or even for encyclopaedic coverage; instead the goal is to identify some important developments of German scenography in the hope of stimulating debate and encouraging further research.

Contemporary German scenography: Identifying key aspects and major trends

A round-trip in three steps

The work on this book began with some 'joyful confusion': How could we give readers an insightful, thorough introduction into such a varied, multifaceted field? As just explained, this study is particularly interested in exploring the inter- and cross-disciplinary dynamics of contemporary scenography. To be able to highlight these, we have not given up on a genre-related view. Accordingly, the book is arranged into three sections. Section I provides the reader with insights on recent developments in the performing arts; section II offers examples from museum and exhibition design, as well as from the fields of temporary architecture, installation, urban intervention and artistic activism. With section III, entitled 'Rethinking Scenography', theoretical and methodological questions are again raised and reflected on. Research *into* scenography (particularly in the chapters by the contributing designers and artists, or in the editor's conversations with these) is combined with research *on* scenography (provided in theoretical treatises, cases studies and analyses).

I Scenography in and beyond the theatre

The first section of this volume, entitled 'Scenography in and beyond the theatre: Aesthetics and epistemes', puts its focus on theatre scenography and set design, while also offering some glances into costume design. The assembled contributions show that artistic practices today have freed themselves from a former dependency on play texts and directing. On the level of production, artistic teams and institutions now call for scenography's equal status (to those previously dominant sign systems) within the collaborative art of theatre making. Significant examples are the sets of Aleksandar Denić; a Serbian set designer born in Belgrade, who works mostly in Germany. Since they first met in 2011, Denić has regularly worked with Frank Castorf, who held the position of artistic director at the Volksbühne in Berlin from 1992 to 2017. In and outside Berlin, they have collaborated on numerous opera and theatre projects, including a scenic interpretation of Wagner's *Ring* cycle in Bayreuth (2013), followed by theatre works in Hamburg, Munich and Stuttgart. Additionally, Denić designed the stage for Castorf's farewell production at the Volksbühne, an adaptation of Johann Wolfgang von Goethe's *Faust* (2017) that became iconic soon after its premiere. Stage designs and sets by Denić are reminiscent – at first sight – of film sceneries; they are multi-part, large-format and multilevel stage architectures (often installed on a revolving stage) and, thus, intricate and complex structures. This is by no means surprising: Denić, as a scenographer, works for both film and television, as well as in the theatre. The most striking feature of his stages, however, is their high density and the overabundance of cultural symbols and signs. In their infamous version of *Faust*, Castorf and Denić decided to relocate the plot of Goethe's tragic play about the scholar who makes a pact with the devil to 1950s Paris, during the time of the Algerian war and liberation struggle. Starting with the topic of annexation and land reclamation (which is anticipated in the second part of the play), their aim was not to restage Goethe's drama as a specifically 'German' tragedy, as has often been done, but rather to take these scenes as references to the history of colonialism, which originated from the Germanic countries and Europe at large. Consequently, their *Faust* was based on only a few elements of Goethe's texts but also integrated texts by other authors (including Émile Zola, Paul Celan and Frantz Fanon). Correspondingly, Denić's stage architecture was a mosaic of quotes from recent history[5]: There was a dark, castle-like architecture that had a hell's gate (resembling the façade of the famous Montmartre cabaret 'Café L'Enfer') and a messy backyard, where one could also see subway stairs (a replica of the Paris Métro station 'Stalingrad') and, as an integral part of the design, a projection screen and a large LED screen. Causing further confusion and generating a loaded, energized atmosphere, the scenery included

Swastika-patterned walls, as well as film and exhibition posters from the 1930s, 1940s and 1950s, some of them carrying irritating, even racist messages (e.g. as within the invitation to the Paris Colonial Exhibition in 1931). The complexity of all of this was propelled by the fact that the whole structure, built on a revolving stage, circulated several times in front of the spectators' eyes. Reflecting on his approach, Denić states, 'I am trying to add more layers to the story' (see the editor's conversation with the artist in this book). One might say that he is pushing the concept of the 'dramaturgically composed' stage set (Brecht, Piscator) and its 'postdramatic' redefinition to an extreme. While Brecht and Neher intended what they called the 'epic' composition of expressive elements, Lehmann describes the (postdramatic) concept of 'writing in space', that is, doing scenography to deconstruct cultural symbols and signs as well as provoking associative, arbitrary signifying processes (2006: 159). Denić's scenographic approach reconceptualizes both tactics and creates a stage that in its complexity reflects on traces of history in contemporary life. From an audience's perspective, the sets seem almost as incomprehensible as the ever-shifting formations of today's social, political and economic reality.

It has become a widely accepted assumption that, rather than being a static image, scenography is a temporal event for actors, viewers and makers alike. Consequently, there's an increased interest in *scenographic materiality*, that is, in the energies and material qualities of scenographed constellations and objects. A prominent example of this is the works by German stage designer Katrin Brack, who, in some regards, might be considered the antipode to Aleksandar Denić. Critics have described her as a 'minimalist', 'atmospherist' and 'landscape designer' and her scenic designs have been labelled as 'worlds beyond history'.[6] In fact, when working with directors such as Luc Perceval, Dimiter Gotscheff, Armin Petras, Johan Simons and, most recently, René Pollesch, Brack does not build a set. Instead, she uses material such as confetti, balloons, artificial rain, foam, fog or snow to fill the space and to evoke particular atmospheres. During the performance of *Prinz Friedrich von Homburg* (The Prince of Homburg; 2006/7), for instance, it rained continuously, while the temperature in the performance space became perceptibly cooler. In all her works, material or matter moves in seemingly uncontrolled ways, like self-guided particles and almost like a natural occurrence. Usually, she chooses only one material for each production, which operates like an abbreviation that conveys the central theme and prevailing mood of the play. But Brack has claimed that '(the material) is never a symbol. And it is not a stage effect. These two aspects are most important' (quoted from Grenzmann 2018). As dramaturge Stefanie Carp observes, in 'her most successful sets or installations, the material does not become an allegory but remains innocent as if radiating energy' (Nioduschewski 2010: 22), which the audience perceives first and foremost on a subconscious, not an intellectual, level. What is most remarkable about these designs is the way Brack employs radical reduction to open up interwoven layers of interpretation, so that the things at play point beyond the order of the semiotic. According to her, the material itself has no symbolic meaning; instead, it unfolds performatively in its material, temporal and atmospheric character. Another important aspect of her work is her method of making the usually invisible relations between human actors, objects and things visible. Scenography manifests itself here not in 'stage design', but rather according to the conceptual thinking that configures ('composes') media, scenographic objects and acting options to 'orchestrate' them within aesthetic processes and performative, multimedial events (see McKinney's chapter in this book). This hints at a paradigm shift: The traditional hierarchy between humans and things is revoked, which corresponds with the academic debate of new materialism, originally sparked by Karen Barad, Jane Bennett and Bruno Latour, among others. This interdisciplinary debate centres on the fact that while we manipulate the environmental conditions of life, such as nature or climate, we do not command them; instead, they have their own 'vital materiality' (Bennett 2010b). Likewise, we do not have control over recent technological developments such as ubiquitous computing, 'smart gadgets' and (social) networks; rather, we are experiencing their increasing uncontrollable influence on our lives.

Another key concept of contemporary scenography, and in some ways connected to this debate, is the attempt to reinterpret theatre as a complex machinery and a 'technical organism'. This practice makes reference to historic stage techniques or technology-based production processes of the twentieth century and/or refers to employment and artistic critique of newer digital technologies. The productions of director and set designer Ulrich Rasche should be mentioned here;[7] his works seem to be driven, or even produced, by high-tech apparatus and technology that is impressive yet intimidating. In Rasche's version of Büchner's revolutionary drama *Dantons Tod* (Danton's Death; 2015), the ensemble was performing on a gigantic rolling mill. As if on a treadmill, the actors moved on the spot, never making any progress at all. For *Die Räuber* (The Robbers; 2016), two enormous black tilted conveyer belts were mounted onto the revolving stage of the Residenztheater in Munich, which rotated like tank treads for the entire duration of the performance and altered direction between pointing upwards and downwards or, as it were, towards the heavens or the abyss. Like the schemes of Franz Moor and the tragedy of his brother Karl the belts followed an unstoppable course. The monumental machine (whose design and construction took the Munich theatre workshop over a year to finalize) became the main actor: the machine drove this scenic composition of space, movement and sound, in which the twenty or so actors trod along the belts like galley slaves. They moved rhythmically and in sync and delivered their texts either in choral chants, as in the theatre of Einar Schleef, or accentuated by the live orchestration of the percussionist Ari Benjamin Meyers and his band members; the words, movements and sounds were perfectly timed.[8] Rasche's machines make life's challenges physically palpable (and not only for the characters in the play). Their historic inspiration or precursors might be found in the sets of twentieth-century avant-gardist Friedrich Kiesler, who, as early as 1923, formulated that the stage is a 'completely independent organism with the laws of technologies of our time. And this animation of stage technique gifts us with [the possibility of] a supra-individual and dynamic composition of the space' (Zillner, Bogner and Bogner 2017: 37). While there are similarities between the two approaches, Rasche obviously does not share Kiesler's faith in technology. Instead, he seems to suggest that the 'technical organisms' of today generate rather dystopian spaces. Within these, human beings are but tiny cogs in the giant clockwork of time. Rasche explains that the machine is an 'expression for a certain run of events, for a historical situation on repeat, for the experience, both personal and historical, which says that things don't ever really take a turn for the better'.[9]

A further notable, even notorious, development that has been discussed widely elsewhere is the employment of video and film in contemporary theatre, where technological media act as 'scenographic extensions' to the visuality (as well as the acoustics) of theatre. This extension happens both on stage and beyond (e.g. in environmental performances, on-site scenography or scenographic interventions). Of course, Fluxus, the influential video and multimedia art group, as well as guest performances by international, predominantly American artists and collectives (such as John Jesurun, the Wooster Group and The Builder's Association) during festivals such as *Theater der Welt*, have been influential within the German context even before the turn of the millennium.[10] Nonetheless, under Frank Castorf's artistic direction, the Volksbühne radically championed such media experiments by consistently including them in their programme. They also mobilized Erwin Piscator's historic experiments with set design, which had taken place in the very same theatre, to imbed this artistic choice. Specifically, the Dostoevsky series (2001–15, direction: Frank Castorf, stage designs: Bert Neumann)[11] became noted for the specific manners in which film or video became part of the performance process both dramaturgically and scenographically. This approach had initially been developed during the rehearsals for another piece, *Endstation Amerika* (2000, based on Tennessee Williams' *A Streetcar Named Desire*), for which Neumann, channelling Hitchcock, built a set with a bathroom included, which was closed on all four sides. Neumann refused to open the space, even when the director (Castorf), who wanted to use the room for several scenes, protested; the idea then was to install a camera in the room to film everything that was not directly visible from the auditorium and to livestream it to the audience. Since then, many of Neumann's stages function on the principle of visual fragmentation between what is visible and what is invisible, what is on the inside and what is on the outside. This is especially true for his intricate container architectures which he built during the 2000s. In the 2002/3 season, the playing space for Dostoevsky's *The Idiot* required the complete remodelling of the interior of the theatre to build an urban landscape from container modules, scaffolds and staircases, the so-called 'Neustadt' ('New City'). This three-storey-high structure also had a mobile tower, from which the audience watched as the action unfolded; the stage action materialized from an intermedial combination of live-action on stage (or rather the multiple performance spaces within the container architecture), the projections of live video, as well as the constantly changing constellation of these elements within each scene. One can call this practice of scenography *'hybrid compositing'* (Boenisch 2010: 198; Wiens 2014a: 255–61). The audience members found themselves in a visually multifaceted and de facto incomprehensible spatial configuration, in which they constantly had to reorient themselves.

Bert Neumann was the head of the set and costumes department from the early 1990s until his untimely death in 2015. During this time, the Berlin Volksbühne became one of the most influential theatres in the German-speaking countries. It was a convergence point where new ways of theatre making were pioneered and coined; the cultural tensions between East and West (Berlin) as well as the emerging internationalization of the city lead to an artistic explosion which polarized the audience as much as it united it. Alongside Neumann, who without a doubt most shaped the visual language and identity of the theatre, many other eminent scenographers of widely different artistic styles worked at the Volksbühne, including Anna Viebrock, Hartmut Meyer, Penelope Wehrli, Katrin Brack, Aleksandar Denić and many others. Moreover, visual artists such as Jonathan Meese and the artist duo Vinge/Müller were invited to join the theatre's team. Renowned filmmaker and performance artist Christoph Schlingensief, who also passed away prematurely in 2010, had been working there since the 1990s.

In 2011, Schlingensief was posthumously awarded the renowned Hein Heckroth Prize for scenography.[12] Although his oeuvre is rarely discussed with regard to this category, his scenographic works indeed were remarkable and even groundbreaking. His 2006 installation *Kaprow City* and the long-term artistic project *Animatograph* were among the most pertinent of his scenography career. 'Animatography' refers to a concept – as well as an apparatus he later developed – which he used to radically transcend artistic genres and combine film, theatre, installation art and painting into hybrid and idiosyncratic visual compositions. An 'animatograph prototype' emerged during his work for the set of his staging of Richard Wagner's *Parsifal* at the Bayreuth

Festival in 2004. Schlingensief presented (and substantially reinterpreted) this opera, centred around the quest for the Holy Grail, the ruler of the kingdom Amfortas and Sir Parsifal, as a near-death experience and a meditation about dying. To translate this directorial vision, he placed a multipartite installation onto the revolving stage and projected different films and videos onto the moving stage. Using large-format and multiple projections, Schlingensief succeeded in simultaneously projecting various visuals (geometric animations, coloured patterns, symbols from different religious and cultural contexts) from numerous perspectives. This formed an ongoing and multilayered flow filling space; leaving the singers and the markedly multiethnic ensemble in a dark atmosphere most of the time. By introducing his animatograph ('soul-writer') onto the stage, the artist tasked himself with generating a strong scenographic equivalent to Wagner's music. Quoting Joseph Beuys' famous iconography, the last scene displays a dead, rotting hare and then the audience sees Parsifal disappear into a tunnel of light. This production, taking up Wagner's famous lines 'Here Time becomes Space', might be described as a kaleidoscopic multiplication and dynamic sampling of space. Schlingensief continued his *Animatograph* series for another two years, employing its technique both in the theatre (for productions at the Burgtheater in Vienna and at the Berlin Volksbühne) as well as outside. It travelled to Iceland and to a township in Namibia (further stops in Bhaktapur in Nepal, Jamaica, Buenos Aires, New York and Tokyo were planned but never came to fruition: Berka 2011; Biesenbach et al. 2014). The central theme behind this journey was the idea to charge this multimedia apparatus with culturally diverse images (hopefully void of cliché) to recontextualize these visuals. Schlingensief's artistic and increasingly social approach last found expression in his visionary *Operndorf Afrika* (Opera Village Africa), which was to be built near the city of Ouagadougou in Burkina Faso.

Artistic approaches, as far reaching as those by Schlingensief or, in different ways, those by Bert Neumann, are emblematic for the observation that scenography today has the potential to happen everywhere, especially in regard to its cross-disciplinary dynamics. In the case of theatre, it is notable that theatres have not only opened their doors to other art forms and media since the 1960s, but that the reverse is true as well. There has been an outward migration from the theatre (buildings) into the public space: productions have been staged in parks, streets and public squares (Kaye 2000; Aronson 2018 [1981]); museums, galleries and former cinemas have been used temporarily or permanently (a popular example is the Schaubühne am Lehniner Platz, which used to be a movie theatre), and vacant factory halls and teardowns have been repurposed for new public contexts. These interventions into different spaces which stretched and, at times, suspended the limitations of the stage, brought new audiences and changed the ways of viewing theatre and of the perception of art at large. At the same time this expanded concept of art lead to an exploration of the urban environment and discovered it as a 'dynamic piece of art' or 'an artwork that lives' (Klein 2005: 13). So, today, it is no longer strange when, for example, the Schauspiel Dortmund spends almost two years playing in the former warehouse of the local football club's merchandise store, the BVB Megastore (in this case, not for artistic reasons but because restoration work is taking place in the actual theatre). The theatre (artistic direction: Kay Voges) did manage to gain critical attention when it staged a series of intermedial projects, which took up the far-reaching theatrical, site-specific and topographical context of the space. Their proclaimed aim was also to become pioneers of the experimental field of digitality and theatre within the German context.[13] Among their most notable productions was the 2013 theatrical adaptation of Thomas Vinterberg's film *Festen* (1998), which grappled with the manifesto of the Danish Dogma movement (*Dogma 95*), and advocated updating the movement's demands through the means of live-art theatre and the artistic exploration of the relationship between theatre and film worlds. Other productions attended to the concept of 'augmented reality'. *Borderline Prozession* (2016), for instance, reflected on the increase in sensory overload triggered by digital and social media online: 'We read about the war in Syria, while checking football scores on the side and hearing that mother is sick – How is all this possible at the same time?' (quoted from Wildermann 2017). Set designer Michael Sieberock-Serafimowitsch scenographically responded to this paradox by building an apartment building with ten rooms into the hall of the Megastore, including a bus stop, a kiosk and a parking lot. During the whole performance a camera team circumambulated the installation, like a procession, and captured the various scenes and actions in a sheer endless loop. The scenes became part of a composition of images, shreds of films, quotes and short outtakes from daily TV news shows visible on the large projection screens placed around the room. The audience members had a free choice of seats and could opt to follow the action from two different perspectives within the performance space or explore a virtual version of this theatrical installation (produced by the artist group CyberRäuber) in the antechamber of the hall. In order to take these experiments further, Voges' next project (stage design: Daniel Roskamp), *Parallelwelt* (Parallel Worlds; 2018), happened simultaneously in two theatres, the Schauspiel Dortmund and the Berliner Ensemble, and was conceived as a joint project between the two theatres connected via digital technology.[14] These developments and their interest in networks, multiple locales and simultaneity, however, require a new conceptual approach to scenography. Scenography is no longer and not predominantly a singular set, an installation or a materialized form but a coded structure; a programme and dynamism in an actor–network constellation operating between theatre and other spaces, both real and virtual, simultaneously and in different places at once.

Recent discussions on hybrid spaces, or 'augmented scenography', as it were, have reflected on the intermedial versus immersive aspects of such constellations and on the audience involvement they foster. Various works by Rimini Protokoll, for example, bring up the question of how scenography addresses an audience. Particularly their interactive installations and multiplayer video pieces (e.g. *Situation Rooms*, 2013; *Nachlass/Heritage – A Play without Actors,* 2017) as well as their audio walks, 'documentary truck rides' through public urban spaces, and other formats (e.g. *Remote X,* 2013; *Cargo Sofia X,* 2006/2018) seem to explore scenographic potentialities to make spectators participate and even trigger their actions and spatial perception. In the course of these projects the audience becomes confronted ('alienated') and/or surrounded ('immersed') by scenographed spatial effects, and therefore it becomes their task to 'navigate' through the respective environments. Similar but different to that, the production *Nationaltheater Reinickendorf, Container 1–9* by the German-Norwegian artist duo Vegard Vinge and Ida Müller was a twelve-hour performance and installation project. Part of a curated program series entitled *Immersion – Limits of Knowing* (2017), organized by the Berliner Festspiele and the Gropius Bau museum in Berlin, the project evoked immersive effects not predominantly through means of technology but rather by excessively using collages, street art, comic strip drawings and lots of paint applied all over the walls, ceiling and floors. Within their fictitious 'national theatre', which was only temporarily established in an old factory complex in the district of Reinickendorf, Vinge/Müller seemed to trace the history of immersion back to Wagner and Shakespeare. By translating these references into their own grotesquely distorted visuals and through a very raw and loud aesthetic, they created a heterotopic world, based on its own rules (see Thomas Irmer's chapter in this book). Matt Cornish, who has already been referenced several times in this introduction, seems to be right in his assertion that history – be it sui generis or even ex nihilo – remains a central point of reference for contemporary German scenography even its most advanced experiments (Cornish 2018), but, as the outlined examples also have shown, it moves beyond this through its various cross-cultural practices and discourses.

Many more works of theatre makers and scenographers could be mentioned here. And yet, as this brief overview has shown, the outlined developments are not fundamentally different regarding their approaches to scenography when compared with other European countries. Nonetheless, the particular artistic styles may differ, as may the underlying questions. Even when just looking at the field of theatre on its own, it is obvious that there is a diversity of forms at hand and that there is not one school or style dominating the artistic production within German-speaking countries. One of the leading artists, who shaped the landscape of scenography for many years and whom younger artists often reference or draw from, is Bert Neumann, and many of the key developments in the contemporary practices and discourse can be seen in his design work at the – now legendary – Berlin Volksbühne. His last design work at the Volksbühne, towards the end of Castorf's appointment, was a so-called durational set: It was a basic black space that was meant to remain in place for at least one season. Neumann had the rows of seats removed from the auditorium and the floors cemented; the whole room was painted in a monochrome black (Figure 5.1, page 95). Comparable with Malevich's *Black Square* (1915) in the visual arts, this move seemed to be a literal and metaphorical overpainting as if designed to set the spatial and scenographical parameters of the theatre back to 'zero'. However, due to the very complicated history of the Volksbühne, there can be no 'point zero', as it were, inscribed within this place as a cultural memory. Therefore, taking the example of Dieter Mersch, one could see a gesture of negation in this, which, at the same time, becomes productive in that it gives the audience pause 'to think' and thus reveals the process of scenography as art as well as an ongoing and (self-)reflexive epistemological practice (Mersch 2015: 123).

II Circulation of scenographic knowledge and cultural transfer

As shown by these examples, the practices and discourses of theatre scenography have spurred much debate in recent years. The same is true, maybe even more so, for related fields, such as exhibition and museum design, performative architecture, scenographic art and design for public urban contexts, as well as the scenography of commercially orientated events. The second part of the book, entitled 'Circulation of scenographic knowledge and cultural transfer', offers some insights into these fields. Transgressions of scenographic approaches across the genres have increased and intensified since the 1990s and particularly since the new millennium (with the EXPO 2000, the World Fair in Hannover), marking a 'scenographic turn' taking place within the various fields of the German-speaking regions. The starting observation – or hypothesis – that the authors of this section work from is that many of recent developments regarding scenography in the field of theatre and performance, as discussed in section one, can similarly be observed in neighbouring fields. Briefly summarized, these are: (1) The (re)definition of scenography as 'writing in space' ('narrative spaces') or as a compositional process (scenographed spaces as 'artistically manipulated and orchestrated environments'). Here scenography is thought of as being a process, not as static sets. (2) The reconsideration of scenographic materiality and the agential potential of things. (3) The various reinterpretations of scenography as 'technical organisms', including networked constellations and 'augmented scenography'. (4) The numerous attempts to activate audiences and involve them in the scenographic constellation intellectually as well as physically and sensually (e.g. by triggering participatory processes, interaction and immersion). From today's range of approaches, the contributions to this section discuss major developments of the past decades, which have taken up, employed or creatively transformed theatre scenography in fields away from the stage. These are projects by artists and designers from various disciplines (including dance, film, installation, media art or architecture) who work across disciplines between stage, gallery and public space. Here one can see artistic, curatorial and dramaturgical practices born from a reflection of the various art forms and their institutions, representing different modes of production and presentation (for instance, the 'black box' vs. the 'white cube'). By reinterpreting their various spatial configurations, social frameworks, institutional rules and aesthetic parameters, new modes of creation and transmission emerge and a temporal offset of previously defined borders occurs. One of the many eminent examples is the work of the Swiss-German artistic group Rimini Protokoll, which is at all times focused on being cross-disciplinary. The group was already mentioned in the last section. Here once again, the group becomes interesting because of how many of their projects meander both on a conceptual level and a scenographic level between the various disciplines. They take place in the theatre, often also in a museum context or within public spaces (they also perpetually travel and tour worldwide; see, for example, their project *Remote X*, Figure I.2).

Based on various, but different, additional examples and by adopting the concept and discourse on 'expanded scenography', as sketched out above, the contributions in section two employ case studies to trace what kind of creative dynamics, knowledge transfers, translational processes and adaptations occur between the arts and the field of design. According to the findings of this section, mainly four developments can be identified within scenography's extended field. First, there are various performing arts projects that are being produced for a museum or gallery space instead of a stage. In turn, these projects ask the question: What place can ephemeral art forms such as theatre, dance and performance art have in a museum? Notably, there are the numerous crossover projects in dance, which, on the one hand, ask how theatre and dance performances can be documented and archived and, on the other, interrogate the situation of an exhibition itself. These pieces explore the museum space as a space where movement happens, is observed and even choreographed (i.e. the curated directional flow through a museum gallery). Prominent examples include the exhibition *Move. Choreographing you!*

FIGURE I.2 *Rimini Protokoll,* Remote X, *Houston edition:* Remote Houston *(2016). Photo © dabfoto creative for the Cynthia Woods Mitchell Center for the Arts at the University of Houston.*

(curated by Stephanie Rosenthal, London, Berlin and Düsseldorf, 2010/11), *Tanz! Wie wir uns und die Welt bewegen* (*Dance! Moves that move us*, Hygiene Museum Dresden, 2013/14) and the solo show of the artist and choreographer William Forsythe, *The Fact of Matter* (Frankfurt am Main, 2015). Such projects, which simultaneously resemble performative installations and interactive environments, involve the visitor intellectually, physically and kinaesthetically. In these projects, scenography and choreography are understood and explored as being interdependent. One such hybridized artefact is Forsythe's work on the 'choreographic object'. The artefacts are constellations without dancers, where audience members become the players of a composed, yet open, 'spatial score' (see Kirsten Maar's chapter). By referencing practices of dance and movement rotation, as well as compositional techniques of organizing space, sounds and movement introduced by John Cage, Allan Kaprow and the Fluxus movement (graphic notation, scores, scripts, instructions for performance), Forsythe's works prompt all participants to reflect on the question of how space is brought forth in each and every moment of the actual event. In other words, it asks which cultural practices, media and spatio-temporal codes are at play within the design, production and reception of space and movement and which epistemological framework is at work during these moments.

Beyond the thematically specific projects that oscillate between exhibition, art project and artistic practice as research, a more general shift in the relationship between art and performance can be observed within the German context since the 1990s. Propelled by spectacular events, such as the EXPO 2000 in Hannover, or mammoth projects, such as the *Sieben Hügel* (Seven Hills; Gropius Bau, Berlin 2000), a show that aimed at presenting the history and future of technology as if in a 'cabinet of 21st century curiosities' (Sievernich et al. 2000), scenographic design was broadly introduced and translated into the field of exhibitions, museums as well as into public urban spaces, corporate design and commercially oriented events. This process was prepared and accompanied by the founding of numerous design studios specializing in scenographic and spatial design, for example TRIAD Berlin (since 1994), ART+COM (since 1988), Tamschick Media+Space (since 1995), Chezweitz Berlin (since 2000), and others.[15] A particularly prominent example of this trend is the Stuttgart-based studio Atelier Brückner. Founded in 1997 by Uwe R. Brückner, himself a trained stage designer, and his team, the studio has since grown to about 100 employees. The studio realizes scenographic designs for exhibitions and museums in Germany and around the world. One of their recent (and probably largest) projects is the interior design and exhibition concept of the Grand Egyptian Museum (Gizeh 2018). Further, their portfolio includes commercial projects, that is, corporate environments and spaces for brands. Contemporary scenography, thus, encompasses all of these practices. What one also notices is that many of the design studios do not just inform about the portfolio of their projects (and design awards if applicable) or the self-initiated book projects on their websites; they also give us extensive insights into the methods of how they work scenographically. Through this, their interdisciplinary competence and skills come to the fore and are made clear for all to see (Tamschick and Tamschick 2015; Atelier Brückner 2016 [2011], 2019). This is very different from what we know from the field of art in general; here, concepts and even design methods are named and dealt with.[16] Regardless of their mainly commercial focus (or maybe also driven by this), these activities see themselves as being at the interface of new technologies, of art and design as creative research. In their contribution to this book, Uwe R. Brückner and Linda Greci from Atelier Brückner discuss the question of how their studio positions itself within the scenographic field and current discourse. Based on case studies from their own work, their focal question is: 'How does one develop narrative architectures, experience-oriented exhibition and synaesthetic scenographies?'[17] By often (and sometimes even explicitly) referring to theatrical means in their scenographic work, they have developed their own design approach, which is continually revised and always connected to research, theoretical debate and what they call their 'design philosophy'. Reflecting on the studio's international reach, they also remain mindful of keeping an inter-/transcultural perspective and ask whether there is a 'cultural specificity to scenography' or whether we can conceive of a 'globalized form of art and design' and, if so, what are the dynamics of this cross-cultural exchange (see their chapter on this)? Referencing German design theorist Susanne Hauser, these processes of reflection can be called 'redesigning design' (Hauser 2016).

Contemporary debates on scenography, be it in the performing arts, museums or profit-oriented firms, are obviously in flux. At times, they can be costly and showy, especially when it comes to their high-tech iterations in business contexts, as is the case for cross-media advertising or staged commercial events. It would be conceivable to discuss this expansion and adaptation of scenographic practices under the umbrella of a 'theatricalization' of the everyday (Warstat 2014 [2005]) and to note the performative character of contemporary (Western) cultures, where everyday life is endlessly produced as a visual and experiential spectacle. Considering the wide range of 'expanded scenography', however, these explanations seem neither sufficient nor particularly illuminating. The various artistic or design-oriented approaches, be they aesthetic concepts, critical interventions or commercial endeavours, are too diverse for this singular line of argumentation. This is even more so since experimental architecture recently provided a different basis from which to understand quasi-scenographic practices attempting to generate different and, crucially, temporary rooms outside of previously defined institutional frames. In Germany particularly, the reclaiming of and the demand for free spaces for artistic and social use has been a burning topic since the reunification of the early 1990s, where, combined with the phenomenon of 'shrinking cities' in eastern Germany, a process of gentrification has started in most of the larger German cities (East and West), including Berlin. Run-down city centres and urban areas were luxuriously renovated, making them more attractive to private investors, thus driving out former residents. Here, scenography and temporary architecture intervene to point out the dynamics taking place and to create heterotopic spaces for a certain amount of time. In addition to these economic shifts, which very obviously affect public spaces, certain ecological developments also need to be taken into account when discussing contemporary scenography, such as the observation that today, even in nature, there are very few – if any – areas not yet subjected to human intervention; areas that have not been technologically shaped, manipulated or regulated. Further, due attention must be given to the digital turn and the ubiquitous presence of digital media, particularly as these forces permeate and shape our cultural and social lives. Spatial art, architecture and scenography have responded to this shift. Joachim Sauter from the Berlin-based studio ART+COM, for example, posits: 'The big difference today to the communication within a space of the pre-digital times is that people have become aware of the qualities of new media – such as interaction, collaboration and networking – and they also have come to expect them in an actual communication space' (Sauter 2011: 224). All these factors affect design practices since artists and designers need to position themselves with regard to these developments, confronting them critically or affirming them positively. Whether they act as critics, generators of new ideas or a combination of the two, the differences between 'art' and 'design', between 'free' and 'applied' are no longer easily distinguishable. In light of this, others are looking for a third way. In her work, Berlin-based artist Annett Zinsmeister, for instance, attempts to address the changing contexts and structural shifts in artistic and commercial production on a meta-level. Her chapter in this book gives insights into her long-term artistic research on serial structures and the so-called *Plattenbau* (which refers to the industrialized Soviet-style apartment buildings of the GDR), which she translates in media art and installation works (that are exhibited in galleries and museums). Finally, the architecture and artistic collective raumlaborberlin pursues yet another creative approach; their work crosses the disciplines between experimental architecture, urban planning, artistic intervention and activism. Their scenographic work is neither tied to artistic nor commercial endeavours; instead, they focus on 'radical social design' which uses scenography as an intervention method into public spaces. Their audiences (or perhaps collaborators is the better word) do not only become involved during the actual happening of the event but are called upon earlier to participate in the design and construction phases (see Benjamin Foerster-Baldenius' chapter in this book). In other words, 'expanded scenography', in these cases, means that the audience themselves become largely responsible for the designing, planning and realization of their imagined spaces.

III Rethinking scenography

By examining a choice of significant design practices and positions, the case studies and analyses assembled in this book once again raise the question of a theory of scenography. Looking at this range of practices, we need to ask ourselves what theories and methodologies are productive when dealing with this field. This is what the third part of this book, titled 'Rethinking scenography', attempts to answer. To this day, a definition of scenography is being debated; however, there is some consensus around the basic premise of scenography being a 'cultural technique' (Gethmann and Hauser 2009; Siegert 2015). As it has been made clear, this new premise sees scenography – notwithstanding its previous iterations as backdrop, scenery or decoration – as a discursive formation through which space is created, produced and reflected; under this principle it has gained significant cultural relevance in recent decades. The case studies in section one and two have exemplified how contemporary scenography operates in various fields. To identify and explore the varied scenographic processes and scenographed constellations within their respective artistic, epistemological and discursive contexts, the chapters take up, and also move beyond, the analytical methods and tools provided by theatre and performance studies (such as semiotics, performativity and media theory), by combining them with more recent theoretical approaches, such as relational aesthetics, affect theory and new materialism. In addition, they also define principles, such as technological space, architectural space, materiality, participation and agency, sketching them out, and introduce more appropriate methodological frameworks as in McKinney and Palmer's seminal study on 'expanded scenography' (2017: 4–18). Part three of this book aims to focus on this theoretical debate. One of the main theses of our book, though, is that scenography cannot be primarily understood through performance analysis, audience experience and theories of perception. Instead, the analyses of the various scenographic concepts, 'art as research' projects and scenographic interventions in this book observe that the production and reception of scenography cannot be viewed as being separate from each other. As these analyses show, contemporary scenography, in its diverse forms, is often better understood as a performative event or, more precisely, a production process unfolding so that its own aesthetic parameters, media, tools, epistemes and cultural references become apparent or even highlighted during the moment where production meets reception; that is, during the moment of the performance. Thus, scenography is not a constructed artefact but, as Dieter Mersch suggests in his chapter, should be thought of as being a 'composition', constellation or network of things, matters and actions; as such, it is inherently incomplete and dynamic, which – according to Mersch – makes it both ungovernable and uncontrollable and speaks most clearly of its close relation to art. Wolf-Dieter Ernst's contribution postulates tools for analysis by combining Bruno Latour's actor-network theory with performance analysis. Ernst's approach connects to Mersch as well as to McKinney and Palmer who, in their 2017 study, also claim that scenography needs to be rethought and explored 'as a network or an organism – a whole with interdependent parts – a matrix of individuals, ideas and things that might produce scenographic agency' (2017: 17). With his case study, and by using Rimini Protokoll's installation and multiplayer video piece *Situation Rooms* (2013) as an example, he contributes to the shift in analysis and research perspective that this book attempts to undertake. According to this perspective, a visitor to a multimedia constellation, such as the one that can be found in *Situation Rooms*, is a human actor, who is – in situ – in a symmetrical relation with a non-human scenographic constellation. It can be assumed that this theoretical approach and way of thinking about scenography is not yet very widespread in Germany. To find out more about the current standards in education, Thea Hoffmann-Axthelm and

Robert Kraatz have undertaken an analysis of the scenography degree courses that are currently being offered at universities and art academies in Austria, Switzerland and Germany. According to their survey, the discourse here is very much in motion while, obviously, there are considerable differences between the individual courses and study programmes. In the last chapter of this volume, Serge von Arx, a Swiss-born architect and scenographer who works and teaches internationally (i.e. at the Norwegian Theatre Academy, Fredrikstad, at Robert Wilson's Watermill Center in New York, Long Island and at Zurich University of the Arts) offers his thoughts on contemporary (German) scenography, coming from a cross-cultural and comparative perspective. In his conversation with the editor – which also is a preliminary resume of the book's discussions – he pleads for an ongoing rethinking and understanding of scenography as a research-oriented practice, a context-based analysis and a cross-cultural discourse. In this sense, he envisions scenography as being an 'open field': Instead of trying to define it, he suggests that scenography 'finds quality in openness and the indefinable', a potential that posits an even greater challenge for the formation of tools for analysis and a body of theory.

Rethinking scenography: Scenography as *dispositif*: Notes on the analytical and methodological approach of this book

I don't build spaces, I think spatially
WILFRIED MINKS 2011: 247.

This edited volume provides insights into contemporary Germany scenography and it is addressed to an international readership. The case studies and analyses presented move beyond artistic and aesthetic criteria to explore how scenographic practices relate to traditions, cultural discourses, and institutions as well as to epistemological histories and the recent social and political shifts, such as globalization, migration and the intercultural transfer. Beyond the analysis of individual projects or artistic styles, our study conceptualizes scenography as a *dispositif*; scenography is thus seen as a praxis and a discourse within a cultural and social framework. The French term *'dispositif'* (meaning 'apparatus', or a device in general) was introduced by Michel Foucault to describe a concept of social (self-)description, a tool to observe and differentiate various networks and 'heterogeneous ensembles' of institutions, persons, discourses and practices (quoted from Gordon 1980: 194). Accordingly, our volume proposes to analyse scenography as a process of both production and reception while taking into account its institutional contexts and discursive settings. The contributions to the volume represent scholarly perspectives of both art and design theory, while also giving a voice to practitioners of stage design and scenography coming from different occupational fields. Furthermore, these analyses aim at tracing the ways in which scenography's cross-disciplinary expansion within the various fields changes its modes of artistic production as well as the way it is perceived and understood by different audiences. The contributions, particularly those by the practitioners, reflect on processes of scenographic creation and make their diversity and respective differences visible – when it comes to the artistic approaches taken, designs as well as 'modes of thought' (see the chapters by Aleksandar Denić, Sophie Rois, Klaus Grünberg, Uwe R. Brückner and Linda Greci from Atelier Brückner and Benjamin Foerster-Baldenius/raumlaborberlin). By giving glimpses into their own creative work they identify scenographic concepts, design methods (including the media used) as well as the various work steps, starting from the first drafts all the way up to the realization. The impact of scenographic design tools, particularly models (scale models, 3D modelling) and the various forms of scenographic notation (scores, scripts, storyboards, graphic composition), is reconsidered and discussed (see the chapters by Denić, Brückner/Greci and Maar). As these chapters argue, these tools – that for a long time were considered to be mere by-products – now demand that they be considered both aesthetically and theoretically. This is especially the case as these tools have become artistically reinterpreted. It has become a widely applied practice to present such artefacts in exhibitions or on stage as 'autonomous objects', to reflect on them on a meta-level and to point to their communicative function, mediality and creative role within design processes.[18] Clearly, this approach – which can be termed as being 'meta-scenographic' (Scorzin 2011) – is about analysing scenographic aesthetics and, moreover, identifying epistemes. The aim is to explore the conditions, effects and critical potentials of a specifically artistic generation of knowledge: How is scenography's epistemological repertoire produced, reinterpreted, presented and disseminated? Recent debates on 'research in the arts' (see for example Biggs and Karlsson 2011) have touched upon similar questions, yet not many have focused particularly on scenography. To fill the gaps within this debate, the approach of this book operates from the assumption that studios and rehearsal rooms are *not* places of 'different knowledge' or even another type of laboratory – as is often asserted in discourses of *art as research* (see Borgdorff 2012). Similar to Borgdorff, the performance studies scholar Annemarie Matzke has suggested using the term 'experimental system' for the analysis of studio work and theatre rehearsal processes in order to examine how 'individual artistic questions cross-over with the institutional ramifications of the theatre as well as its production techniques and instruments' (Matzke 2015: 191). The term 'experimental system' was introduced some time ago to epistemology and the history of science by the theoretician Hans-Jörg Rheinberger; by using this term he expressed the idea that to judge the results that come from laboratory work, one always has to discuss the instrumental and material conditions of laboratory situations (Rheinberger 2001). Transferred to the discussion of theatre, the arts and design, this research approach seems fruitful since it allows one to explore the usage of, for example, scenographic scores or of modals as a cultural technique, or even a 'phenomeno-technique' (Bachelard 2002 [1938]: 70). Yet, it is questionable whether experimental systems can be applied sensibly to artistic research and design practices. Philosopher Dieter Mersch, a contributor to this book, succinctly states that 'despite the obvious experimental character of aesthetic practices, they are not experimental *systems* as defined by Rheinberger. In the latter, tools, log books, and observation aid systematic research; art, however, tends towards the faltering, the chaotic, and the erratic' (Mersch 2015: 19). It is exactly these disruptions, ruptures and countereffects from which creation and aesthetic reflection arise. Thus, artist's ateliers, design studios and rehearsal rooms are not to be thought of as 'laboratories' but as heterotopic places for creative experiments and for the search for the unknown (see von Arx and Wiens in this book).

'Design never starts from point zero': this thesis was put forward by Serge von Arx during our Munich conference (2016) and while we were working on this book. It hints at the multiple cultural contexts, artistic inspirations, epistemological histories, institutional framings and economic conditions of scenography and thus it became one of the *leitmotifs* of this book. Following this approach, this volume presents contextualized and in-depth analyses of some of the most recent developments, which the contributing artists, designers and scholars have identified as the most influential practices in Geman-speaking countries. It showcases contributions from practitioners within the field, while also offering some outside perspective on the German context. Indeed, scenographic practice – as well as the theoretical discussion of it – does not start from 'point zero', and we are hoping that we can continue these discussions as a dialogue with an international readership.

Notes

1 Patrice Pavis' handbook articles have been seminal in describing this shift: Pavis 2015/1996, 2007.
2 See the conferences of the European Initiative Scenography and the annually occurring (since 2000) scenography colloquia of the DASA with the respective publications (www.scenology.eu, www.dasa-dortmund.de).

INTRODUCTION

See also the event that takes place annually in Ludwigsburg: *Raumwelten (Spatial Worlds – Platform for Scenography, Architecture and Media)*, www.raum-welten.com.

3   Foucault introduced the term in the late 1970s in 'The Confession of the Flesh' (1977), interview in Gordon 1980: 194–228; cf. Wimmer, 'Dispositiv', in Frietsch 2012: 123–30.

4   In 1994, the Centre Pompidou in Paris dedicated an individual exhibition to the artist (1930–2017): *Wilfried Minks – Scénographe*; see Union des Théâtres de l'Europe 1997 (exhibition catalogue).

5   For a photo of the scale model, see the built model on page 43 in this book.

6   See Nioduschewski (2010) and her portrait of Katrin Brack on pp. 15 and 20.

7   In the assembled contributions for this book, Rasche's works are not discussed further. They are of course relevant and, just as the scenographic approaches of Christoph Schlingensief, Kay Voges/Michael Sieberock-Serafimowitsch and others, they are briefly mentioned.

8   A video of Rasche's production *The Robbers* is available online, www.youtube.com/watch?v=5LyU-J1mCAA.

9   Quoted from www.residenztheater.de (accessed 30 August 2018).

10 *Theater der Welt* was founded in 1981 by the German centre of the International Theatre Institute (ITI) as a biennial festival. It became triennial in 1993; each festival edition takes place in a different city in Germany and with a different artistic director. See www.iti-germany.de.

11 The series included plays such as *Erniedrigte und Beleidigte* (The Humiliated and Insulted; 2001), *Der Idiot* (The Idiot; 2002), *Der Spieler* (The Player; 2011) and, finally, *Die Brüder Karamasow* (The Brothers Karamazov; 2015).

12 This prize, named after the stage designer and film scenographer Hein Heckroth (1901–79), is awarded every two years by the city of Gießen; www.hein-heckroth-ges.de (accessed 30 June 2018).

13 See also their 'Academy for Theatre and the Digital', founded in February 2018, in collaboration with the Folkwang-Schule Essen and other partners; www.enjoy-complexity.de (accessed 30 June 2018).

14 Of course, such projects have precursors in the media arts of the last few decades and are particularly indebted to telematics; see Daniels 2002.

15 For a more thorough overview see Kiedaisch, Marinescu and Poesch 2019.

16 See the design approach of the agency TRIAD Berlin, sketched out on its website, www.triad.de/en/company/method/ (accessed 10 October 2018)

17 www.atelier-brueckner.com/en/atelier (accessed 10 October 2018)

18 For observations of these (meta-)reflexive practices see for example Brejzek and Wallen's *The Model as Performance* (2018), and Amelunxen, Appelt and Weibel's comprehensive study on *Notation* (2008); the term 'meta-scenography' was coined by Pamela C. Scorzin (Scorzin 2011).

PART ONE

Scenography in and beyond the theatre: Aesthetics and epistemes

PART ONE

Scenography and beyond the theatre: aesthetic and existence

1

'I am trying to add more layers to the story': From the model to the stage

Scenographic thinking and artistic practices in Aleksandar Denić's theatre works with Frank Castorf and others

A conversation between Aleksandar Denić and Birgit E. Wiens

Stage designers play an important role when it comes to the development of theatre productions; their work is an integral part of the productions, of the artistic conceptions and of the aesthetic form of a staging that they often decisively influence. Usually, however, the theatre audience only experiences the result of their work in the framework of the actual staging itself. The creative impact that stage design has – in other words, the entire process that takes place in the studio, within the theatre workshops and during rehearsals until the opening night – is rarely ever reflected in theatre reviews or even discussed in academic publications;[1] moreover, it has also been largely marginalized within the ongoing debate on 'artistic research' and 'research in the arts'.² Within this book, the various chapters focus, from different perspectives, on questions of scenographic design processes, artistic practices, tools and 'scenographic thinking' as well as 'knowledge production'. This chapter – very much practice based – presents a workshop discussion with one of the most acclaimed scenographers in contemporary German theatre, Aleksandar Denić. In the course of the conversation, we will introduce some of his major works; thus perspective on the 'making-of', on the scenographic process from the model to the stage, is at the centre of the discussion.

Denić, who is based in Belgrade (Serbia), is a scenographer who, since the late 1980s, has mainly worked as a production designer in the film industry; within the German-language theatre world, and also internationally, he became known in recent years for his ongoing collaboration with the theatre director and former artistic director of the Berlin Volksbühne at the Rosa-Luxemburg-Platz, Frank Castorf.³ In their numerous renowned and award-winning productions, Castorf and Denić carry out a type of collaboration that is principally non-hierarchical and fuelled by artistic dynamics in which both – the director and the scenographer – understand the other to be a partner on equal terms. This form of artistic collaboration, which Castorf also shared with Bert Neumann (his long-time stage designer since the late 1980s, who passed away in 2015), had its historic prefiguration in the research-based production mode that Bertolt Brecht and his stage designers, mainly Caspar Neher, had developed (de Ponte 2006). With their so-called model productions, they had not only searched for a 'new type of performance', but also aimed at implementing a decidedly modern 'work sharing' collaboration model within the theatre.⁴ Castorf's theatre, in a certain sense, can be seen in this tradition. Since, on the aesthetic level, his productions at the Berlin Volksbühne were typically marked by a non-linear, radical and multi-perspective narration, they were often described as 'postdramatic theatre' (using the term coined by Hans-Thies Lehmann in 1999). The term also implies that, in these kinds of theatrical forms, scenography (or 'visual dramaturgy', as he also puts it) can actually become as important – or sometimes even more important – as the play text (Lehmann 1999: 158–61). As influential as Lehmann's term had been for quite a long time in German-language theatre discourse – and beyond it – it is after all, as Matt Cornish states, 'not always useful' for understanding twenty-first-century scenographic aesthetics (Cornish 2018: 465). Also, it does not say much about the changes in artistic production forms and the ways in which they question standardized schemes of theatrical production. Thus, when we talk about what we have termed the 'scenographic process' in the theatre, we need particularly to describe the creative process, the decision-making, the rehearsals and the various modes of collaboration; nowadays, they are complex, often experimental, so they have become nearly as diverse as the artistic signatures and the aesthetics themselves.

The stages of Aleksandar Denić, a few of which will be discussed in the following, are probably best described as hybrid spatial structures loaded with references to our urban surroundings as well as to the history of our recent past. Denić's years of experience in the film industry are definitely noticeable when looking at these spatial compositions. But instead of designing 'sets' or 'backdrops', he creates multi-storey, labyrinth-like stage architectures that are accessible and often take up the entire height and width of the stage. Typically, these constructions are full of small details, which at first glance can barely be recognized or deciphered. Preferably, they are set on a revolving stage, so that they are moveable and can even be turned in front of the audience's eyes. Like in most productions with Castorf, there can also live film sequences being played as well as an excessive use of cameras on the stage, which again exponentially adds to the aesthetic complexity of these designs. In terms of semiotics, Denić's spatial setups are multilayered and ambiguous while, phenomenologically, they seem to be highly energetic and expressive. 'At first glance all of it seems familiar. But if you look closer then you realize that such constellations would never exist in reality' is how he himself describes his designs.[5] Compared with the feature- and equipment-oriented film scenography with all of its requirements, theatre work obviously allows for more artistic freedom. Nevertheless, Denić does reuse a lot from film when it comes to the drafts and design practices and the technical tools. For example, he uses – much more than most other stage designers – computer programs, animation as well as 3D simulations, during the creative design process. The following discussion gives insights into his artistic way of thinking, and explains how he actually works.

Aleksandar Denić, your stage settings have been described as being 'monumental nightmares' (Cornish 2018: 468), in which – at the sketching level – different historical contexts and location references are intertwined. They are complex structures; with their oversupply of signs, they are not easily readable and often they spread a threatening atmosphere that cannot be rationally grasped by a theatre audience. An explicit example here is the stage that you designed for Journey to the End of the Night *(Residenztheater Munich, 2013), a theatre adaptation of Louis-Ferdinand Céline's semi-biographical novel* (Voyage au Bout de la Nuit, *1932). It is set in the First World War, colonial Africa, post-war America and Paris, and deals with the traumatizing events as well as the misanthropy and world weariness of the protagonist.*

The stage design for this production, an assembly of Céline's text with scenes from Heiner Müller's *Der Auftrag* (*The Task*), was a courtyard located in Congo, combined with the entrance of the Auschwitz concentration camp. During the Second World War, Ferdinand Céline collaborated with the Nazis, then he went into exile, later returning to France, and was celebrated as being one of the best French writers of his generation. Nobody approached him, but when he died, only a few days later, someone burned down his house, as if to say that his art work can be respected but not his political attitude and what he had done. For a similar reason, I quoted the Auschwitz entrance door, but replaced the inscription *Arbeit macht frei* ('Work sets you free') with *Liberté, Égalité, Fraternité*. What happened to these ideals, to 'liberty, equality, fraternity'; where have those postulates of democracy gone? Scenography, I think, has to be thought-provoking. To achieve this, I use various elements, in this case a photo of Céline and various objects that connect to his biography, for example a first aid box, since over the years, he had worked as a medical doctor specializing in epidemic control and disease protection, aside from writing books and articles. The scene was located in the African jungle: a troublesome camp, built of bare wood and scrap metal, and above all of it, there was a large screen, which was used for projecting live videos. On the scene, there was a van, like the mobile hospitals used by Médecins du Monde or Médecins sans Frontières, after whose humanitarian interventions, only flags and banners remain. I also included advertising posters for movies, especially the so-called blaxploitation movies that were released in the 1970s, and Cassius Clay's famous 'Rumble in the Jungle', which was a boxing match but also a huge, liberating event for black people, African people and African American people at the time. But where are we now; what is the situation today? My aim is, here and now, to raise such questions using artistic means. Like in this production, my designs usually are structures composed of strong symbols, small emblems and heterogeneous signs; in other words: they are 'scenographic allegories'. Parts of these sets are hyperrealistic but all in all, in the way they recontextualize and combine things, they are hugely imaginary – in fact, they are impossible constructions. My task is not to be provocative or rude but to provide, with the means of scenography, some 'food for thought'. The creative potential of this approach becomes particularly obvious in opera productions. In opera, as we know, the libretto is set – you cannot escape, you can't change the storyline. But as we showed with the *Ring* at the Richard Wagner Festival in Bayreuth (2013) or, more recently, with our staging of Charles Gounod's *Faust* at the Stuttgart State Opera (2016), you can add more layers to the story and thus open it up.

Castorf's staging of Wagner's Ring des Nibelungen (The Ring of the Nibelung) *and your stage designs were described as being a kaleidoscope of references, locations and associations. In this production, the Nibelung myth was reinterpreted as a parable of our contemporary fixation on the quests for power, financial profit and world domination through the control of 'liquid gold' – oil. Your designs, placed on a revolving stage, led the audience from an American motel on Route 66* (Das Rheingold) *to the early days of oil*

FIGURE 1.1 *Aleksandar Denić*, Reise ans Ende der Nacht *(Journey to the End of the Night), directed by Frank Castorf, Munich, Residenztheater, 2013. Photo © Aleksandar Denić.*

production in Azerbaijan (Die Walküre), *and from there onto Mount Rushmore* (Siegfried), *to Alexanderplatz in Berlin, then to a run-down GDR apartment block, and finally to the Stock Exchange of Wall Street* (Götterdämmerung).[6] *Reviewers complained that, with the 'essentially non-Wagnerian' approach of the staging, you were all too rigorously doing away with Wagner's concept of the* Gesamtkunstwerk,[7] *while others, however, admittedly valued it as being a 'provocative, irritating yet fascinating production'.*[8]

It is pretty obvious what we did in Bayreuth with Wagner's *Ring*, and indeed, it became much debated. By tracing the history of oil, we did indeed add more layers to Wagner's opera, and the stories were even conveyed on a parallel basis. With my designs, I am sending out a lot of messages. At first, that was difficult for parts of the classic audience in Bayreuth – there was a lot of booing; later on, our approach became more accepted and in the end, it was celebrated.

These stage designs are attention seeking but also disorienting, thought-provoking and on the conceptual level quite complex – not only with regard to their rich visual facets but also in terms of materiality and spatial dimensions. How are they conceived and created, and what can be said about the artistic collaboration, rehearsals and the production processes? Could you give us some insights?

First of all, it might be important to mention that I work both in film and in theatre, and I don't make any distinction about how I approach projects in these different fields. I work in my studio. I have my own team, which is organized akin to the production companies in the film industry and, within this team, I have several assistants who are responsible for their own parts (e.g. model making, drawing and construction plans). All this work also supports the production process in the theatre. We prepare a lot in advance to make it easier for the theatres to apply our concepts.

Still, for the theatres and their workshops, this can become quite challenging. For instance, in Bayreuth your interpretation of Brunnhilde's rock in Siegfried, *the third part of the* Ring *cycle, became a communist version of Mount Rushmore, featuring Karl Marx, Vladimir I. Lenin, Joseph Stalin and Mao Zedong.*

This mountain, of course, does not exist, but for *Siegfried*, transforming Mount Rushmore and playing with these icons go well with the story. During the past century, the world was divided mainly into two parts, two systems, and the battle over energy, that is, oil, was a major component of the Cold War. Accordingly, I built that Western monument (or my version of it) on one side of the revolving stage, and on the other side I set up a replica of Berlin Alexanderplatz, with the world clock and all of the other things located there, as Berlin used to be the symbol of the once-divided world, East and West. Those heads of Marx, Lenin, Stalin and Mao were relatively big, 15 metres high and about 22 metres wide, and making them was a particular challenge (and quite an unusual task for the theatre workshops). But my sculptor in Belgrade is an expert in these kinds of tasks. He used photos during the production process. Based on these, he built a sculpture, or to be more precise, a model at the scale of 1:20. Using the model, we found out what exactly these four heads should look like. For instance, I told him that when they are onstage and people in the audience are looking at them, there should be no direct eye contact. That is to say no one can tell if these four guys were right or wrong, if they were lying or even if they were criminals and what they had to hide, so no eye contact was a prerequisite. The sculptor did a great job, and with his model, we went to Ingolstadt and got in touch with Jürgen Uedelhoven from Uedelhoven studios, who is a production designer specializing in car design – he works for Audi and Bugatti, among others. There, our model was scanned in high resolution and, by using the most advanced computer program for 3D surface calculations, a huge milling machine and several tons of polyurethane foam, basically our Mount Rushmore was built. To bring it to Bayreuth, it had to be subdivided into smaller parts. At the festival theatre, they were assembled and brought into shape, and finally the whole object was painted. Of course, all these efforts went far beyond the conventional work process of stage design and what is usually required from the theatre workshops and technical departments. But – and even though Frank Castorf and I had only one year of preparation time for the *Ring* (which is even less time than you would usually have for one opera) – we managed to realize this project. A catalyst in the process was definitely the way we understand technology and how we make use of it. In our opinion, it should not be about producing stage effects or even claiming new aesthetics; we consider technology to be merely a tool.

A discussion of the Ring, *which Castorf and you as the stage designer produced and staged collaboratively, could probably fill an entire book. Maybe we should talk about other theatre productions and sets a bit more, using another example. In 2016 you designed, together with Austrian director Martin Kušej, the stage for the production of Goethe's* Faust *at the Munich Residenztheater.*

The initial idea for the Munich production of *Faust* was to build a very large and dark structure, a structure with several archaeological layers, that would reference the political, historical and social dimensions of Goethe's tragic play, as well as the ballast of interpretation and ideological appropriations that affect this piece. Faust's world is dreary; the only contrast in the fully black construction was to be a white room in the centre of the stage: Gretchen's home, which at the very beginning was clean and innocent and in the course of the action became splattered with blood and then destroyed.

You have worked as a scenographer and production designer for film as well as a stage designer for the theatre and, as you have mentioned, when approaching these two fields, you make no distinction. Still, German theatres and opera houses particularly – on the institutional and organizational level, as well as on the level of artistic work and collaboration – predefine certain working conditions, in terms of traditions, hierarchies but also when it comes to funding and the financial means one has at one's disposal. With regard to this, how would you describe both the creative process and the production process, taking Faust *as an example?*

First of all, I meet the director – in this case it was Martin Kušej – and make suggestions. After we agree on a direction – and both of us think we are going in a good direction – I make sketches. I prepare a computer model in accord with the sketches, then the 3D model and some small animations, and, at that point, the presentation is ready. Then I meet the director again and we talk about the design and its potential. Basically, this should be a collaborative process on equal terms, sharing the decision-making. I am not interested in a process with somebody telling me, 'We need two doors here and two chairs over there'. That would not be a job for me. As a stage designer, I work intuitively, set goals and play for the team, but I need to have my hands free;

there has to be artistic freedom. And, most importantly, there has to be a high level of trust between the director and myself.

With your designs you forego abstraction and illusion and they are no set designs in a conventional sense but the designs can, if you will, best be described as being complex, multilevel architectural constructions, which open up for many different situations. The abundance of detail is striking. To the director and the actors or actresses of a theatre production, these stages seem to offer almost unlimited possibilities for scenic activity, interaction and movement. Most of it is on the table before the start of rehearsal. Do you discuss these options with the director and with the members of the ensemble beforehand?

When presenting my designs, I try to keep it short. My job is to draw and to design the structures, but not to talk. Indeed, the aim is to create playgrounds that offer a variety of options. But then it depends on how the director and artistic team use their imagination; it is very rare that I tell them: 'You can do this or that', because it's obvious. Before this, during the phase of design work, drawing and model making, I undertake a lot of research, and usually there is not much left to be developed at a later stage. My designs are somehow finished, they are worlds of their own, and when I present them to the director and artistic team, it's like we are travelling to some other planet: you enter the new world and the planet is ready to be explored. From then on, it is up to the director to survive on that planet. Not every theatre director agrees with working in this manner, but Frank Castorf especially appreciates such a challenge. He told me many times how difficult it is for him; still, we both like this creative work process and our intuitions often run parallel. Of course, it depends very much on whom you are working with. Artistic dynamics can't be controlled, other than the artisanal and technical production processes. Due to my work experience in the film industry, I am used to coping with large productions. When I worked on *Underground* with Emir Kusturica back in 1995, we had film sets of about 70,000 square metres and three years of preparation time. The technical drawings, for instance, were all done by hand, which was a really tough school to go through. Today, using the computer is so much easier and faster. But even more than that, it became important to keep control of the situation both in the studio and in the workshops, for example if I want a stage object to be made of a certain material or colour, I have to be in touch with the workshops and keep control of what is actually being built and produced.

You mentioned the computer; again, what are the tools that you use during both the design and the production processes, and how do you use them? With Frank Castorf, you did another staging of Goethe's Faust *at the Berlin Volksbühne, only a short time after your Munich production with Martin Kušej;*

the Berlin *Faust*, which premièred in March 2017, also became Castorf's farewell production from the theatre of which he had been the artistic director for twenty-five years. Maybe we could focus on this production as a case study?

This production was later also invited to a festival, the 'Theatertreffen 2018', presenting the 'ten most remarkable productions of the last season' from theatre houses in Germany, Austria and Switzerland; that was a real honour. When designing the stage, I first of all – as I always do – made sketches by hand. The next step, using the computer, is to develop so-called 'white models' (Figure 1.2) that allow for the testing of spatial proportions and positions and to see how the design fits on a given stage. The computer program even allows us to go to each seat in the audience and check what the view onto the stage will be like. Then, the following steps are about lighting: we can simulate what it will look like and where the light sources will be and then also try out some atmospheres created by means of colour, composition and light. This feels almost as if we were doing this in the theatre, but everything happens onscreen and via computer. Of course, we also build a physical 3D model as this is still the most important tool during the conceptual discussions with the director and the team. Usually, my model maker in Belgrade builds them to a scale of 1:50; they are relatively small but highly detailed and easier to carry than larger models. This makes perfect sense because I work at theatre and opera houses throughout Europe and have to travel a lot. Sometimes we use a 3D printer. Depending on who we work with, we also built 1:20 models, which is more conventional. All of this happens before presenting the first designs to a director.

Models are both artefacts on their own and design tools that take over certain communicative, operative and aesthetic functions within the respective production processes (Reichle, Siegel and Spelten 2008; Brejzek and Wallen 2018). I'd like to look at these a bit closer. Stage design models are akin to architectural models, but also differ from these. As you said, they are probably the most important medium, or tool, for drafting all the visual elements of the stage and, similar to architectural models, embody construction and design thinking. Stage design models, drafting spaces for the ephemeral art of the theatre, help artistic ideas to be developed and formulated. So they seem to oscillate between replications (e.g. of forms, structures, sign systems to which they can potentially refer) and a future product not fully tangible through the model. Their function is to turn these ideas into something materially concrete and, moreover, to communicate and to present them, namely to the director, the actors and the theatre's technical team, so that they can all discuss their feasibility. Built in miniature, models – as you have described it – provide the possibility of trying out acting potentials, proportions and visual axes (sight lines), simulating atmosphere and light effects, varying the proposed concept and, if necessary, changing it, before the first design is tested during the Bauprobe *(building rehearsal). The final step then is to realize the spatial conception for the stage, in the original size. In general, one could say that stage design models envision spatial concepts and provide hints for the visual, aesthetic and performative potential of the respective concept; by means of a model, artistic thought and design knowledge are condensed in a quite complex manner (and in a way in which language on its own cannot).*

During the design phase in the studio as well as for presentation purposes in the theatre and during the early rehearsals, the model is indeed a key tool. And as a side result of how I work, the *Bauprobe* has become mostly unimportant for me, since we check most of the parameters (spatial dimensions, proportions, views of the stage from the auditorium, etc.) in advance via computer. Our computer-generated models go directly to the design engineer and the workshops; based on the quite accurate information from these (virtual) models, they can start building the set.

A physical model of your Faust *stage design was also built in the workshop of the Berlin Volksbühne and, later on, did not remain in the depot of the theatre*

FIGURE 1.2 *Aleksandar Denić, computer-generated 'white model' for Frank Castorf's staging of* Faust, *Berlin, Volksbühne am Rosa-Luxemburg-Platz, 2017. Screenshot © A. Denić.*

FIGURE 1.3 *Scenic design for Frank Castorf's staging of* Faust *by Aleksandar Denić (2017), physical scale model (model construction: Stage Design Dept. at the Berlin Volksbühne, based on the computer-generated 3D model by A. Denić). © DTM Deutsches Theatermuseum / German Theatre Museum, Munich.*

but was recently even publicly presented under the aegis of an exhibition at the Deutsche Theatermuseum in Munich.⁹ Models are not only design tools, but also documents, 'witnesses' of past performances, and this model (Figure 1.3) tells just about all one needs to know about the stage architecture, the spatial structures and the various locations, that were intended with your design for Castorf's Faust. When starting work on the production, you both had decided to interpret Goethe's drama not first of all as a German narration but as a reflection on European cultural dominance, misogyny and colonialist expansion; thus, the plot – by combining Goethe's text with fragments from Frantz Fanon's The Wretched of the Earth *(1961),* Zola's Nana *and other texts* – is set in twentieth-century Paris during the time of the Algerian war. Based on this idea, the collage-like design combines fragments of historic architectures: a hell's gate (the copy of the façade of the famous Montmartre cabaret 'Café L'Enfer' which in reality existed until 1950) with illuminated letters spelling L'Enfer (hell); next to that there is a kiosk and a cage (the 'human zoo'); above this, the castle-style architecture of the historic 'Café L'Enfer' (including magic figures on the façade); in addition, emergency staircases that lead to various rooms and the balconies on the second and third storey of the structure.

On the ground level: subway stairs (a replica of the Paris Métro station 'Stalingrad'), a pulling cart, numerous beer kegs and, as integral part of the design, a projection screen and a large LED screen. This stage architecture (in some aspects reminiscent of stage constructions that Erwin Piscator had experimented with in the late 1920s)[10] covered the entire circumference of the revolving stage. Scenographic means and in particular the limits of the technological possibilities seemed to be exhausted here as far as possible. During the actual performance the whole stage turned a total of twenty-five times,[11] and in some scenes, it was even a trigger for the stage action. This visual complexity and the spatial dynamics were even exponentiated by video projections of filmed live-action sequences (a camera team was also onstage) or of preproduced material (e.g. short cuts from Gillo Pontecorvo's movie The Battle of Algiers, 1966).

This production is a good example of what I aim at: scenography – or scenic design – should be thought-provoking; that's what I claim at as a stage designer for theatre as well as a production designer for film. Indeed, it became apparent, for example with *Faust* at the Volksbühne, that the stage design can even become another actor – a non-human actor, which performs and conveys its own messages. Just imagine how many messages can be sent to the audience. When appearing onstage, all of these signs and symbols are loaded with history and cultural meaning. Some might feel like they were being poisoned, even radioactive, and some messages might be conflicting and controversial. All of my stage designs operate like this, be it *Journey to the End of the Night*, the *Ring* cycle, *Faust* or other projects. Potentially though, they leave strong impressions and the audience does not even need to grasp every detail. What they will perceive, however, might stick in their minds after the performance and maybe, at a later stage, they will continue interpreting and reflecting. This is what I mean by claiming that stage designs can and do provide 'food for thought'.

Notes

1 Here in fact we have – both within theatre criticism in German-speaking countries as well as in academic theatre and art research – a blind spot. Yet one can also observe that in the past, say, fifteen years more and more publications have come out that have been commissioned by artists themselves or have actually been published by them, with which they, monographically, have given insights into their work methods and creative approaches (viz. Maack and Minks 2011; Nioduschewski and Brack 2010; Müller-Tischer, Ubenauf and Viebrock 2011; SAM and Viebrock 2011; Carp and Ehnes 2015; Audick, Bärenklau and Dresenkamp 2018; or the workshop book Bert Neumann planned with Hatje-Cantz before his death, which was therefore never realized; for 'exhibition scenography', viz. as an example Atelier Brückner 2016/2011, 2019). Thus we currently have a clear and vested interest on the part of the artists in, as it were, opening up their ateliers and inviting audiences to understand how they work.

2. For example, the *Routledge Companion to Research in the Arts*, aside from Catharina Dyrssen's chapter on 'architectural thinking and art-based research', contains no chapter on scenography; also, the terms 'stage design' and 'scenography' cannot be found in the index (cf. Biggs and Karlsson 2011). An exception, elsewhere, is the article by McKinney and Iball (2011).

3. Aleksandar Denić studied film and set design at the University of Arts in Belgrade. Since the late 1980s he has worked on numerous theatre and film productions, including Emir Kusturica's movie *Underground* (1995), *Deathwatch* (directed by M.J. Bassett, 2002) and *Chernobyl Diaries* (by Bradley Parker, 2012). His work includes also more than 100 TV commercials. After meeting Frank Castorf in 2011, their ongoing collaboration began in Paris (*The Lady of the Camellias*, Odéon-Théâtre de l'Europe, 2012), followed by numerous productions at major theatres and opera houses in Germany and internationally.

4. Viz. Wiens 2018; see also A. Matzke: 'Contingency and Plan: Working in Theatre', in Buchmann, Lafer and Ruhm 2010: 58–70.

5. Quoted from: Artist talk with Aleksandar Denić, on the occasion of our conference 'The Art of Scenography: Epistemes & Aesthetics', Munich 2016 (unpublished transcription).

6. For a more detailed description of the production, see Skramstad (2013).

7. Richard Wagner introduced this term in his 1849 essay 'The Artwork of the Future' to describe his vision of an artwork that combined music, poetry, performance and visual arts. Certainly, Castorf's work is much influenced by another aesthetic principle, the 'separation of the elements', famously formulated by Brecht (first in his 'Notes on the Opera *Rise and Fall of the City of Mahagonny*', 1930), which stands in diametric opposition to that of the 'integrated work of art' proposed by Wagner. 'One can understand why some directors, especially Germans and Marxists, may feel uneasy about tackling Wagner's vast work in his own theatre, but that's the challenge', Martin Kettle wrote in his article on Castorf's *Ring* (Kettle 2013).

8. See Skramstad 2013; all in all, the press reviews of both the German as well as international press have been highly controversial (for a synopsis also see Skramstad 2013).

9. See Blank 2018: esp. 136–60.

10. Erwin Piscator, along with Brecht a pioneer of the 'epic theatre', introduced the concept of stage constructions, mechanized sets and movies during his time as stage director at the Volksbühne (1924–7) and, later on, also in his own theatre (the Piscator-Bühne on Nollendorfplatz): 'The scaffolding construction was predominantly purpose-oriented, in order to support the play, to enhance it and to convey meaning. The autonomy of the construction, which is – placed on the revolving stage – a world on its own, eliminates the proscenium of the bourgeois theatre. It could also stand in the free, open space …' (Piscator, quoted from Boeser and Vatkova 1986: 63).

11. According to the director's notes; we would like to thank Carl Hegemann, former dramaturge at the Berlin Volksbühne, for providing a copy of the script of Castorf's *Faust*.

2

Notes on Bert Neumann's stage and costume designs

Scenography as a co-player and counterpart in theatre performances and rehearsals

A conversation between Sophie Rois and Birgit E. Wiens

'Art production is a state of emergency on a permanent basis.' These are the words Bert Neumann chose to describe theatre work and how he defined it.[1] Neumann, born in Magdeburg and raised in East Berlin, became widely known as the long-term artistic partner of Frank Castorf at the Berlin Volksbühne on Rosa-Luxemburg-Platz, where he was head scenic artist from 1992 until his untimely death in 2015.[2] 'Stage designs are social habitats, film studios, living laboratories and, if necessary, entire towns'[3] is how he described the spectrum of his designs by using – almost in the sense of an aesthetic programme – a notion of scenography that extends far beyond the theatre stage and expands into real space, other media, public realms and discourses, namely architecture, urban life and everyday culture. In addition to stage and costume design, the entire visual image campaign of the Volksbühne (including the graphic designs for the posters, programme leaflets and the theatre's famous 'walking wheel' logo) became part of his scenographic work.[4]

When he started working as a scenic designer at the Volksbühne shortly after the fall of the Berlin Wall, Neumann's works were, first of all, artistic reflections on a cultural landscape in transition in which post-socialist experiences clashed with Western lifestyle and consumerism. By combining provisional architecture, plastic chairs, neon lamps, flowery wallpaper, cheap clothing and other low-cost goods from contemporary mass production with quotes from pop songs, advertising and political symbols and signs, he created designs that, in their rawness, ambiguity and ironic dreariness, were unsettling. Thus, these works did not merely operate on an aesthetic level but also implied critical perspectives on shifting political and socioeconomical conditions. Artistically compelling and complex, these scenographic designs reached beyond the 'given' theatre space while, at the same time, they were also reflecting and commenting on contemporary as well as historic stage forms and staging conventions (examples are the Volksbühne *Amphitheatre* project, 2009, the *New Globe*, 1999, or his *Neustadt*, 2002/3, inspired by the theatre works of Erwin Piscator).[5] 'For me, scenic design does not end at the proscenium, but encompasses the whole theatre space including the auditorium. Experimenting with different forms, to me, is exciting', Neumann once explained.[6] Apparently, he considered the theatre as being a heterotopic space and explored it as such (in the Foucaultian sense). 'Doing scenography' meant that the parameters, references and artistic rules used in the artistic processes had to be constantly negotiated and reflected on. This applied not only to the work in his own studio but also to the collaborative work in the rehearsals room and onstage.

The following conversation with Sophie Rois allows for some insights into these processes. Sophie Rois, who is an actress and one of Germany's most acclaimed performing artists, has been a long-term member of the ensemble of the Berlin Volksbühne. As one of this theatre's leading performers, she has collaborated with Bert Neumann for many years. 'As an actress, I am often asked questions about the director or my colleagues, but hardly ever about the scenic designer. Obviously, not many people are aware of how important they are and how much they contribute to the theatre and the productions' was one of her initial observations before this talk.[7] Sophie Rois, born in Austria, moved to Berlin after studying acting at the Max-Reinhardt-Seminar in Vienna. Since 1993, she has been member of the Volksbühne ensemble, which, for almost twenty-five years, she considered to be her 'artistic home'.[8] Being involved both in theatre productions and in productions for television and film, she has worked, among others, with movie directors Detlev Buck, Tom Tykwer and Vanessa Lapa, as well as with theatre directors such as Christoph Schlingensief, Frank Castorf, Christoph Marthaler, Herbert Fritsch and

René Pollesch, to name a few. Compared to other theatres and production contexts, the Volksbühne ensemble and staff, strongly affected by Bert Neumann's approach, thought of their playhouse as a laboratory where theatre work would potentially transform into a 'research journey', according to a type of research that uses so far 'unknown procedures', so that the results were always 'fully unknown' beforehand. 'One has to go and see what one can find and what one can discover. It's very open …'.[9] 'For me, it was the encounter with Bert Neumann that became essential … the way he thought and how we collaborated, and the way in which … all of this became artistically expressed', recalls Sophie Rois.[10] In return, Neumann had emphasized on numerous occasions that, for him, much of the creative work depends on a dialogue: 'The most exciting thing about theatre is: finding the right partners that commit to this way of working and collaborating' (Neumann 2013).

Scenic design became a crucial factor for the Volksbühne's works and the formation of the theatre's aesthetics – with Bert Neumann's designs and also the different scenographic languages and works by guest artists such as Anna Viebrock, Hartmut Meyer, Penelope Wehrli, Katrin Brack, Jonathan Meese, Vegard Vinge and Ida Müller, and Aleksandar Denić. These experiments and the particularly research-oriented attitude not only affected the Volksbühne's aesthetics, but notably implied ongoing reflections on the shared practices and techniques and on how collaborative work should be organized. 'A long-lived but false idea is the belief that theatre work is structured as a hierarchy, in other words, that there is the director, whose instructions are based on a given drama or plot and must be followed and carried out by the scenic designer, the actors and all of the team members. But this is not how we proceed', Neumann once stated (2013). He added, 'Instead, artistic work ought to be carried out as a collaboration on equal terms and a shared decision-making process' (Neumann 2013).

Regarding his own professional profile, he saw himself as a 'visual artist who works at the theatre' (Kümmel 2010: n.p.), and although being involved in the inevitably collective work processes of this art form, he called for 'creative freedom' and even 'artistic autonomy' (Kümmel 2010). Usually, he conceived his designs fully independently before presenting his drafts to the director and the team, but during rehearsals they often became a trigger for improvisation, dialogue and artistic invention. This is why he preferably described his designs as being 'open systems' for a joint production of the performance space (instead of 'set designs' or 'stage designs'). 'I try to avoid making stage designs that are hermetic and too pre-defined … because then, there would be no space left for the others (i.e. the actors and the director) to bring in their own ideas', he once explained. 'Of course, this is an aesthetic decision, but perhaps also a political one, and it depends on the choices you make in life. I am not interested in closed systems or things that are seemingly perfect, because I have lost faith in such systems' (Laudenbach 2002: 112). In the following, Sophie Rois talks about selected theatre projects in which she collaborated with Bert Neumann and provides insights into the mutual dialogue that the two artists – the actress and the stage and costume designer – had on these occasions.

Sophie Rois, when preparing for this discussion, a scene in a film documentary on the Berlin Volksbühne struck me, in which Bert Neumann explained to the actor Herbert Fritsch, with the aid of a model, the spatial structure of his 'Neustadt'.[11] This space was used for an entire season for many different projects, among others for Castorf's production of The Idiot *(2002) in which you play the character of Lisaweta Jepantschina. In the film, we do not see Neumann in a conceptual rehearsal scene (where a stage designer normally presents his model to the entire team) but rather – much more informally – in a dialogue with an actor. In particular, you yourself were again and again intensively discussing matters with him. What function did these discussions have?*

This has a lot to do with the very specific work practice that developed at the Volksbühne over the years. This has a lot to do with managing director Frank Castorf, in particular, with his method of not getting involved. If a director, for example Christoph Schlingensief or René Pollesch, got the go-ahead for a production, then he or she could do, more or less, what he or she wanted. It was then the problem of the director to get the actors together for a production or it could even be no problem at all. In any case, no one was forced to do anything they didn't want to do by the management of the theatre. The artistic arrangements made all came about without the influence of any hierarchical structures. This felt very grown up and everyone was comfortable with this way of working. Bert Neumann was also involved in these processes.

Here is an example of how it all worked. At the end of 2006, Bert Neumann called me, stating that, 'Next year, the Russian revolution will have its big anniversary. There are no plans in the theatre at the moment regarding this event. I've agreed to sit down with Pollesch and talk about working on a project. Do you want to join in?' I said, 'The role played by the dictator's spouse is what I find fascinating and one seldom has a chance of playing it. I really would like to perform the role of Elena Ceauşescu, just because of her style, the headscarves and fur coats!' Then he designed the marvellous stage set for *Diktatorengattinnen* (Wives of Dictators), the three of us together debated what actors we would like to involve in it and then we started developing the piece.

Bert Neumann, as quite often, did not just design a stage set but he also made changes to the architecture of the actual theatre: in this case, certain elements on stage reflected on and interacted with the wall panelling of the Volksbühne auditorium, which has been kept in a late-1940s style. Back then, one dictatorship supplanted another and for a very long time rumours circulated that for the post-war reconstruction of the Volksbühne marble from Hitler's Reich Chancellery was used for the building process. The stage set plays with all of these related aspects. In René Pollesch's production Diktatorengattinnen (2007) the relationship and the balance of power was highlighted. The piece by Pollesch – he is both author and director – came about, as all of his play texts, only during the rehearsal stage. In a conventional sense, these are not dramas but rather material for plays. This meant that for the mutual work and rehearsal stages the stage set and, where applicable, the costume designs – as an artistic setting – is there first, and always first. That is why René Pollesch described Bert Neumann, the scenic designer, as the 'first author' of his plays on numerous occasions (viz. Pollesch 2015). Neumann in turn was quoted as saying that 'A stage set should have a setting, it should make a statement, be concrete, but the story should be never fully told to the end', and 'as a principle I make something which is unfinished, incomplete' (Müller-Tischler 2010: 8). This is due to the fact that his design only comes to the fore – depending on what the director and the actors do with it – during the rehearsals or even when being performed, and sometimes in a very different manner to what he actually thought would happen. The 'risk' that is inherent for all those participating in such an open process is 'important' (Müller-Tischler 2010). How can one imagine that when taking the perspective of the rehearsals into account?

As an example, for the production Ein Chor irrt sich gewaltig (A Choir Is Totally Wrong), which took place in the Prater of the Volksbühne, there was a wooden stage with boards at the start with steps underneath. The old building structure of the Prater was laid open and reinforced in parts. It was a very open situation. A large part of the stage set does actually come about due to the actors present – how we actually physically use and perform within the space. Bert Neumann did indeed avail of something akin to an 'artistic vocabulary' that he was always able to augment and mix. What I also noticed was that, depending on the director, his design approach varied. For Frank Castorf he produced quite varied spatial designs, just looking at the materials used, than for example Luc Bondy, and totally different again were the designs for René Pollesch. The stage sets designed for Castorf could easily be taken apart or disassembled – it wasn't a problem if an actor ripped open a wall. These designs could be used in manifold ways and could be interpreted quite differently. For Luc Bondy, however, he would never have built something like this as his stage; for example the production of Genet's Die Zofen (The Maids) rather had the look of an old film set. What I want to say here is: he was able to do both. He was able to work with different artistic approaches and he really enjoyed doing both. This included reflecting on what he was actually doing.

At the same time, he was fully autonomous as an artist. During the rehearsal stage this could at times also lead to altercations – Bert's stage sets were, so to speak, 'resistive'.

For us actors, his stages, if they were designed as 'open structures', were at the same time resistive (a counterpart), as well as being a co-actor, a non-human actor on stage. Using this concrete material, the actors were able to play out their roles and yes, there were risks and moments of surprise when it came to the actors' interaction with one another. Bert had been working together with René Pollesch since 2001;[12] in the Prater back then, and together with him, we rehearsed our very own way of making theatre over many years. It was a new way of producing theatre where there was – as you rightly mentioned – no play text at the start (and no other basic material, such as a novel) but rather first and foremost the stage set and then, second, a title for the project. The title was usually quite open and could be associated with a lot of things just like the film titles Luis Buñuel came up with (e.g. *An Andalusian Dog*). Pollesch titles have names such as *Heidi Hoh arbeitet hier nicht mehr* (Heidi Hoh Doesn't Work Here Any More), *World Wide Web Slums 1-10*, *Diktatorengattinnen* (Wives of Dictators) or as with the project for the reopening of the Prater, *Ein Chor irrt sich gewaltig* (A Choir Is Totally Wrong).

The Prater of the Volksbühne is the second production venue apart from the big theatre itself. When the Prater was converted in 2010, Bert Neumann hung up a large neon sign on the outer facade of the building and it immediately had the appearance of some sort of boulevard theatre or a version of a boulevard theatre. The Prater, a 'Vergnügungsgaststätte' (a place of leisure and all-round enjoyment) set up in 1850, in which theatre and variety productions were shown for many years, was already used as a location by Castorf's ensemble beforehand, but Bert Neumann was the first person to bring the hidden architecture, the old historic theatre stage with the stage portal, to the fore in the wake of the redevelopment process. He, so to speak, brought it into the present. For the reopening the challenge was to produce a fitting play without any folklore; rather, it was to be a type of popular theatre ('Volkstheater') which was up to date and for our times. The stage for this project, Ein Chor irrt sich gewaltig, *was as you mentioned made up of wooden boards with steps, connected to the old building structure, which was now viewable. This constellation had something of a vaudeville stage to it, even though it was quite empty at the same time, something very atypical for the works by Bert Neumann. The play – it deals with a woman who leaves her husband after he has an affair and criticizes gender-specific power structures and relationships – used, very loosely, motifs from a French film comedy,* Ein Elefant irrt sich gewaltig *(An Elephant Is Totally Wrong; 1976), as well as text fragments from a socially critical polemic pamphlet written by Dietmar Dath. In this play only women acted out the parts, except for the dancer and actor Jean Chaize.*

Using this example, one can really demonstrate how we worked: In the beginning, there was the stage and the ensemble – in this case, there were three actresses, as well as Jean Chaize and the women's choir, headed by Christine Groß, who has worked with Einar Schleef in the past. The idea with the choir came from Tine and myself, just as René Pollesch develops his plays together with the actors. He, however, is the person who writes the piece. One could say that the play, in all of its elements (text, stage, music, movement, etc.), was mutually composed during the rehearsals; they were, so to speak, experimental arrangements. Stage set and acting do not reciprocally illustrate each other. It was always the case that we wanted to kick-start a process in which things have a performative relationship with each other, where a text has a relationship with a costume or a costume to a stage design.

Bert Neumann, unlike many other stage designers that I know, was almost always present during rehearsals; it was part of his practical work method that he – depending on how the rehearsals were going and what was being developed therein – modified his stage design and settings. Already during the production process, his designs were active co-players and counterparts. During the rehearsals for *Ein Chor irrt sich gewaltig*, he stated, 'We don't need a stage design here, you are the stage design, with the costumes.' In fact, there was only a flowery curtain present and for the actors and the choir he designed clothes in a Rococo style but sewn from African fabric. That looked really fabulous, especially when the choir with the swarm of women moved

FIGURE 2.1 *René Pollesch,* Ein Chor irrt sich gewaltig *(A Choir Is Totally Wrong), Stage and Costume Design: Bert Neumann, Volksbühne Berlin, Prater, 2009. Photo © Thomas Aurin (in the centre of the picture: Sophie Rois).*

about. Indeed, the costume design here became the stage set design simultaneously with all of the forms, colours and the playful dynamics of the acting.

Just as with the costumes, Bert Neumann's stages are almost always related to everyday materials, fashion, known structures and design forms that come from the most varied of contexts (container architecture, cheap functional designs, funfair glitter, quotes from pop culture, trash), so that they seem to play with the meanings and potential ambiguity of cultural signs and symbols. One example of this is the Coca Cola lettering, which he – in Cyrillic letters – scenographed as a huge neon sign and popular emblem of Western lifestyle for the single-entity staging area of the Die Brüder Karamasow *(The Brothers Karamazov; Vienna, Berlin 2015) (see Figure 5.1 in this book). One can add here the conflict that he had with typography and fonts, which he undertook as if it were a research project, including the blackletter typefaces that he used last for posters, programmes, theatre banners and as visual stage elements. In other words: Bert Neumann's way of dealing with cultural signs – the practice of how he deconstructed them and reassembled them in a scenographic manner – was never just purely associative or random, also never nostalgic but always historically aware. And even though the whole process was rather playful, there was a highly differentiated design thinking going on behind this way of quoting. Visual sign systems, languages of forms, cultural materiality: all of this he seemed to be researching in an almost systematic manner and not only considering their aesthetic dimension but also in reference to their social and political significance.*

Here Bert Neumann was definitely formative and the Volksbühne aesthetics had, if one takes an overall look at the many theatre productions staged, a high level of inner logic as well as stringency. No other theatre had this and sharing this really was a great joy. There was an artistic position being taken and certain principles kept to. Among other things, he said, 'In my spaces there is only illusion if one is allowed to also see the backside of the stage scenery and its construction'. In many respects, he was heir to Bertolt Brecht. The last production that I worked on with Bert Neumann and René Pollesch was based on a real-life altercation between Brecht and Caspar Neher. It was not produced in Berlin but at the Schauspielhaus in Zurich. In 2015, we had a contract with that theatre and the play's location was the Pfauen, the premiere being on 1 April 2016. As always, at the beginning everything was open. Only the line-up was clear and Bert designed the stage scenery.

The idea was to relate to Brecht's *Antigone*, his first theatre production after returning from exile. He planned it in Zurich together with his stage designer Caspar Neher and then staged it in 1948 in a little theatre in Chur. Bert's stage for the later Pollesch production was more or less a readymade, a reproduction of Caspar Neher's stage set. We met and he showed me the *Antigone* model book (Brecht, Neher and the photographs by Ruth Berlau documented the rehearsals back then in this book)[13] and related the story of how he, as a student at the art academy in Weißensee in East Berlin, had had the original stage set model of Caspar Neher in his own hands and that he even restored it. Therefore, he knew it very well. For our production, he also had a first version of his stage set model, which he had assembled himself. And he told me a lot about how Brecht, Neher, Weigel and the ensemble had rehearsed back then and how they had developed a totally new form of theatre rehearsals. However, the production, with Helene Weigel in the main role, has gone into the history books as being the most well-documented flop in theatre history. Beforehand, Brecht had got into some political problems in Zurich, so the production, with the help of the theatre producer Hans Curjel, could only be realized in Chur in the end. Bert Neumann's idea – and a personal delight of his – was to help in getting this set design staged after seventy years, the one that couldn't be seen back then in the Zurich Schauspielhaus.

The title that René Pollesch invented for this Zurich play was Bühne frei für Mick Levčik! *(Clear the Stage for Mick Levčik!) and – in a comparable but rather quite different sense, as with Brecht's and Neher's* Antigone *by Sophocles (based on Hölderlin's German translation), which they brought into their present around 1945 – they reflected on their* Antigone *project*

FIGURE 2.2 *René Pollesch,* Bühne frei für Mick Levčik! *(Clear the Stage for Mick Levčik!), stage design (after Brecht/Neher): Bert Neumann, Schauspielhaus Zurich. Photo © Thomas Aurin (on the left hand side: Sophie Rois).*

from today's point of view. The stage that Bert Neumann had in mind, in the assembled realization, was actually a 1:1 model of Neher's stage design. The recording of the staging concept back then, which is clearly fixed in Brecht/Neher's model book with a score-like notation that includes text and pictures, was supposed to be a role model for future productions. They both, together with the Pollesch ensemble, however, threw out the role model because they had their own particular way of doing things, their quite different and open production and acting method.[14] What is actually true is that they didn't stage the play as such and didn't present a reconstruction or re-enactment of it either. On the contrary, they – in a sort of meta-reflection or even commentary – posed the question as to why Brecht in the end failed with this model concept. The production, using the text that you and Pollesch worked on, did actually focus especially on the question to what extent artistic work is even possible without any relation to historical models, texts and pictures and if culture, communication and even the projects and processes dealing with art do not also mean that we are actually constantly quoting what already exists, reassembling it in new ways and reinterpreting it at the same time. Accordingly, art or the theatre – this you actually highlighted quite strongly – is always related to its point in time, its location, the cultural context and to historical discourse relationships.

That's right. What I have to say about the Volksbühne and what it was during the twenty-five years under the directorship of Frank Castorf I have already stated elsewhere: This could not have taken place everywhere.[15] It is, in my opinion, a real quality of the theatre that it is something local and that it is connected to a real place. Of course, one can also tour with it, going on international trips, but to begin with, one does not produce plays that have a universal claim. For an evening to get its very own special expressiveness, it needs a connection to a real place at a concrete time. The stage and costume designs by Bert Neumann and his entire visual design for the Volksbühne functioned in this manner. And that is how, as an example, the plays by René Pollesch operate. Within these, the awareness of the time and the relationships in which one lives is quite strong and very present, not only on an emotional level but also on a reflective level.

Notes

1 See the panel discussion with Bert Neumann, 'Kunstproduktion ist permanenter Ausnahmezustand: Die Theaterbühne als "Gegenort"' ('Art Production is a Permanent State of Emergency: The Theatre Stage as a Counter Space'), LMU Munich, Studio Stage, 28 October 2013 (unpublished manuscript).

2   After studying stage and costume at the Art Academy Berlin-Weißensee in East Berlin, Bert Neumann first worked with Frank Castorf in 1988. When Castorf became the artistic director of the Berlin Volksbühne in 1992, he became head of the scenic design department, and also worked as a guest artist at theatres and opera houses both in Germany and abroad, collaborating with the directors Leander Haussmann, Jossi Wieler, Peter Konwitschny, Alain Platel, Johan Simons and René Pollesch. He received numerous awards, including the prestigious Hein Heckroth prize for stage design in 2015. In 2010, the Viennese museum Augarten Contemporary presented his works in a solo exhibition, entitled 'Setting of a Drama'. In the summer of 2015, he unexpectedly passed away at the age of 54.

3   Quoted from Laudenbach's portrait of Bert Neumann, in Initiative StadtBauKultur NRW 2005: 26.

4   Blievernicht, Fehrmann and Neumann 2004; for an in-depth discussion, see Wiens 2014a: 191–226 and Wiens 2014b.

5   For a photographic record of his works, see Hurtzig 2001 and Hegemann, Aurin and Witt 2017.

6   Quoted from Neumann 2013.

7   Sophie Rois, 'Wer ist das, vor dem man sich da ausbreitet?' ('Who is That Audience Watching When Actors Spread Themselves on the Stage?'), in Raddatz 2016: 130.

8   Sophie Rois left the Berlin Volksbühne in 2017; since 2018 she has been an ensemble member at the Deutsches Theater Berlin. For her work as an actress for theatre, television and film, she has received numerous awards, including the prestigious Gertrud-Eysoldt-Ring (2017).

9   Bert Neumann in an interview for the jubilee publication on the occasion of the Volksbühne's 100th birthday (2014), cf. ibid. 'Das Projekt Volksbühne – Wiederabdruck' ('The Project Volksbühne – Reprint'), in Raddatz 2016: 27.

10 Sophie Rois in an interview, conducted by Ulrich Seidler for *Frankfurter Rundschau* (25 April 2018), www.fr.de/kultur/theater/sophie-rois-spielen-bedeutet-befreiung-von-der-arbeit-a-1493156,2 (accessed 15 May 2018).

11 See the documentary movie *Zeitspuren, oder Die Vermessung eines Theaters* (Time Tracks, or the Surveying of a Theatre) by Jan Speckenbach (2004), 90 min., https://vimeo.com/227943924.

12 René Pollesch, who studied Applied Theatre Science in Gießen, Germany, with Heiner Müller, George Tabori and John Jesurun, started to work as dramatist and director at theatres in Frankfurt, Berlin, Leipzig and Stuttgart during the 1990s. From 2001/2 he collaborated with Bert Neumann on a regular basis, and he also worked with stage designers such as Janina Audick, Barbara Steiner, Wilfried Minks and Katrin Back.

13 Their model book was published one year later: Bertolt Brecht and Caspar Neher, *Antigonemodell 1948*. Editorial collaboration: Ruth Berlau. Berlin: Gebr. Weiss, 1949.

14 After Neumann's death it was completed by Barbara Steiner in collaboration with the workshops in Zurich.

15 Rois, quoted in Raddatz 2016: 135.

3

Scenographic materiality
Agency and intra-action in Katrin Brack's designs

Joslin McKinney

Katrin Brack is an influential and acclaimed German stage designer,[1] who has become known for her minimalist approach using materials such as fog, confetti and snow for 'a new style of space-forming' where 'the visual arises from the material' (Irmer n.d.). Her work reflects new ways of thinking about scenography and how it happens. Whereas many stage designs are solid and often static constructions, Brack's designs are fluid, responsive and ephemeral. Her sets are not visual interpretations of textual themes or fictional locations in the way that much mainstream scenography is. Rather, they are 'atmospherically charged';[2] active, vibrant spaces that make a distinct contribution to the performance as it unfolds, even to the extent that they can be experienced as another 'actor' on the stage. Brack's approach is a challenge to traditional thinking about scenography, where, as Rebecca Schneider points out, most theatre scholars assume that props, costumes, lighting and other stage 'paraphernalia' are there only to serve or support. In the 'dominant (scholarly) Western imaginary', humans are considered the sole agents (Schneider 2015: 10). But this trenchantly anthropocentric view of theatre limits accounts of how scenography such as Brack's works.

Anthropocentricism in general is currently under some scrutiny. The role of materials and our relationships to them in all areas of our lives is being questioned by 'new materialism', an emergent, transdisciplinary discussion[3] that is engaged in a reappraisal of materiality in areas such as climate change, bio-technological engineering and 'the saturation of our intimate and physical lives' by various technologies (Coole and Frost 2010: 5). Jane Bennett, a prominent new materialist thinker, asks:

> What ... if we took more seriously the idea that technological and natural materialities [are] themselves actors alongside and within us – [are] vitalities, trajectories, and powers irreducible to the meanings, intentions, or symbolic values humans invest in them? (Bennett 2010a: 46)

Brack's scenography provokes similar questions. Considered through the lens of new materialist thinking her designs prompt a reconsideration of the agentic potential of materials and how 'matter comes to matter' (Barad 2003) in the theatre.

Scenography and new materialism

Although the contribution of scenography and the 'props, sets, lights, sound, makeup, and all the backstage machinery supporting the fretting and strutting about' (Schneider 2015: 14) have long been understood by practitioners, it is only recently that theatre scholarship has given it much serious attention. In the past decade or so, several publications on scenography have moved beyond the practicalities of design and analysed the dramaturgical contribution that scenography makes to theatre (e.g. McKinney and Butterworth 2009; Baugh 2013; Aronson 2018). Some have focused on the significance of specific materials including light (Palmer 2014; Abulafia 2016), sound (Brown 2009; Kendrick and Roesner 2011), costume (Maclaurin and Monks 2015; Barbieri 2017) and space (Brejzek 2011; Hannah 2011). However, as Schneider implies, this work has not yet made an impact on the wider field of theatre and performance studies. Her reference to stage 'paraphernalia' points to a widespread assumption that the non-human in theatre is superfluous or merely instrumental. In new materialist thinking, these anthropocentric views can be seen as part of a much wider picture that applies across all our dealings with matter, both natural and technological, where it is figured as

> essentially passive stuff, set in motion by human agents who use it as a means of survival, modify it as a vehicle of aesthetic expression, and impose subjective meanings upon it. (Coole 2010: 92)

And even where the contribution of scenography is recognized (e.g. in publications on postdramatic and immersive theatre[4]), it is human agents that are generally considered to be in full control of the scenographic material and what it can be made to do or to mean. Lately, scholars have turned to new materialist ideas to examine the work that scenographic materials do in performance and to examine the consequences for aesthetic practices. For example, Minty Donald (2014, 2016) takes a new materialist approach to reflect on her own environmental, site-specific performance practice. Meanwhile, Maaike Bleeker (2017) has analysed the creation of Kris Verdonck's scenographic performance, *End*, as a process of material thinking.[5] New materialism is being called on to examine the fundamental role of non-human material in the making, performing and reception of scenography.

Three interlinked ideas that emerge from new materialism provide a framework for the development of a theory of 'scenographic' materialism. The first is that all matter, including non-human matter, is agential: Even so-called inanimate objects and materials have what Bennett calls 'thing-power' (2010b: 4). This prompts questions about the agency that scenographic materials might have above and beyond the meaning conferred on them by designers, playwrights or performers. The second idea is that agency is distributed across assemblages of human and non-human material and that agency emerges from the operation of these assemblages (2010b: 20). This allows a closer look at the reciprocal relationship between materials and bodies of different kinds in scenography. The third idea is that matter is discursive in that it can define what is meaningful without necessarily defaulting to language (Barad 2003: 819). Another prominent new materialist thinker, Karen Barad, challenges the 'excessive power granted to language to determine what is real' and explores matter as 'an active participant in the world's becoming' (2003: 802–3). For scenography, this idea is a way to address meaning-making processes that emerge from the material as a central rather than peripheral dimension of theatre experience. Stimulated, provoked and inspired by Brack's designs, I want to use this new materialist framework to develop an account of scenographic materiality that attends to creative agency in the design, performance and reception of scenography and recognizes the active role of materials in those processes.

Katrin Brack – a brief introduction

Brack's work, especially since the early years of the new millennium,[6] is marked by the use of single materials that usually fill the entire stage area. The objects and materials she has used (including tinsel, balloons, artificial fog, sleeping bags, wind machines, confetti, live plants in pots as well as theatrical snow) are often commonplace or even tawdry things, but in Brack's designs they take on a new aesthetic and poetic potential.

In *Kampf des Negers und der Hunde* (Black Battles With Dogs; 2003), bright, multicoloured confetti fell thickly and constantly across the whole stage for the duration of the performance. For *Anatol* (2008), there was a dense forest of giant-sized silver tinsel garlands hanging from the flies to the stage floor. The set for *Iwanov* (Ivanov; 2005) consisted of a vast amount of fog hovering (mainly) over the stage. In *Prinz Friedrich von Homburg* (The Prince of Homburg; 2006/7), water spray rained down on the actors throughout the performance. In *Ubukönig* (Ubu Roi; 2008), hundreds of party balloons covered the stage while large helium-filled balloons drifted around and above the actors. Balloons appeared again for *Radetzkymarsch,* (Radetzky March; 2017), this time they were pushed into the auditorium, inviting audiences to hit them back. The use of these materials in theatre is widespread and normally unremarkable or even clichéd. But the uncompromising application and abundance of them reveals new possibilities, not only in terms of signification and symbolism, but also as materials in themselves, not limited to intentions invested in them by humans.

Dramaturg Stefanie Carp says that in Brack's most successful work 'the material does not become an allegory but remains innocent as if radiating energy'.[7] For example, in *Hermannschlacht* (The Battle of Hermann; 2010), the stage set consisted of many large pastel-coloured blocks of solid foam that actors stacked and heaped into different configurations during the performance. The soft, pale blocks contrasted with the staged battles, underlining the anti-war theme of Kleist's text, but the foam blocks themselves had a dominant presence. Their unwieldy bulk (solid but wobbly) informed and shaped the whole atmosphere of the performance. A key feature of Brack's work is the apparent independence of the materials from other elements (human and otherwise) on the stage; they seem to be, as Carp puts it, 'indifferent' to the human situation (Nioduschewski 2010: 20). Abundance and material excess form another notable tactic. The snow started falling at the beginning of *Molière* (2007) and continued for four hours. In *John Gabriel Borkman* (2015), there was already deep snow (knee-deep) on the stage before the performance started. Actors in *Das grosse Fressen* (Blow-Out; 2006) were deluged by soap bubble foam, and assaulted with sudden eruptions and explosions of confetti in *Tartuffe* (2006). The exuberance and extravagance of these 'cheap' materials used in large quantities can be thrilling in the manner of the circus or a spectacular show, but they are also challenging and sometimes difficult to work with: fog irritates throats and eyes; rain and foam are cold and slippery.

Although Brack's work is sometimes described as an installation, architecture or sculpture (Nioduschewski 2010: 19), Brack herself says:

> I don't see stage design as an autonomous work; my work only makes sense in interaction with other agents in a production and only then does it develop its effect. (Nioduschewski 2010: 179)

In Brack's own view, the materials she uses are fully part of a conglomeration of 'agents' that includes actors and other stage materials. Collaborating with directors such as Dimiter Gotscheff, Luk Perceval, Armin Petras and Johan Simons, her aim during the production process is to create a space that is 'atmospherically charged and makes it possible to generate precise but far-reaching associations, as well as physically intense impressions' (Nioduschewski 2010: 175). The designs do not prescribe particular meanings, but instead they facilitate the generation of ideas and discoveries through performance.

Agential material and 'thing-power'

Brack's designs are capable of producing metonymic and metaphorical effects. The falling confetti she used for *Kampf des Negers und der Hunde*, set in a failing French-owned construction site in Africa, seems to suggest a place of shimmering heat or swarming insects. The gradual accumulation of a thick layer of the coloured paper on the stage floor also suggested debris and waste of late capitalism which the play also deals with. Brack says she was thinking of the bright sunlight, heat, people, music and landscapes of Africa as well as colonial exploitation, poverty, disease and rubbish – the multicoloured confetti seemed to her to unite these diverse reflections (Nioduschewski 2010: 174). However, the confetti was not merely a medium for the conveyance of meaning; it was also an active component in establishing the atmospheric conditions of the performance and its reception. Twirling paper discs filled the whole space of the stage, blurring and reacting to gestures of the actors. The fluttering, flickering movements of the paper, like static interference, informed the experience of seeing and sensing the performance. It exhibited what Jane Bennett refers to as 'thing-power' or 'the vitality that is intrinsic to materiality' (2010b: 3), which operates independently from human intention.

The tendencies and propensities of confetti, as a manufactured material, are in part determined by the size, shape and weight of the paper and how it is discharged. Nonetheless, action of the colour, texture, form and movement of the coloured paper discs filling the stage, thickening and disturbing its volumetric space, are 'a decisive force' (Bennett 2010b: 9) in the way actors inhabit the stage and the way individual members of the audience experience the performance. Brack refers to the power of materials that follows from using them in abundance to completely fill the stage:

> I'm trying to fill the space with the material and to a certain extent to define the space ... if it really fills the space, [the material] has a completely different kind of power. (McKinney and McKechnie 2016)

FIGURE 3.1 *Stage design by Katrin Brack for Dimiter Gotscheff's staging of* Kampf des Negers und der Hunde *(Black Battles with Dogs), Volksbühne Berlin 2003. Photo © Thomas Aurin.*

According to philosopher Gernot Böhme, it is the perceptible power of a thing's presence in space or 'the ecstasies of the thing' that forms atmospheres. The characteristics of a thing (e.g. its form, extension, volume colour, smell or sound) can exert 'an external effect' as well as simply define the thing itself as a discrete object (Böhme 1993: 121). In *Kampf des Negers und der Hunde*, each piece of confetti was both an object taking up space and, at the same time, a thing that articulated its presence perceptibly and externally, 'radiating', as Böhme puts it, into the theatre. Through this ecstatic process, a thing can intervene in 'the homogeneity of the surrounding space', filling it 'with tensions and suggestions of movement' (Böhme 1993). The confetti's twirling movement, its flickering colours and gentle pattering sound as it landed on the floor established an atmosphere, that is, a particular, perceptible and affective presence in space.

Böhme has described atmosphere as being vague, indeterminable and inexpressible while also being something that 'takes possession of us like an alien power' (Böhme 2013), which seems to fit Brack's scenography very well. So it comes as a surprise when Böhme cites 'the stage set' as a paradigm for the creation of atmosphere and makes it clear that he does not consider stage design to have anything more than a supporting role in performance:

It is ... the purpose of the stage set to produce atmospheric background to the action, to attune the spectators to the theatrical performance and to provide the actors with a sounding board for what they present. (Böhme 2013)

Böhme's notion of set design follows the predominant view of theatre objects that Schneider refers to, but the atmospheres that Brack's designs create are not merely background for action. They do not do what Böhme sees as a chief virtue of a stage set, that is, to rid atmospheres of 'the odour of the irrational' (Böhme 2013) to create atmospheres with a clear directive and purpose. Rather, they productively engage with the irrational, emergent and even antagonistic dimensions of atmospheres as 'quasi-things', as Tonino Griffero calls them. These are 'entities that, without being full objects, are present and active on us' (Griffero 2017: viii). Quasi-things include constructed entities such as images and melodies and also naturally occurring phenomena such as fog and twilight that 'generate a deep and intimate felt-bodily resonance' (Griffero 2017: xv) regardless of the guiding hand of a human agent. There may well be a cultural dimension to the impact of quasi-things, but crucially they exert their affects through a bodily and prereflexive experience (Griffero 2017: viii–ix). The cultural meaning of confetti in Brack's designs is less significant than the multisensorial impact – visual, kinetic, haptic and sonic – that it makes on a spectator. Thinking of scenographies as atmospheric quasi-things accords materials an active and determining presence in performance, especially at the level of the felt-body of the spectator. In contrast to Böhme's suggestion that it is the intention of stage designers that generates and determines atmosphere (Böhme 2013), Brack's designs leave room for the materials themselves to establish a 'quasi-thingly' presence and, in that way, to exert some level of 'thing-power' in the way that they make a difference or become a 'decisive force' in the performance (Bennett 2010b: 9).

Matter engaging with other matter: The agency of assemblages

For the performers, these materials can be considered as

another actor on stage, one that wasn't on the cast list – unpredictable, stubborn, doesn't stick to arrangements, makes you angry. You have to take him as he is, not force him, then he cooperates.[8]

For Wolfram Koch, an actor who has worked repeatedly with Brack, the material is decisive in some sense and the actors have to work with it, not impose themselves on it. This goes against expectations that it will be 'the actor who confers meaning upon the object' (McAuley 1999: 205). McAuley's position reflects what Tim Ingold terms as being a 'hylomorphic model of creation', a deeply entrenched theoretical view in Western thought, where human agents impose form on inert matter (Ingold 2010: 92). In practice, however, artists and craftspeople have always understood the need to 'join with and follow the forces and flows of material that bring the form of the work into being' (Ingold 2010: 97). In puppetry, for example, there is a recognition that the relationship between humans and objects is more symbiotic and founded on a process of 'listening' to materials, following their lead through 'respectful handling' (Margolies 2014: 323–4). Earlier, Koch described a bodily experience of working with and alongside materials, improvizing with them during the performance so that he and the materials are co-creative. The dramaturgical meaning is discovered, rather than imposed by the designer or the performer; it can only emerge through the materiality of the performance.

The materials in Brack's designs often draw attention to themselves as independent forces. They can be imposing and even confrontational in the way they take up space, leaving little room for actors. Some can be physically challenging and uncomfortable to work with. In *Das grosse Fressen,* adapted from the 1973 Marco Ferreri film *La Grande Bouffe*, four middle-aged men resolve to kill themselves through gastronomic and sexual excess. Beginning with a virtually bare stage, Brack had a foam cannon shooting jets of soap bubbles up into the air and these gradually filled the stage with foam. Over time, this exuberant, even joyful gesture became something rather more threatening as it continued to pump out torrents of foam, soaking the actors, making them slip and slide as they became progressively wetter and colder (despite neoprene suits under their costumes). They were eventually overwhelmed by the foam.

It is not Brack's intention to simply impose conditions on actors; rather, the aim is to create situations where actors 'can experience new things and might – ideally – develop new forms of acting' (Nioduschewski 2010: 178). One way that these new forms might arise is through the way that stage space is reconfigured through the dominant presence of material. Paradoxically, this can give the arrival and the presence of actors an added importance. Making their entrances through forests of tinsel or banks of rolling fog, or even, as in the case of *John Gabriel Borkman*, from beneath a thick layer of snow almost an hour into the performance, actors can slowly materialize from the depths of the stage or else appear quite suddenly. Brack says that 'the actors and directors decide for the most part how to act with the material' (Nioduschewski 2010: 176). Finding creative ways to work with the material on the stage is a process of discovery and improvisation that is common to other forms of art and craft where skilled practitioners are not imposing form but 'intervening in the fields of force and currents of material' in an ongoing and reciprocal process (Ingold 2010: 92–3).

Nonetheless, the unpredictability of some of the materials that Brack uses is especially challenging for actors. For *Iwanov*, stage technicians at the Volksbühne, Berlin, pumped out enormous amounts of fog across the stage. Brack first conceived the fog as a manifestation of the way Chekhov's characters seemed to her to be both there and not there, wishing they could disappear (McKinney and McKechnie 2016). The fog allowed actors to play with degrees of their own visibility. But, extremely sensitive to changes in heat and air movement, the fog was unpredictable in its movements. This meant that actors could not rely on the fog to be there to facilitate entrances, exits or even frame key moments in the play; instead they had to work alongside, and sometimes follow, the fog. But through an acceptance of the material on its own terms, new creative possibilities for the actors opened up:

> The material carries you along, drives you forward, transforms you, makes you invisible, visible, naked; it strips you, hides you, buries you, makes you disappear, vanish, makes you vulnerable, lonely, isolated.[9]

The collaboration of materials and actors is actually part of a larger assemblage that includes other materials such as costume, light and sound, the stage space – its architectonic qualities and technical infrastructure, stage technicians, the auditorium as well as the audience members and so on. As Bennett admits, the danger of a concept of 'thing-power' is that it might suggest that materiality is stable and immutable (Bennett 2010a: 20) whereas the agentic capacity of matter is revealed through 'the collaboration, cooperation, or interactive interference of many other bodies and forces' (Bennett 2010b: 21). The collaboration of these various entities in a 'volatile but somehow functioning whole' can be thought of as 'assemblages' or 'ad hoc groupings of diverse elements, of vibrant materials of all sorts' (Bennett 2010b: 23).

> Each member and proto-member of the assemblage has a certain vital force but there is also an effectivity proper to the grouping as such: an agency *of* the assemblage. (Bennett 2010b: 24)

Any one of the parts of the assemblage might, in combination with other parts, produce a distinct effect while operating towards an overall outcome. Heiner Goebbels describes how this might work in the composition and reception of theatre where conventional hierarchies of bodies and objects are set aside and the various means of the stage, human and otherwise, 'all maintain their own forces but act together', where, for example, a light can be so strong that you suddenly only watch the light and forget the text, where a costume speaks its own language or where there is a distance between speaker and text and a tension between music and text. (Goebbels in Lehmann 2006: 86)

The idea of a theatrical event as a 'volatile' assemblage containing 'active and powerful nonhumans' (Bennett 2010b: 24) might seem far-fetched when we consider the carefully controlled environment of contemporary theatres, which are, as Paul Rae points out, 'underwritten by a significant hinterland of expertise and stabilized technologies'. Yet it is also the case that theatre events 'retain a multifarious capacity for instability, be it as an aesthetic strategy, an equipmental or psychic breakdown' (Rae 2015: 120) and it is in this that the limits of 'human-centred theories of action' in the theatre can be identified (Bennett 2010b: 24).

In several of Brack's designs, materials, through their propensities and characteristics, instigate instability and uncertainty in the theatre assemblage. Furthermore, the staging of the designs brings into focus the delicate and volatile cooperation of all kinds of matter on which theatre is based. For *Ubukönig* Brack imagined the stage space full of balloons. She hoped that large balloons full of helium would hover over the stage, rising and falling gently like the wax in a lava lamp. However, the heat from the theatre lanterns made the balloons rise right up into the grid. Technicians found a solution: station people in the grid with water pistols to squirt the balloons, cooling the helium enough for them to sink again. Balloons, performers, the heat of the lanterns, technicians with pistols, water droplets and water vapour operated as a shifting, unstable assemblage. Active components of this assemblage extend to the auditorium; heat, noise and movement of audience members all contribute at a micro-level.

Discursive matter, or how matter comes to matter

Brack says that her designs are 'nonsynchronous' references to the play, which allow 'an increase in new connections made by the public' (Nioduschewski 2010: 178). As part of the theatre assemblage, audience members engage with the materiality of the designs, not just with their signification. This implies that the audience might, like the designer or the performer, be alert and responsive to the forces and flows of materials in the performance rather than just trying to read backwards from a design to identify an originating artistic intention in the mind of the designer. As Ingold puts it, 'the work invites the viewer to join the artist as a fellow traveller, to look with it as it unfolds in the world' (Ingold 2011: 216).

Whereas designer and performers have a physical relationship to the materials, Brack's audiences are mostly seated observers, rather than active participants. There are notable exceptions though. The fog in *Iwanov* was not always confined to the stage and in some performances it enveloped audiences too; in *Prinz Friedrich von Homburg*, water spray dampened the first few rows of the audience and in *Radetzkymarsch*, the balloons were deliberately sent into the auditorium. But even without a direct physical experience of the materials, audiences are a part of the same atmosphere as those various bodies on stage are, as Erika Fischer-Lichte has discussed:

Through its atmosphere, the entering subject experiences the space and its things as emphatically present. Not only do they appear in their primary and secondary qualities, they also intrude on and penetrate the perceiving subject's body and surround it atmospherically. (Fischer-Lichte 2008: 116)

The 'ecstasy of things' that Böhme (1993) describes in the formation of atmospheres lends itself to a physical and bodily experience for audiences that is 'distinct from the visual or aural perceptions' (Fischer-Lichte 2008: 116). Sound, light and smell, for example, contribute to the way atmospheres can enter the spectator's body and 'break down its limits' (Fischer-Lichte 2008: 119). But what is particularly important in Brack's designs is the way that the movement of each material makes itself felt to the watching body. The detection of movement or a kinaesthetic awareness of the 'flux' of energies in the environment (Gibson 1968: 319) is an important means by which spectators sense changes in sound and light, the movement of costumes and objects (McKinney 2012). These changes are often matched with a corresponding feeling in the observing body. The meandering drift of the fog, for example, has a different bodily impact than fluttering confetti or gushing jets of foam do. This is partly related to a spectator's capacity to empathize with actors who are working directly with the materials and to their capacity to imagine what the plastic snow would feel like on their own skin or how it would feel to lose their footing and slip on a soapy stage. But it also comes from bodily impressions, feelings of expansion or contraction, lightness or weight, calm or agitation, that emanate from the materials themselves and make themselves felt through a spectator's whole body through muscular, vestibular, cutaneous and visual means (Foster 2011: 116).

According to Fischer-Lichte, the ecstasy of things provokes sensual impressions that are not commensurate with linguistic expression and only 'very inadequately describable', yet they form the basis of understanding where the perceived thing triggers associations and becomes 'interlinked with ideas, memories, sensations and emotions' (2008: 142). As a semiotician, her concern is tracing chains of thought through which linguistic meaning might emerge from sensual impressions. Nevertheless, she concludes that

> the concretely perceived bodies, things, sounds, or lights, however, are robbed of their specific phenomena; being if one condenses them into language retrospectively, whether during or after the performance. (2008: 160)

Instead, she proposes that the phenomena that appear through the performance need to be understood as an 'autopoietic feedback loop' or a shared circulation of energy emanating from the actors and from the ecstasy of things that 'impresses itself particularly intensely onto the perceiving subject' (2008: 166). According to this idea, impressions feed back into the ongoing and self-generating interactions between spectator, actors, space and the things in it.

Fischer-Lichte's notion of autopoiesis seems to be compatible with agency that is distributed across an assemblage of things, including non-human materials (2008: 206–7). Nonetheless, she stops short of the new materialist project of giving 'matter its due' (Barad 2003: 803) by evoking the 'mysterious elusiveness' of invisible forces (Fischer-Lichte 2008: 206–7). Bennett's 'thing-power', for instance, is intended to draw attention to 'an efficacy of objects in excess of the human meanings, designs, or purposes they express or serve' (2010b: 20) and to identify the particular contribution of the non-human. However, it is, as Bennett admits, impossible to 'name the moment of independence (from subjectivity) possessed by things' (2010b: 3). And in attempting to decentre the role of human agents and give credit to materials, Bennett seems to fall back into dualist notions of subject and object that new materialism aims to undermine.

Barad takes a different route, one that dispenses with binary divisions between non-human and human or material and meaning. By focusing not on separate and distinct entities in dialogue (interaction), but on the relationships or 'intra-actions' that give rise to meaning, Barad's account of agency is not as a pre-existing property of things, human or otherwise (as Bennett seems to suggest) but an enactment that proceeds through 'agential intra-actions' (Barad 2003: 815), where

> *matter comes to matter* through the iterative intra-activity of the world in its becoming. The point is not merely that there are important material factors in addition to discursive ones; rather, the issue is the conjoined material-discursive nature of constraints, conditions, and practices. (Barad 2003: 823)

Barad's proposal is that matter and meaning are intertwined in an ongoing process. Applied to performance, this concept of intra-action suggests that engaging with or attending to the material dimension of theatre is the foundation of the aesthetic experience. It is a way of 'knowing' about a performance that challenges 'exclusively human systems of comprehension and communication' (Donald 2016: 254). In Brack's designs, intra-action through feelings, impressions, associations and meanings can only arise when materials of all kinds (including human bodies) combine and interpenetrate. Scenographic materials are mysteriously elusive only if we always insist on translating them into language to recognize their contribution. If, following Barad, we consider scenography as materially discursive or as Bleeker has suggested, a material mode of thinking (2017), it is possible to see scenographic materials as being active and necessary participants in agential intra-actions and scenography as a process of matter coming to matter.

Scenography reconfigured

One could ask what new materialism has to offer, given the fact that theatre habitually trades on blurring distinctions between the animate and the inanimate (Schneider 2015: 14). However, the lack of attention paid to materiality impinges, in particular, on our understanding of scenography. A new materialist perspective invites reconsideration of well-worn tropes such as the designer being the interpreter of the text, or generator of visual metaphor, or provider of props and supports to actors or director or manipulator of audience responses. New materialist thinking provides a spur to explore the expressivity and instability of theatre materials as part of their contribution to aesthetic experience. Moving humans out of the spotlight, for a moment at least, gives a fresh perspective on the processes of making, performing and attending to theatre.

Brack's designs are unusually bold, although by no means unique,[10] in the way that they foreground materials. However, across the body of her work, her designs consistently and insistently make the case for materials as an active part of performance. Brack's sketch for *Iwanov* conveys these basic ideas: there will be fog (lots of it) and there will be bodies. The fog will be moving. In this sketch, this is all that is required to convey the potential for scenographic intra-action. The focus of the drawing is on scenography in its forward trajectory. It does not invite us to read backwards from the intention of the designer but rather to imagine how the fog might creatively commingle with the actors' bodies.

This drawing underlines the fundamentally co-operative nature of all kinds of materials, within theatre. As well as the bodies and the fog on the stage, the drawing implies machines to generate the fog, technicians to operate them, to decide when enough is enough. It suggests that the fog might not

FIGURE 3.2 *Katrin Brack, sketch for* Iwanov, *dir. by Dimiter Gotscheff, Volksbühne Berlin 2005.* © *K. Brack.*

be contained by the stage. It also underlines the idea that an aesthetics of scenographic reception is founded not in a spectator reading a stage picture but that it arises as part of a temporal and experiential process that emerges from the intra-action of materials. As Bleeker proposes:

> Performance design is not a practice of inscribing matter with meaning, nor of putting together independent entities, but proceeds through setting up intra-actions that allow matter its due in the performance's becoming. (Bleeker 2017: 128)

A designer's role can be seen to be initiating conditions for intra-action, for setting in motion an ongoing process of formation where scenography is a gathering of lively matter coming together in an assemblage or a meshwork of 'material flows' (Ingold 2011: 88). This challenges ways we have traditionally thought about theatre materials and realigns assumed relationships between theatre makers, audiences and materials. It helps us to understand scenography as an experiential and emergent event rather than a static image or a self-contained artefact; something that manifests itself fully at the moment when an individual spectator senses it working, when meaning congeals through the intra-actions of their sensing body and the vibrant materials on stage.

Scenographic materialism clears a space for us to look specifically at the work that materials do in scenography, to move away from ways of talking about scenographies as objects that need human agency to bring them to life. It opens up a way to think about the discursive, yet non-linguistic, nature of scenography and to the embodied nature of the way in which audiences engage with it. A strict divide between human and non-human no longer seems tenable as part of a theory of how scenography works. Following from this, divisions between materiality and signification are also unhelpful for scenography where matter and meaning are intertwined. Scenographic mattering is a continuous process, through making, performing and attending to performance where materials have a continuous and active influence. This way of approaching materials will not be novel to many designers, but it has implications for the way scenography is figured in theatre scholarship. This is not simply a case of claiming recognition for the often overlooked work of designers, but of finding a way to foreground the fundamentally material-discursive nature of theatre.

Notes

1 Katrin Brack has received numerous awards for her stage designs in Germany and Austria (several times 'Stage Designer of the Year', awarded by the journal *Theater Heute*; 'Faust' award in 2006; Nestroy prize in 2007

and 2017) and her lifetime achievement in theatre was recognized at the Venice Biennale in 2017, but until the publication of *Bühnenbild/Stages* in 2010 (in German and English, ed. Anja Nioduschewski), her work was not widely known in the English-speaking world.

2   According to the artist's own reflections on her work, one of her most important goals is 'to create a stage set that is atmospherically charged and makes it possible to generate precise but far-reaching associations, as well as physically intense impressions' (Nioduschewski 2010: 175).

3   Rick Dolphijn and Iris van der Tuin noticed the first use of 'new materialism' in the late 1990s to identify a cultural theory 'that does not privilege the side of culture' and radically rethinks dualisms 'between nature and culture, matter and mind, the human and the inhuman' (Dolphijn and Tuin 2012: 93).

4   For example Hans-Thies Lehmann's book on *Postdramatic Theatre* (2006), which includes accounts of scenographic structures and materials as performance in the work of pioneers such as Robert Wilson and Tadeusz Kantor, as well as Josephine Machon's (2009) analysis of the visceral and '(syn)aesthetic' impact of immersive theatre; both offer the possibility of scenography as a central rather than peripheral aspect of theatre experience but still reinforce anthropocentric accounts of the how scenography operates.

5   Tanja Beer (2016) has also drawn on new materialism to develop her practice of eco-scenography and Kathleen Irwin (2017) has explored questions of ethics and responsibility in scenography using Karen Barad's ideas. I have also reflected on the agency of scenographic objects in my own practice research (2015).

6   Brack began her work as a designer in the mid-1980s after studying stage design in Düsseldorf and, since then, has worked at theatre houses such as the Volksbühne am Rosa-Luxemburg-Platz Berlin, Schaubühne Berlin, Centraltheater Leipzig, Thalia Theater Hamburg, Schauspiel Frankfurt, Kammerspiele Munich, the Burgtheater Vienna, Het Toneelhuis Antwerpen and NT Gent.

7   Stefanie Carp, 'Worlds beyond History' (Nioduschewski 2010: 22).

8   Wolfram Koch, 'Gorillas in the Mist' (Nioduschewski 2010: 240).

9   Almut Zilcher, 'Risen from the Foam' (Nioduschewski 2010: 241).

10 Other performance makers who have foregrounded the performance of materials include Philippe Quesne, Heiner Goebbels, Kris Verdonck and William Forysthe.

4

Composing scenography

Reflections on Klaus Grünberg's collaborations with Heiner Goebbels and others

David Roesner and Klaus Grünberg

For this chapter, the notion of 'dialogue' is a central pivot: it has been written as a continuous exchange between a theatre scholar and a stage designer, but it also investigates the interplays between practice and research, between director and scenographer, and between music and scene. It is also 'dialogic', not just in the sense of a to and fro between two or more speakers, but also in Mikhail Bakhtin's sense (developed in his seminal work of literary criticism *The Dialogic Imagination* from 1975[1]), in which works of literature (and we would argue other works of art, too) are always in communication with each other and mutually inform each other, both forwards and backwards in time.[2] A second perspective that informs this text is the recent scholarly interest that has been directed towards creative processes and rehearsal practices. Under headings such as 'genetic research' (Féral 2008) or 'rehearsal ethnography' (Buchmann, Lafer and Ruhm 2010; McAuley 2012; Matzke 2015), theatre practices have been analysed through field research within the rehearsal space, qualitative research through interviews or even quantitative research based on surveys or various data collections.

With this in mind we present this chapter as a dialogue on process(es) to underscore the dual authorship as well as the reluctance to arrive at one coherent argument. It is, to stay with Bakhtin, a *heteroglossia* (in the sense of distinctly different 'voices', idioms, even jargon) of reflections, hoping to both give insight into Klaus Grünberg's work as well as its theoretical contexts and consequences.[3] We have structured the dialogue into three sections, which highlight different aspects of the problem at hand: the fluid relationship between music, composition and scenography, none of which can be seen as being fixed and discreet categories. First, we look at 'music with images', then at 'composing with scenography' and, finally, we will explore the notion of the instrument as an entity *on* stage as well as a metaphor *for* the stage.

'Music with images' *(Bebilderung)* – beyond a practice of *Bebilderung*

David Roesner – *No more décor*

The relationship of music-theatre and scenography has often been a complicated one. From early forms of extravaganza, exuberant spectacle and stage machinery that sought to 'wow' Baroque audiences and help to sell tickets to more recent practices of what has been called *Bebilderung* or *Ausstattung* in German theatre (i.e. providing merely décor and furniture as a backdrop), there was always a danger that seeing and hearing, scenography and composition would compete with each other, eclipse each other or even imitate and duplicate each other. This much maligned practice of the *Dopplung* (doubling) of sound and image is, according to most German directors and dramaturges, something that has to be avoided at all costs.

In the twentieth century, this relationship was continually under review: early on, Adolphe Appia introduced notions of 'rhythmic spaces' and a musical sense of lighting design that revolutionized our thinking and was echoed in the works of Einar Schleef, Robert Wilson and Heiner Goebbels. Appia's scenographic vision was very much about musical qualities in the visual and spatial design of theatre staged, as Richard Beacham explains:

> In the spring of 1909 Appia created about twenty designs which he termed 'Rhythmic Space'. ... Because of the qualities of architectural harmony and proportion with which Appia imbued them, though lacking any element of time or movement themselves, as the eye surveyed them they could nevertheless visually provide a strong sense of rhythm. (Beacham 1994: 79)

And in relation to light, Appia puts it this way: 'Light has an almost miraculous flexibility ... it can create shadows, make them living, and spread the harmony of their vibrations in space, just as music does' (Appia 1993 [1919]: 114). By use of a musical analogy, Appia thus realizes light's formal potential and rhythmic quality. By applying musical thinking, Appia liberates light from its mere pragmatic and narrative/atmospheric functions: light no longer only helps us to see the actor and the painted scenery better or to identify the location, general atmosphere or time of day in an imitation of realistic light settings.

Ninety years later, composer Helmut Lachenmann took another turn when calling his landmark opera *Das Mädchen mit den Schwefelhölzern* (*Little Match Girl*, 1988–96) (based on the Hans Christian Andersen fairy tale) a *'Musik mit Bildern'* (music with images),[4] which deliberately challenges conventions of staging and the respective roles of music and image:

> Could not the fact that I depict everything in my music, which means: occupy the imaginary, narrative part, maybe even obstruct it, be a challenge for a director, challenge him/her to creatively respond or resist? ... The theatrical has to redefine itself, which is exactly what I ask of myself in composing. Of course: if trombone glissandi imitate a vehicle racing by, you cannot also show that on stage. But this action needs to be theatrically counterpointed by whatever means. Music and scene can cast a different light on to each other, reinforce each other. Structures can be revalidated by counter-structures, and the imagination, that has been occupied by me, maybe put into a different light, complemented, cracked open and enhanced again by theatrical imagery. (Lachenmann 2001: 30–1, trans. D. Roesner)

This idea of the autonomy as well as the independence of image and music and the challenges this presents struck me as being a particularly relevant theme when discussing Klaus Grünberg's work. Now follows his perspective.

Klaus Grünberg – Scenographic designs in the rehearsal and production processes: Autonomous role and heterogeneous interactions

Set design also tells the story, but in its own, maybe different way.
RUTH BERGHAUS

It was probably this statement and the experience of working with her as Erich Wonder's assistant that brought me to my perspective on the relations between different media in a theatre production: image, space and light need to play independent roles, and they need to do that in the production process. They each have their own rules of composition, they follow their own grammar and they need to be designed and played according to these rules, just like in a music ensemble where every instrument has to be played in its own specific way to be able to harmonize with the other instruments, or perhaps like in a piece of music that is made up of various heterogeneous, independent voices, and where *unisono* parts only occur as interesting exceptions.

Whenever several theatrical elements come together (music, text, light, space, visual elements, media and props, acting, dancing, etc.), I prefer them not to all tell the same story at the same time, but rather to enter into a conversation of different voices, telling us more than any single voice could possibly tell. I find it problematic when the different media are in unison too often. This issue arises especially when directors design their own set. They will want to design something that is practicable for their directing ideas and then their staging will be confined by the framework of their design. In most cases, this leads to a lack of resistance, surprise, friction and contrast. The result is often too logical, too consistent and too plain and therefore one-dimensional. When, in contrast, members of a production team determine a direction to aim for and then choose independent paths to follow, their heterogeneous interactions generate synergy that often leads further than any goal they might have formulated beforehand. Therefore, I believe it is necessary to keep the different media separate while they are being developed and to bring them together at a later stage, when they are mature and fully formed. In this way, they evolve as strong and independent partners that can enter into a dialogue with each other.

In the opera and theatre productions that I am involved in, there are usually three phases of collaboration:

1 A content-related orientation phase: Discussion with the entire production team where I quite strictly make sure that we don't talk about visual ideas but determine the fundamental issues in terms of thematic content.

2 Independent design period: Here, the design team experiments and develops the visual and scenographic form of the production as a scale model, working alone, without the other leading team members, for several weeks.

3 Presentation of the scenography in the form of precise scale models including lighting and movements or scene changes. In complex cases, modified photos of the scale model help to simulate the ideas. In this phase, the rest of the team can react to our concept and make their own suggestions.

Six weeks before the opening night, all of these elements are elaborated on and can then be built and rehearsed with.

This is not meant to be a rigid, linear system – there are many detours, shortcuts and exceptions – but the phase of independent scenographic conception, during which its specific qualities and inherent rules can unfold, is very important to me. For instance, in productions with Heiner Goebbels, the first phase is not only a discussion at the table but also includes a few days of a hands-on jam session on stage with elements that can be suggested by any member of the production team. It is crucial that these rehearsals include all forms of media: image, costume, light, sound, actors, musicians, text and so on, so that we can judge our ideas by trying them out in practice instead of discussing them abstractly. Of course, this method can only work when the collaborating artists trust each other and communicate with openness, curiosity and respect with regard to the results of their partners. Also, it can only work when the producing theatres are aware of these processes. The production conditions must adapt to the needs of this kind of collaboration. If scenography is to play an autonomous role as well as acting and reacting as an independent partner, it must be given space in the production schedule: technical rehearsals, days on which the possibilities of the room can be explored, and sufficient time for lighting rehearsals. In many theatres, this is still very problematic and sufficient working conditions must be fought for, every single time. The repertoire system in most subsidized theatres in Germany, for example, allows for comparatively little time to rehearse on stage and operates with technical crews, which work in shifts, rather than for a particular production. Most of the rehearsal time takes place with rehearsal costumes in rudimentary rehearsal sets and without lighting, which prevents the mutual development of these elements. This makes productions that deviate from the standard production process and chronology very difficult.

As a good example of a production that was developed simultaneously from different directions (scenography, music, staging, acting, dancing, etc.), I will give some insight into the production process of *De Materie* at Ruhrtriennale (2014),[5] which was conceived in the much less restrictive context of a major arts festival.

The making of *De Materie*

Even though the music of this opera had already been written by Louis Andriessen in 1988 and could therefore not react to our ideas (which of course would have been a wonderful thing), its form of four separate and very different parts makes it very open to both the designer and director's autonomous creation process.

We chose the huge former industrial hall Kraftzentrale in Duisburg as the location.[6] Thanks to its enormous dimensions (200m long, 34m wide and 18m high), I could make its architecture disappear into darkness if need be. As we began, we discussed extensively what this opera is about (sung and spoken texts from the thirteenth to the twentieth centuries of seemingly incoherent historic figures, circling the topic of matter, and the orchestra music that at times is very closely connected to the text sometimes adds a completely independent voice) – but also what our production of it would be about (emphasizing the opera's structure of four heterogeneous chapters and an associative investigation of the opposing subjects spirit and matter, science and emotion, religion and eroticism, nature and nuclear physics). Then we made a list of what we would like to try out at our so-called jam session a year ahead of the premiere.

Heiner wanted to work with a flock of sheep – an idea that I quite liked because sheep (and animals in general) refuse to be directed. I wanted to experiment with remote-controlled luminous zeppelins, not so much because of the zeppelins themselves, but rather to have a tool allowing me to scan and explore the immense interior of the Kraftzentrale. In our jam session, we tried out the zeppelins together with all of the other elements that we had available, and it turned out that a combination of sheep, a luminous zeppelin and

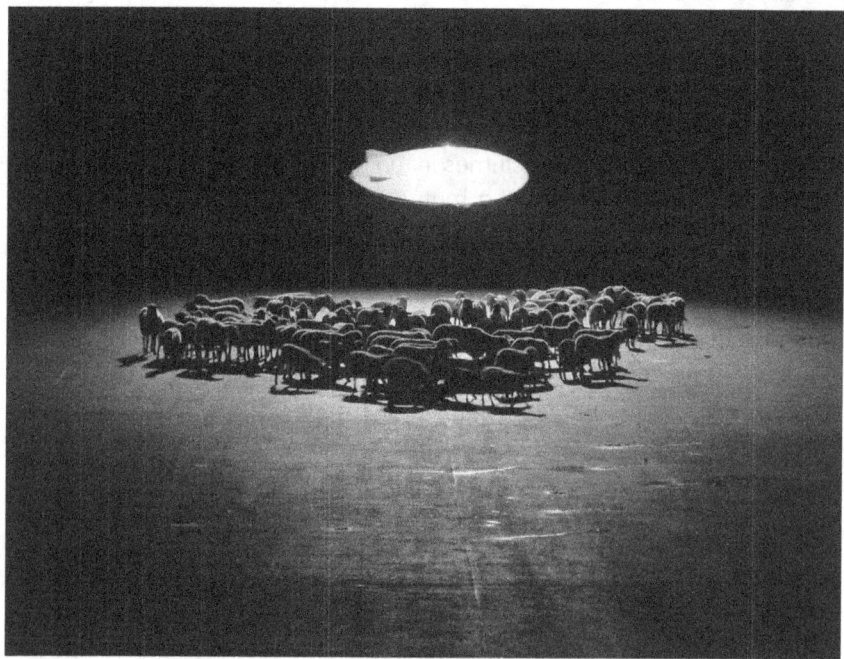

FIGURE 4.1 *Klaus Grünberg,* De Materie, *dir. by Heiner Goebbels, Ruhrtriennale 2014, sheep and zeppelin.* © *K. Grünberg.*

fitting backlighting was just the right thing for the fourth act of *De Materie*. No one was directing or designing this scene: the sheep decided where they wanted to go, the zeppelin led or followed them and the scene just emerged from the ingredients that were given. Thanks to this method, we discovered solutions that we couldn't have expressed or imagined beforehand.

Back home with all of the input from the jam sessions, the design team built a scale model and went on experimenting with the scenographic form of the show, independently from the rest of the team. We built a flock of illuminated tents in the shape of the Kraftzentrale – forming a counterpoint to the immensity and darkness of the space housing the production.

The other element that I felt was worth experimenting with was a double pendulum that I first tried out as a scale model (1:10) and, at a later stage, at full scale.[7] The movement of double pendulums is utterly unpredictable. Even mathematicians are unable to calculate what will happen, and that is precisely why I chose it. I can design the pendulum – but I cannot shape or design its movements. I really like this idea: I don't want to draw my movement in the air; I want to create a device that draws on its own.

We designed the show without following a dramaturgical masterplan but through several days of experimenting and exploring the venue, the objects, visual elements and Louis Andriessen's music. This happened very intuitively and with great openness on our part to each medium's inherent qualities. We also let coincidence play an important role. Consequently, the staging emerged from all ingredients simultaneously: the visual, the spatial, the choreographic and the musical, giving each medium its autonomy and allowing them all to tell the story in their own way.

Composing with scenography – *Europeras*

David Roesner – Theatre and compositional thinking

The relative autonomy and contrapunctal relationship between music, staging and scenography, which Klaus Grünberg described above, can clearly be contextualized in a particular kind of music–image relationship and a compositional practice, which Matthias Rebstock and I have sought to capture under the heading of *Composed Theatre* (2012). I will outline some of the key characteristics of this field at this point. Composed Theatre describes a process of theatre making, where the act of composing (in a musical sense) extends beyond the mere organization of audible events. All elements of the theatre are now potentially subjected to compositional thinking and become material in a polyphonic score of sounds, space(s), architecture, design, gestures, lights, colours, props, video and so on. Compositional techniques, such as motivic or thematic development, permutations, rhythmical forms of shaping time, thinking in parameters such as pitch, duration, volume and timbre, but also jamming, sampling, looping and improvising are applied to potentially all elements of the stage. While this field of practice has flourished over the past two decades and is associated with practitioners such as Heiner Goebbels, Dieter Schnebel, Manos Tsangaris, Carola Bauckholt and Christoph Marthaler, earlier examples can also be found, for example in John Cage's and Mauricio Kagel's compositions.[8] A brief example by the latter may illustrate the point.

In 1965, Kagel wrote *Die Himmelsmechanik* (*Celestial Mechanics*), a composition for moving scenographic elements. According to Rebstock, it

> provides a particularly clear exemplification of how composition shaped by the experiences of serial music goes beyond its influences and leads to its own form of Composed Theatre. The piece is identified by a subheading in the score as a *Composition with stage sets*. In an Italian-style theatre the parts of a stage set move about: 'At first, grey-pink clouds drift by, then a blue vapour appears in which the sunrise totters upward. As if by accident, the moon appears for a brief moment. He comes back though, marries the sun, such that only the full moon remains' (Schnebel 1970: 173). And all the movements of these set pieces are precisely notated in the score, where they follow a compositional and not a narrative logic. (Rebstock 2012: 40)

Composed Theatre has since found a wide range of expressions, which we in turn may associate more strongly with music theatre, concerts, installations, dance or performance. What they have in common is that music and stage, composition and scenography are much more intertwined here, their hierarchies no longer predetermined, their notation sometimes directly meshed together, their cuing often digitally connected through software, which can trigger acoustic, visual or robotic events, their authorship often shared or densely interwoven.

With a sense of humour similar to Kagel's (but with otherwise altogether different intentions, or non-intentions), John Cage undertook another deconstruction of music theatre with his *Europeras 1–5*. Parts 1 and 2 are the most discussed, and premiered in Frankfurt in 1987. Stefan Beyst describes the work:

> The musical material of the *Europeras* consists of fragments of operas from the eighteenth and nineteenth century. No music made by the composer, but 'found' music: 'ready made music', or 'musique trouvée'. In *Europera 1 & 2*, this material is brought by 19 singers performing the song parts from opera fragments, 28 instrumentalists playing isolated parts form the orchestral accompaniment, and by the 'Truckera', a tape with

101 aria's [sic] superimposed … . The original concept of *Europera 1 & 2* in Frankfurt comprised wrestlers, acrobats and zeppelins. In the final version, John Cage restricted himself to dancers, singers and instrumentalists. The costumes and the decors are borrowed from old encyclopaedias – again: 'objets trouvés'. There are all kinds of props and a kind of scenario for the movements on the scene. … Also the 'light events', the movement of the actors and the props over the numbers of the grid are determined by a chance operations generator. Just like the choice of the arias, also the choice of the costumes is relegated to the discretion of the wearers. (Beyst 2005)

William Fetterman explains further that all elements of the *mise-en-scène* were 'selected and composed according to chance procedures using an *I Ching* computer program designed by Andrew Culver' (Fetterman 1996: 167). Instead of a conductor, singers and performers follow a 'videotaped digital time-display' (Fetterman 1996: 170). Their position as well as those of stage elements and flats was also determined by chance, according to a chessboard-like floor plan with sixty-four squares. The 3,726 light cues are also composed and available from the music publisher – interestingly the colour palette is restricted to a large number of different whites, with hardly any coloured lights at all. As often with Cage's music-theatrical compositions, but never quite at this scale, there is a great sense of playful contradiction between the required accuracy and sheer precision in performing something deliberately arrived at through chance. It also means that our basic instincts as semiotic animals, as meaning-seeking audiences, are completely sidelined. It is, as Heinz-Klaus Metzger (who commissioned the work) called it, an 'irreversible negation of the opera as such' (Beyst 2005).

What becomes evident in these practices of transferring or transposing compositional principles to other media and materials is that not only is the nature of what composing means interrogated, but also the ontological conditions of its 'material' and the ways in which we phenomenologically sense the composed theatre at play. Beyst put it this way:

> The generalisation of the principle of composition also changes the nature of composition itself. Both an octave and the colour spectrum can be divided in twelve, but the colours thus obtained do not therefore relate like tones: there is no such thing as a colour that would be the dominant of another that would be its tonic. The mathematical relation that expresses such a relation looses every musical concreteness when it is generalised to the domain of colours. (Beyst 2005)

During the 2012 Ruhrtriennale, Klaus Grünberg and Heiner Goebbels staged *Europeras 1&2*, and here Grünberg reflects on this experience.

Klaus Grünberg – Europeras 1 & 2

Creating *Europeras* was a fascinating but also ambivalent experience. In my work, I often explore ways to let art generate itself. I want to make the hand of the artist disappear. For me the impact of an artwork is much stronger when I, as a viewer, do not constantly sense the artist's intentions behind it – especially in my own work. I want to interact with the work, not the artist. This is why I like John Cage's use of chance operations. In *Europeras 1* (1987) he creates a system that generates a meta-opera out of the material fed into it. Instead of writing an opera, he wrote the recipe for its creation and gave some instructions on how to select the material to be used. He dissected the theatrical language into different categories: music, singing, gesture, props, set design, costume, light and so on. The production team's task is to fill these categories with their choice of material from existing operas and then let the system rearrange it. This concept presupposes that it is indeed possible to dissect theatrical language into separate entities. However, I personally don't believe this to be possible.

This raises interesting questions concerning the independence of these theatrical elements. When we imagine a room with a lamp, does the lamp lighting the room belong to the category 'light' or 'room'? Does the light falling through a window belong to the window or does the window belong to the light? Does the wall with a window in it belong to the category 'light', since it is blocking the light that does not fall through the window? To which categories should we assign lamp, window and wall? It is amazing to watch the art form theatre writhing and wriggling, reluctant to be sorted into such a system. Because they consist of so many different parameters, set designs are very difficult to deal with in such a way. This is why feeding Cage's system requires an authority that sorts and organizes, and makes decisions – the kind of authority that Cage was trying to avoid.

Perhaps for this reason, Cage himself, in his staging of *Europeras* in 1987 in Frankfurt, left out set design and reduced the visual aspect to two-dimensional pictorial quotations printed on flats (covered frames). In our production at Ruhrtriennale in 2012 we were fortunate enough to play in the famous Jahrhunderthalle.[9] This former machine hall of the steel industry with its industrial architecture could serve perfectly as an image producing structure. The vast building seemed very suitable for us to manoeuvre and change the large opera images, so we decided to reinclude set design as a category in this production.

We filled Cage's set-design category, the so-called flat cues, with thirty-two set designs quoting European theatre history of the past 400 years and visualized them in a timeline (on average three set designs in ten minutes)[10]: Due to the complexity of the opera art form, this approach quickly leads to impracticable and even dangerous chaos, if it is not very cleverly organized.

COMPOSING SCENOGRAPHY

FIGURE 4.2 *Klaus Grünberg*, Europeras 1, *dir. by Heiner Goebbels, Ruhrtriennale 2012, the scenographer's table* © *K. Grünberg.*

In practice, the organizational, logistical and technical (and of course artistic) necessities are so demanding that Cage's guidelines are very difficult to follow. At some point, certain decisions had to be made so that I am not sure if, in the end, we succeeded in applying the chance-operated methods that Cage proposes.

Composing space and light according to musical criteria

I often find musical language very useful to describe scenographic processes. The design of my sets follows rhythmical patterns and musical expressions. The criteria of visual design are quite similar, especially regarding rhythm and dynamics.

The parallels to music are particularly striking when it comes to lighting. Perhaps this is because light is as immaterial as music. I am interested in the temporal dimension of light: light can fade, expire, flash, flicker – all temporal events. Lighting cues have a fade time, a rhythm. I realize that I often emanate sounds to describe lighting ideas in the theatre, for example I 'sing' lighting cues. And I find it a pity that light does not actually make these sounds! In *Stifters Dinge*, I managed to make light audible by putting a mechanical shutter on a 5kW fresnel light, which was then amplified, so that the light made a loud shutter noise every time that it went on or off and one could not tell if the light produced the sound or if it was actually vice versa.

The instrument on stage – the stage as instrument: *Stifters Dinge*

Klaus Grünberg – *Creating a performance without a performer*

Our production of *Stifters Dinge* (*Stifter's Things*; Lausanne, 2007)[11] was an experiment to find out if we could stage a performance without a performer. In our earlier production, *Max Black* (Lausanne, 1998), Heiner Goebbels and I discovered how inanimate things on stage exert a great fascination when being treated as performing elements. Even though we see that these objects are controlled through cables attached to them, we still paradoxically think they follow intentions or even emotions. This illusion works despite us knowing that we are watching remote-controlled dead matter. This in turn surprises us, which intensifies the effect. Perhaps an illusion is even more convincing when we can see how it is done. I have always been fascinated by the phenomenon of technical or abstract representation having an emotional impact. This was our starting point for our production of *Stifters Dinge*.

Working on this production, my first steps were to structure the room and propose visual elements to work with, such as a water basin, illuminated water tanks or gauze curtains coming in from above. Goebbels' starting points were automated pianos, table guitars and more unusual instruments or sound-producing objects. In our collaboration, it has always been essential that sound objects should be visually interesting and visual elements should sound interesting.

After a few days of exploring all elements together in our jam session, I wanted to make some notable changes: instead of using one large water basin, I preferred a series of three equal smaller ones to give the room a basic rhythm.

Furthermore, I wanted to switch the colour of the water basin's surface, alternating between black and white for the duration of the performance. The piece begins with a black tarp in the water basins. Later, they are covered with white salt, which reflects light and projections very well. Then water flows into the basins, dissolving the white salt, turning the surface black again and allowing reflections of the objects surrounding it. Next, a machine under the travelling bridges drops pieces of dry ice into the water, turning the surface white again, and finally, the dry ice dissolves, once again blackening the

FIGURE 4.3 Stifters Dinge, *Théâtre Vidy, Lausanne 2007, basic rhythm.* © K. Grünberg.

surface.¹² According to this concept, rhythm constitutes an elementary part of the scenography. Rhythm does not exist without time – it is a temporal sequence. Thus, time is a fundamental element of scenography.

At the same time, developing *Stifters Dinge* reminded me of creating a garden: you design a ground plan, choose the plants and affect the conditions. However, the garden will have to grow and develop on its own. The only things left for you to do are a little watering or cutting off some branches. You can only wait and let it happen on its own. I often apply this idea to theatre. There are many examples in *Stifters Dinge* where the material itself acts, where, inside a designed and organized environment, the images draw themselves. Water finds its own way through the salt. A growing black surface erases the white salt landscape. Light reflects on agitated water without being designed by anyone. Dry ice bubbles at random.

Related to this principle of 'letting things grow', Heiner Goebbels had a slightly different approach:

Let me describe how we created this: I had a keyboard, which was designed by my friend and colleague Hubert Machnik as an interface to all the engines (via MAX MSP) On this keyboard I could control nearly everything in a musical way: one key to set the stone in motion, another key to move the stone backwards. F sharp was used to make it go faster and G sharp stopped it. Another key was used to start the rain, one for the light shutter to go on and off, etc. and all that in addition to providing the musical access to the mechanical pianos. This made it possible to work in a musical way, composing the visual, the space and the sound elements from this keyboard. A keyboard was used to direct like a composer. Probably this musical approach represents a way of working, probably all these decisions (when to emphasise a light or when to move something) go through my body as a director as much as they went through my body as a keyboard player in the rehearsals of this piece. I did music theatre before the keyboard. But it allows you to do things rather uncontrolledly or to let your body (as a composer/director) react to a material or an image. (Goebbels 2012: 118)

Goebbels and I both share a musical approach to theatre: while working on *Stifters Dinge*, we both had equipment available that gave us a direct control of everything that happened on stage.

With his keyboard, the sound designer's desk, the video technician's computer and the lighting desk that let me control not only the light but also – through a control device developed by Thierry Kaltenrieder – the movement of the piano bridges and the gauze curtains, we were able to stage the installation on the spot and in real time. Without preplanning and almost without speaking to each other, we could enter an intuitive dialogue with the objects on stage and with each other. This non-hierarchic jam session went on for several days (machines do not need a break …).

While Heiner Goebbels emphasizes his visceral, pianistic aspect of this process, I expressly do not want this direct physical connection to the proceedings on stage. I value that which he would probably describe as an impediment: for me, breaking down an idea or a process into parameters, numbers and commands is a fundamental process while creating art. I find it very helpful that I must translate ideas and intuition into an abstract language. A large part of my design is done by typing commands into a lighting desk, which results in the movements of objects or light. This creates a distance between me and the proceedings on stage. I like that operating the lighting desk is not intuitive. This interface then translates the abstract language into something I can watch. The result is then presented to me as if I were just any other spectator and I can be as objective and critical as if I hadn't designed it at all.

David Roesner – Stage as instrument

As we have seen in Grünberg's account, he and Goebbels present an entire stage in their production *Stifters Dinge*, which functions as an instrument. This is an idea that resonates throughout the theatrical avant-garde movements of the twentieth century (Appia, Bauhaus, etc.) and is also beautifully expressed by director Peter Mussbach in reference to Lachenmann's opera, which I mentioned at the beginning of this chapter:

> *Little Girl with Matches* provokes a scene, theatre as an instrument. This instrument is double-headed: it is imaginary, hardly visible and is played by no-one except the orchestra itself. The stage is the instrument, played by the orchestra. In that sense the stage depends on the orchestra. Without the orchestra it wouldn't exist. The scene alone is nothing without it. This instrument follows its own laws, though. But this remains invisible. (Mussbach in Lachenmann 2001: 48, trans. D. Roesner)

Mussbach's notion is a more metaphorical one, however, whereas Goebbels and Grünberg, also due to advanced technology, literally 'play' the stage much more as an instrument. The result is a hybrid performance, which combines elements of theatre, installation, radio-play and exhibition – with hints of a physics or chemistry lab. It facilitates a contemplation of nature, culture, technology and voices for the spectator and is characterized by an almost complete absence of human performers.[13] The continuous soundtrack of the piece is produced by five automated pianos, stacked on top of each other, as well as cymbals, tubes, wires and other mechanical constructions that produce ticking, grinding, crashing, thumping, cracking and humming sounds. The stripped-open pianos have been rigged with different complex robotic mechanisms, which extend the pianos' expressive range from 'normal' playing to different techniques of scratching and plucking their strings directly. All of this is programmed and operated from a bank of computers via MAX/MSP software – low tech sound production[14] (e.g. a stone being drawn over a rough surface) meets high-end steering technology.[15]

If we look at the scenography of *Stifters Dinge* in the context of a history of automated instruments, from the player piano or pianola, via the orchestrion to Yamaha's Disklavier, Goebbels and Grünberg transform the kind of interaction historically associated with automated instruments in significant ways. Historically, it was a key transition in the development of automated instruments when the player pianos, which had populated homes and bars for some time, transformed into 'reproducing pianos' from around 1911 onwards. The transition from arranged rolls to hand-played rolls meant that live performances of an actual pianist could now be reproduced by the instrument, including the individual timing and dynamics of the human performance. The somewhat mechanical and 'noisy' clunking of the player piano gave way to a technology that not only captured a tune but an individual rendition of that tune or even 'the performance of a master' (Armstrong 2007: 3). This audibly brings back the element of intentionality into the mix (and as we have read above, this applies differently to Goebbels than to Grünberg): the instrument now echoes the presence of an interpretive musical mind and renders 'noise' into music by 'emancipating' it, as Walter Benjamin might have described it (Armstrong 2007: 16).

It is particularly the theatrical aspect of this transition I am interested in. The scenography of *Stifters Dinge* is built not to store music, but to recreate the performance of music. Goebbels and Grünberg could have used playbacks of the same kinds of sounds, captured by samplers as digital files, but instead they have gone to great lengths to ensure that the audience does not engage with recorded sounds, but recorded performances, recreated by machines and actual instruments. The key difference to the reproducing piano is that the performance is no longer integral, but that it is assembled from layers and layers of acts of performing, programming and editing. It is, for the most part, not performed on the actual instruments, but consists of a translation from a controlling device – a keyboard for Goebbels, computed parameters for Grünberg – to a plethora of instruments and playing techniques. The machine, one could argue, is built in such a way that it does not remember and reproduce a sound, but remembers the *gesture* that produces a sound.

In addition, the two theatre makers exploit the sheer space needed and the spectacle produced by the both intricate and enormous apparatuses by using them as theatrical set design, as well as instilling them with aspects of theatrical dramaturgy, for example by creating a sense of expectation, entrance and revelation. At some point in *Stifters Dinge*, the wall of pianos glides to the front of the stage like an actor stepping forward to deliver a soliloquy. Grünberg also uses elements of rhythmically synchronized lighting to highlight and pinpoint which parts of the apparatus are currently 'acting' and playing.

The old nickel-operated orchestrions of the 1920s actually mostly concealed the mechanics of music production behind the doors of wardrobe-like constructions. In terms of performance, they played with the contrast of the simple nickel that went in and the abundance and complexity of sound that came out. In contrast, Goebbels and Grünberg have an interest in revealing the sound source and the technology used on them: most of their mechanical devices replace actual musicians and point at their ostentatious absence. At the same time, they draw attention to the 'noise' of 'musicking' (Small 1998) – here, the effort and the materiality of sound production.

All this emphasizes the continued performative 'difference' (in Deleuze's sense (2001)) between the sounds produced, the way they are produced and our expectations. In both cases there is friction between sound source and sound event, like an interfering noise between signal and receiver. But rather than being a disturbance, the performance exploits the challenge this posits for the audience and makes it a central part of the attraction. The audience is forced into a very active mode of investigation, asking itself 'how is this

COMPOSING SCENOGRAPHY

done?' or 'where does this come from?' It needs to employ a dual consciousness, which engages both with what is being said or played and how it is being conveyed.[16] Other modes of performance, such as Hollywood films, realist dramas or blockbuster musicals, seek to reduce the 'signal-to-noise ratio' and allow for a more uninterrupted immersion, but here there is a conscious engagement with noise in the sense of what Douglas Kahn calls 'that constant grating sound generated by the movement between the abstract and the empirical' (Kahn 1999: 25). Goebbels and Grünberg make use of this friction.

In the specific way in which Goebbels (and his team) have programmed the interfaces between stage mechanics and computer software, he makes use of his intuitive and personal relationship with his primary musical instrument, the keyboard, so that the process of inputting data, programming tracks, and controlling elements of stage technology are all connected to his body, his memory and the use of expressive vocabularies as a musician. Grünberg, on the other hand, chooses to take a more mediated and defamiliarized way, which is perhaps today's equivalent of the mechanically produced piano roll; that is, the creation of MIDI impulses on a computer screen via mouse clicks and entered numerical parameters.

While in the early days of barrel organs and orchestrions, a machine controlled the musical instrument, Goebbels now makes use of the possibility that he can again use a musical instrument to control the machine that operates another musical instrument. But other than the reproducing piano, which repeats the identical performance of a human being made on the very same instrument, Goebbels uses the element of translation between instrumental idioms in the search for the sound yet unheard, the image yet unseen. He and Grünberg create a world of sounds that could not be reproduced by human performers, but at the same time give it a 'human touch' in the process of programming it.

On stage then, there are also strategies of anthropomorphism, which allow the audience to see the automated instrument both as man (or beast, as Bell argues) and machine. Goebbels and Grünberg animate the objects and instruments of their stage, arranging their sounds and movements both rhythmically and spatially. The musicality brings forth the live effect of the production.

There is a section where four gauze curtains appear to 'dance' to the water reflections of light on their surfaces (which also look like waveforms of sounds); in addition, a spotlight, whose shutter mechanism is amplified to produce a percussive sound, seems to wilfully interject into a recording of aboriginal incantations.

In a curious way, I would even argue that the animation and emancipation of the instruments as stage and of the stage as instrument in Goebbels' work is supported and enabled by his understanding of theatre as a machine;

a machine, however, whose blueprint we have to redesign and reread with each production, rather than relying on the well-tried, 'well-oiled' mechanism to kick in, which would inevitably reproduce more of the same, but nothing new. Goebbels elaborates:

> The students at Gießen University[17] have called the form of presenting their work 'theatre machine'; this machine includes everything, not just the hardware of the fly tower, but all of the people, materials and means involved therein ... If you like, the whole staging concept of my pieces *Black on White, Max Black* and *Eislermaterial* is that each is a machine, which sets its own, new rules. From these, all of the artistic consequences emerge as well as the aesthetics and the impact of the performance. These rules have to be worked on; all those involved in the production have to learn to read their blueprint. (Goebbels 2003: 23, trans. D. Roesner)

Seeing the theatre on the whole as a machine brings into focus how all of the elements contribute to a final production. This necessitates Goebbels and his team actively reflecting on and artistically shaping their interplay, rather than just relying on established relationships, hierarchies and artistic effects. This in turn affords the audience an 'evenly hovering attention' (Freud 1912: 111) which acknowledges both the novelty and virtuosity made possible by the process of automation as well as the familiarity of the personal theatrical and musical vocabularies of Goebbels and Grünberg, whose signatures remain clearly present.

Goebbels and Grünberg, very consciously, do not attempt to emulate the experience captured in romantic writer Adalbert Stifter's account of a forest in winter time by imitating nature in its simplicity, immediacy and reduction. Rather, they present the audience with a complex and self-conscious version of this experience, which is mediated through a plethora of sonic and visual impressions, for which it is, however, vital that despite the high-end stage technology employed, there is again a sense of liveness, of the analogue vs. the digital. It makes a difference that almost all the sounds are produced live (even if produced by robotic construction), that visual effects such as the beautiful dancing water reflection, bouncing off alternating gauze curtains, are not prerecorded projections and that the chemical reactions that make the water bubble with tiny volcanoes of steam happen there and then, in real time.

I would summarize that, paradoxically, Grünberg and Goebbels use the noisy machinery and the mechanical instruments that they have built with their team as a vehicle to contemplate beauty. They subvert and question some of the common cultural encodings that people have regarding noise as being mechanical, unintentional and unnatural. In contrast, it is characteristic of the performance that, other than many of the more common attempts at beauty,[18] which accentuate the flawless, the impeccable, the crystal-clear, the untouched and so on, it does not 'suppress' or 'filter' the noise of excess, of imperfection. Thus, for the audience Grünberg and Goebbels facilitate a confrontation with something that, by being both alluring and discomforting at the same time, both imbued with a sense of superiority over nature and the realization of the inadequacy of our imagination, touches on the sublime.[19]

Joslin McKinney describes the renewed interest of designers and scholars in the autonomous logic of material(s) and characterizes scenography as a 'process of formation' and as 'a gathering of matter coming together in an assemblage or a meshwork of "material flows"' (see previous chapter). On the one hand, this chimes strongly with some aspects of Grünberg and Goebbels' work: water, mist, sheep and the pendulum are all materials with a strong 'mind' of their own, where the designer has to let the garden grow by itself, as Grünberg put it above. On the other hand, there is a strong compositional sensibility in their work, the will to organize, structure and place materials very deliberately – both in time and space. It is noteworthy that both natural and mechanical metaphors ('garden', 'machinery') are present in their discourse, notions of intention and precision, alongside ideas of emergence and serendipity. There is continuous tension in their work, oscillating between the natural and the man-made, between the virtuoso and the amateur, between materials and their framing. In this tension, not in its resolution, lies the beauty of their theatre.

Notes

1 The four essays that make up the book, were, however, already written between 1935 and 1941.
2 The section on Cage's *Europeras* will provide a particularly good example of this 'dialogic' web of references.
3 Klaus Grünberg began designing in the mid-1990s after studying stage design with Erich Wonder in Vienna; since then he has worked as a stage and lighting designer at theatres and opera houses across Europe as well as in Kuwait and Buenos Aires, with directors such as Barrie Kosky, Sebastian Baumgarten, André Wilms, Christof Nel, Tatjana Gürbaca and Heiner Goebbels. See www.klausgruenberg.de.
4 See also Nonnenmann 2005.
5 The Ruhrtriennale is an international festival for the arts situated in the former mining region of Germany. It is hosted by various institutions which were set up and are funded by several cities in the region, the federal state of North Rhine-Westphalia as well as by national arts funding programmes.
6 See www.landschaftspark.de/rundweg-industriegeschichte/kraftzentrale/ for further information and images (accessed 30 May 2018).

7   A video of the double pendulums can be seen on: https://vimeo.com/104239334.
8   A much more comprehensive history can be found in Rebstock's chapter 'Composed Theatre: Mapping the Field', in Rebstock and Roesner 2012: 17–51.
9   See www.jahrhunderthalle-bochum.de/ for further information and images (accessed 30 May 2018).
10 See www.klausgruenberg.de/europeras.htm for images of this production.
11 This production was co-produced by Theatre Vidy Lausanne with T&M-Nanterre Paris, Schauspiel Frankfurt, Berliner Festspiele – Spielzeit Europa, Grand Theatre Luxembourg, Teatro Stabile Turino and was co-commissioned by artangel, London.
12 See www.klausgruenberg.de/stifters.htm for more images.
13 In one instance, two technicians enter the stage to modify the water basins, but they are clearly meant to be seen as stagehands, not performers. See more detailed descriptions of the piece in Bell 2010 and Eiermann 2009.
14 Gelsey Bell describes this further: 'The pianos reinforce the decidedly steam punk aura of the whole thing – proud Victorian-era instruments shown in Frankensteinian derangement. Mechanical technology that – compared to the sleek digital sterility of today – seems somehow more organic, replete with dirt, rust, mold, even bacteria, as if the gilded-era Armory exists as a greenhouse for forests of wild pianos and steam-powered drums' (2010: 152).
15 An article in the *Bühnentechnische Rundschau* (Anon. 2008) describes the technical setup in more detail. The article is also available via www.heinergoebbels.com (accessed 30 May 2018).
16 Bell's description is interesting here: 'I literally cannot tell how the sounds were being made. Directionally, it is clear that most of them are created live on the stage, but it is not easy to identify the individual parts that make the sonic whole' (Bell 2010: 151).
17 Goebbels was professor at the Justus-Liebig-Universität Gießen from 1999 until 2017.
18 This follows John Danvers' thought that beauty is not a 'quality inherent in particular objects' (nor, I should add, merely in the proverbial eye of the beholder), but a 'mode of engagement, a function of a particular kind of relationship between subject and object' (Danvers 2005: 1).
19 This final thought borrows heavily from Immanuel Kant's notion of the sublime (see https://plato.stanford.edu/entries/kant-aesthetics/#2.7, accessed 30 May 2018).

5

Spatial reorganizations and moving dynamics of the active spectator

Thomas Irmer

Since the turn of the millennium, new concepts for organizing and understanding theatre space have become eminent in the work of various stage designers. By definition, theatre is an art form that occurs within the scope of communicative encounters between a performance and the spectators. By focusing on these encounters, contemporary stage design tends to challenge conventional concepts of the stage, of theatre architecture and of theatre's spatial formation. For most people (and according to Western tradition), the word 'theatre' implies that theatre, as an art form and an event, takes place in a building (or at least a fixed area), in which the stage and the auditorium are separated from each other. However, as opposed to this fixed spatial structure, we know from theatre history of flexible forms that allow for other relations between performers and spectators (Carlson 1993: 67). In contemporary theatre, we witness scenographic approaches with which the given space of a more-or-less conventional theatre building become rearranged, refurbished or otherwise remodelled and redesigned. Moreover, since the 1960s and 1970s, we have seen experimental spatial practices that have come to be described as 'environmental scenography' (Aronson 2018 [1981]) and, with the new media and the 'digital turn' around the millennium, a broad spectrum of spatial aesthetics have emerged that has joined the discussion, coined 'intermedial scenography' (Wiens 2014a). Today, contemporary stage design is not only an art practice, but also connected to a 'meta-scenographic' discourse (Scorzin 2011; Wiens 2016) reflecting on shifting constellations, cultural knowledge and changing perceptions of space.

In this chapter, I will discuss three examples that have been seen as being significant for this artistic debate. First, Bert Neumann's multifunctional arrangement in the interior of the Volksbühne in Berlin that he designed for the last season of Frank Castorf's directorship (2016/17) as an example of total environmental space with various positions of performance and, respectively, the audience. Secondly, a staging of Morton Feldman's Beckett opera *Neither* by the Berlin-based media artist Sven Sören Beyer (Radialsystem Berlin, 2012) as an example of technologically advanced musical theatre for a 'floating' audience in a performance rotunda that was developed by the renowned sound engineering collective phase7. The third project I chose is the most recent work of the German-Norwegian artist duo Vegard Vinge and Ida Müller, entitled 'Nationaltheater Reinickendorf' (Berlin 2017), as an example for how a theatre completely designed by the performers for their own purposes ultimately channels their audiences in unconventional and conceptual ways. One could argue with these examples for the spatially activated, three-dimensional experience of the audience in theatre as one of the developments that prefigure the ever more dynamic use of space beyond the regular stage conventions that also enhance the physical experience of performances. People behave and watch differently when they are asked to stand up and walk around. The physical space is not only experienced through one's gaze but actually through the whole body. Wernher von Braun's famous dictum comes to mind here: 'Soon knowing about space will be as useful as getting your driver's license.'[1] Of course, von Braun, the chief engineer for Nazi Germany's missile weapons and, later on, the mastermind of America's Apollo rockets into space, meant it a bit differently from how we understand it nowadays. Yet he pointed to a changing understanding of space in general and the extension of space more specifically, as we are considering it here for theatre and for performance in general. Spatial organization is now and today primarily focused upon the audience with new possibilities – to liberate the gaze and activate mobility in space. As Anthony Howell stated back in 1999: 'It is very often the case that performance art questions the single-sided view of proscenium arch theatre' (Howell 1999: 175). In the following, I would like to illustrate within the case studies, based on the three named examples, various artistic processes that will, in an innovative manner, reinterpret or even potentially reconfigure the architectural space of theatre.

The theatre space composed as an 'open system': Bert Neumann's 'provisional architectures'

For his last Volksbühne interior space, the late Bert Neumann covered the seating area (stalls) with asphalt, thus in a way 'unseating' the audience. Various interpretations of the uneven asphalt surface covering the space for seating have evolved. There is, of course, the uninterrupted connection with the city outside, its roads pouring into the theatre. Neumann was an expert on the interplay between the space inside and outside the theatre as a complex social exchange. For several seasons, starting with the EXPO 2000 in Hannover, Neumann sent his mobile container theatre *Rolling Road Show* to places on the cultural periphery, such as the Berlin outskirts of Marzahn, Lichtenberg and Neukölln. This was as if the rough surface of such places had returned to its home base.[2] There is, on the other hand, along with the black ribbons on the sides, the aspect of a crypt or an underground cave, which shaped the atmosphere for various productions by Frank Castorf (*The Brothers Karamazov*) and René Pollesch (*Discourse on the Series*). And more so, we can interpret Neumann's space as a reflection on the political developments in Berlin. It was, more than ever, a statement of resilience and protest against a

FIGURE 5.1 *Bert Neumann, black scenography/interior of the Berlin Volksbühne 2015–17.* Photo © Thomas Aurin.

complete failure within the local theatre world; exemplary here is the political decision regarding Castorf's successor and the tumult that ensued.[3]

It is, functionally seen, an open space of obstruction – reminding the audience that being within this space is no convenient service nor can theatre be taken for granted in any manner. For Pollesch, for example, Neumann was as much a co-director; he defined the space before Pollesch actually wrote his performance piece for it.[4] During the latest two Pollesch *Discourse* plays, with their endless titles, the stage is used in almost conventional ways while the space of the audience remains a challenge – of physical effort, of 'unseating' the audience, thus breaking the rules of regular theatre. Strangely enough, people did not move around but rather improvised makeshift seats on the floor, sitting on their coats or bags. But there were also different situations when the asphalt space was used for a proper 'unseating', lifting the barrier between design and disorder. People used this space as if they were at a rock concert. This was the case during a memorial ceremony for Bert Neumann that took place at the Volksbühne a few weeks after the artist's death, in the set of Castorf's *Brothers Karamazov*.[5] The whole setup can be used, experienced and interpreted as an expression of the totality of theatre, going beyond the regular staging designs. We don't know if this was Neumann's intention, or even if it was the legacy he wanted to bequeath, but we do see, within his carefully constructed asphalt crypt, a crowd moving within it in a much different manner when compared to regular theatre productions.

Augmented theatre: Performative constellations of theatre and computer-generated spaces – Sven Sören Beyer

Morton Feldman's 1977 opera *Neither*, with words by Samuel Beckett, has only been rarely staged within the world of musical theatre. Practical reasons can be found in the fact that the fifity-minute piece stands outside the repertoire of opera houses, while for smaller independent productions, it is certainly too demanding when it comes to a staging, especially with the requirement of needing a whole orchestra for the performance. On the other hand, Feldman's spherical music matches the 'hovered' atmosphere of the short prose poem that Beckett sent him on a postcard upon his request for a libretto, unlike any other work of music based on Beckett's prose. That very word 'hovered' was seminal when, in 1976, Feldman first approached the somewhat reluctant Beckett for a text that he needed to be written for his music.

Sven Sören Beyer's new media art collective phase7 was founded more than two decades later, in 1999, to explore the possibilities of advanced computer technologies for staging unusual work outside of the regular theatre. The Berlin-based artist group quickly gained recognition at international festivals such as the New Vision Arts Festival in Hong Kong and the American Dance Festival, all due to their innovative ideas. For *Neither*, Beyer's team developed a surround-sound system that would not only produce the effect of a prerecorded orchestra in full scale but would also impress the listener, if not overwhelm him or her, with the illusion that this virtual orchestra can actually move and, if need be, even spin around. An octagon (about 70 feet in diameter) with seventy-two loudspeakers on scaffolds defines the performance as well as the audience space in order to achieve this striking effect which can appropriately be described as 'hovered' music. The technology uses *Wellenfeldsynthese* (wave field synthesis) for three-dimensional audio effects, in this case that of an entire orchestra. Its program IOSONO was developed by the German Fraunhofer research laboratory in Ilmenau and Oldenburg, an internationally renowned institute for advanced audio technology. The conductors Christian Steinhäuser and Raphael D. Thöne must also be seen as sound engineers and they worked in collaboration with Frieder Weiss, an expert in interactive computer arts. All have taken Feldman's music and ideas to a new level.

Thus, having solved the problem of how to arrange the orchestra in relation to the performance space, they were free to put the singer at the centre of the audience space on a simple block with people standing, sitting or even moving

FIGURE 5.2 *Sven Sören Beyer,* Neither, *3D audio opera. Overall conception and direction: phase7 performing.arts, light design: Björn Hermann. Radialsystem V Berlin, 2012. Photo: Vitoscha Königs, © phase7 performing.arts.*

around it. Hovering above Danish singer Eir Inderhaug was yet another technological device, a cube with rather abstract LED displays on its outside surface that also contained the lighting spots and beams for this nameless figure, emanating from the inside. The whole spatial design, set up within one of the halls of Berlin's Radialsystem V, a new space for the arts on the Spree riverbank (established in 2006) and home of Sasha Waltz's much-celebrated dance company, was organized like a rotunda within the building, which previously housed a power station from the late nineteenth century. This of course made an even more exciting contrast between the history of that venue and a contemporary art production for the twenty-first century.

The most important scenic achievement with this high-tech rotunda was certainly the encounter of Inderhaug's voice with the music, in a way very much reminiscent of Beckett's disembodied voices. As there is no real character or any action, this encounter provides the actual dramatic field with the invisible orchestra and the carrier of the voice. Beyer's stage directions only made the singer visible, with her first words 'to and fro in shadow' just a few minutes into the piece. But then the singing merged with the hovered music and seemed to be in space, all around the venue, while listeners could see the singer in her simple white skirt, centred right under the LED structure hanging from above. It was like some unreal scene, as if from a spaceship, thereby fulfilling Beckett's vague concept with great accuracy in this arrangement for sound and voice. So we can consider this performance as being an example of the extension of new theatre space into new acoustic space. In addition, it has also solved some major problems of how to stage this opera piece in a mode that does not foreground the orchestra but rather the moving listener and spectator.

Immersion experiences created through stage design: Vegard Vinge/Ida Müller

Norwegian-born Vegard Vinge, who studied directing at the Berlin University of the Arts, and Ida Müller, who studied stage design with Achim Freyer at the same school, have collaborated for a number of highly regarded, outstanding performances at theatres in Norway and in Berlin. Their work can be seen as aiming for a new form of 'total theatre' that integrates drama (mostly the canonical plays of Ibsen), film (video material produced in a long process for each work but also extensive use of live videos during the performance) and music (with a complex referential structure from European opera, such as the works of Richard Wagner, Giuseppe Verdi and

Giacomo Puccini all the way to pop music and significant film scores). The case in point here is of course their designs. These are highly organized and original, made for audiences and theatrical spaces that combine models of historical theatres with the open-access freedom that are integral to performance spaces.

For their latest work, *Nationaltheater Reinickendorf. Container 1-9*, in Berlin in July 2017, largely based on Ibsen's *The Master Builder*, they designed and built a theatre of their own that invited the audience to participate in unusual activities during the nine over-length performances that each lasted up to twelve hours. By comparison, the concept of an unseated or floating audience can be found here as the unleashed spectator in a durational space, which is, all in all, marked by the combination of performance, exhibition and spatial experience of the comprehensive setting.

Nationaltheater Reinickendorf was a contribution to the *Immersion* programme curated by the Berliner Festspiele. The focus was on the exploration of new relations between audiences and art works of different kinds with the audience experience in the foreground. Vinge and Müller built, over a time span of four months, a small Italian-style opera house within a simple factory hall, located in the remarkably colourless and unpopulated outskirts of the northern districts of Berlin. The contrast of opera and non-urban sites couldn't be any greater. Their opera, however, was made out of their typical cardboard structure. All of the walls and wings were painted with comic book images and ornaments that Ida Müller has shaped over the years as a signature of their theatre productions. The overall impression of most of her style was a comic book, a graphic novel mode, with reminiscences of Scandinavian children's books such as Sven Nordqvist's *Petterson and Findus* series, or dark Gothic images within the designs, which in turn also connected to the fitting music.

Vinge/Müller's *Nationaltheater* invited its audience to long performances that could be seen on the regular proscenium stage or to watch extensive video sequences that were projected on the curtain. But the whole artistic structure was much more complex than this. In the basement one could find the 'dramaturgical tunnel', an exhibition space with about 100 portraits. These portraits referenced the cosmos of Vinge/Müller, with pictures of Richard Wagner, Henrik Ibsen and, as a special tribute, Bert Neumann. Another 'wing' contained pictures of all soccer teams of the 1982 World Cup staged in Spain. Thus, the material used in the video films for the performance was at the same time an exhibition space for spectators. As the durational performances can allow people to also wander around at any time, this was a chance given to the director/designers regarding the display of further artistic material.

FIGURE 5.3 *Vegard Vinge/Ida Müller*, Nationaltheater Reinickendorf, Container 1–9, Berlin 2017. Photo © Julian Roeder.

Spatial reorganization, audience involvement and changing modes of perception

Bert Neumann's 'black scenography', that is, the complete deconstruction and temporal transformation of the architecturally given space, which was achieved by completely ripping out the theatre seating and covering large parts of it with asphalt, might be quite a special case. This project, as it were, is the culmination of Neumann's ongoing artistic research with which he aimed to reflect on 'different constellations of the stage and the audience space'.[6] Moreover, he was interested in exploring how the audiences of today and their behaviour and expectations change and in which ways spectators, by the means of scenography, potentially can become involved in the performance. As the discussion of the three examples has shown, the spatial transgressions and reorganization of theatre space call for an increased audience involvement, for active participation and 'unseated' mobility. Still, as we know, people as an audience are usually hesitant to move around within the theatre, when having to actively participate in what is going on. This is because they do not want to be co-actors, even if this implies being only casual figures that act out a role, or task, in a given, well-defined space. It seems quite different when the performance project is designed as a 'walking tour' outside of the theatre, as we know it from Rimini Protokoll or Janet Cardiff. There people seem to like to being guided through a more-or-less unknown space with either a plethora of new information or a very little – this all being a new experience. But in theatre spaces themselves audiences seem to feel much more uneasy and find such surroundings uncommon and, hence, unwanted. Therefore, I chose these three examples which, of course, show different options when it comes to theatre audiences becoming physically mobile and involved. This is not about mobility as a performance gimmick. Beckett/Feldman's highly experimental opera *Neither*, which somehow managed to become an integral part of the canon of contemporary musical theatre, was actually revised for staging by the artist network phase7. They developed a concept which would have been inconceivable when it was written more than forty years ago. Likewise, Bert Neumann's scenographic transformations and his deconstructions of the theatre space as well as Vinge/Müller's integration of exhibition space demonstrate how the regular audience situation can be expanded and activated, going beyond the one-sided gaze and actually being dramaturgically significant as well. All of these examples show how new ideas of spatial organization for a performance interplay with forms of new drama and musical theatre that were unpredictable when they were originally conceived and written. The observation that one can make for *Neither* could be that we can already find the blueprint for new staging modes within theatre texts of the late twentieth century. They call, as Beckett clearly does, for a three-dimensional experience without actually describing or prescribing it. So the point I would like to make – with my hat off to Bert Neumann, who definitely was an expert on this, and not just from his collaborations with René Pollesch – is that the spatial reorganization of theatre with a moving observer has a long and historical preparatory phase, but was rarely ever realized and, thus, is still a challenge today. Consequently, it is and will remain a crucial matter within contemporary scenographic practices and discourse.

Notes

1 Quoted from Virilio 1995: 145.
2 Neumann designed also temporary container architectures for his 'Neustadt' environment in Volksbühne (2002/3). At the same time, the *Rolling Road Show (RRS)* explored urban space in outskirt neighbourhoods beyond the downtown districts in order to reach an audience otherwise not exposed to theatre. The purpose for the artists was, according to Neumann, to 'organize social experience beyond the daily routine of theatre' with this meandering between inside and outside (Neumann and Wiens 2013). *The RRS* was also on tour in various international cities such as Belgrade, Sofia and Sao Paolo (2007). Later on Neumann used his concept of a mobile container stage for other

productions such as the open-air stage for René Pollesch's *Ruhrtrilogie* (2008–10), and in autumn 2011 the second part of this trilogy was shown in Japan.

3 For a brief summary of this dispute see https://news.artnet.com/art-world/embattled-director-chris-dercon-is-throwing-in-the-towel-resigning-from-berlins-volksbuhne-theater-1265210 (accessed 30 September 2018).

4 On this particular mode of performance production and rehearsing, see Sophie Rois and Birgit E. Wiens' chapter in this book.

5 'Did you see the Rabbit on the Roof'. Geburtstagsfest/A Birthday Party for Bert Neumann †, Volksbühne Berlin, 8/9 November 2015.

6 Quoted from Wiens 2014a: 195.

PART TWO

Circulation of scenographic knowledge and cultural transfer

PART TWO

Circulation of scholarly knowledge and cultural transfer

6

Notation

On the aesthetic potentials and epistemic functions of scenographic scores

Kirsten Maar

We live in the age of borders being transgressed in which choreographers let their troupes dance through museums, fashion designers stages their shows as performances, product designers let themselves be inspired by artists who, in turn, design jewellery or lamps

SUSANNE KIPPENBERGER (2015)[1]

With the exhibition *The Fact of Matter*, held by the Museum for Modern Art (MMK) in Frankfurt, the first solo exhibition of American choreographer William Forsythe opened in 2015. Forsythe, with his companies Ballet Frankfurt (1984–2004) and The Forsythe Company (based in Frankfurt and Dresden, 2005–15), realized groundbreaking choreographies and experimental dance pieces over several decades. In the course of his research-oriented inquiry into dance and choreography – that he understands as being above all an 'organizational practice' that creates motion and structures movement within space – he developed digital dance scores since the 1990s that are also publicly available via DVDs or online.² Aside from film projects, another part to his interdisciplinary work is his focus on site-specific installations which invite the viewers to become protagonists – or even dancers – themselves. An exemplary project here would be his performative installation *City of Abstracts*. When one entered the Frankfurt Museum through the entrance hall one saw oneself as a visitor in a big mirror screen, but the mirrored image did not reflect the image of the visitors' bodies in a reproductive, identical way. Instead, the visitor's body seemed distorted like in an ancient mirrored gallery, a grotesque image of fluid movement, which blurred the body's contours with a slight delay (Figure 6.1). Very soon all of the visitors started to play with the delayed projection (the video software for this project was developed by Philip Bußmann): they tried to influence the outcome of the distortion and to create configurations, together with other visitors. *City of Abstracts*, a project that was conceived by Forsythe in 2000,³ was first designed for public spaces, streets and public squares to explore how people would react to these kind of 'instructions', how they would interact and actually alter their behaviour in public spaces. Thus, this video installation reflects on the modes of cultural control and regulation as well as having a very playful character at the same time. It reflects on what a *dispositif* of a theatrical framework enables us to do – and what it prevents us from doing. It makes us think about the potentials that the general public has: How do I myself, as a person, perform? How do I

FIGURE 6.1 *William Forsythe,* City of Abstracts, *Museum for Modern Art (MMK), Frankfurt a. Main, 2015. Photo © Dominik Mentzos.*

perceive others? And by a set of quite simple technical devices – the morphing of the body's contours plus the delayed projection – the installation triggers fundamental questions about how to move in space, how to move with others, how to negotiate the given spatial parameters and the common space.

After first having been presented in Frankfurt (Frankfurt Hauptwache) and, later on, worldwide in the streets and public places of more than twenty cities, Forsythe's *City of Abstracts* exhibition space finally moved to become part of his exhibition project at MMK. These kinds of 'choreographic installations', which are produced as process-oriented, context-related artworks, may also be understood as being artistic tools that William Forsythe conceived in order to artistically reflect on choreography and to free it from its close relation to the moving body of a dancer. Of central importance are his works that he defines as 'choreographic objects': 'A model of potential transition from one state to another in any space imaginable … not as a substitute for the body, but rather an alternative site for the understanding of potential instigation and organization of action to reside' (Forsythe 2008: 7). Included in these, formally very different, 'choreographic objects' that were presented at the MMK in 2015 is the piece *Instructions 2015*, which Forsythe described as a proposed 'method for realizing an immaterial object'.[4] The work presents instructions for a course of movements – a notation, so to speak – that has been inscribed on the museum wall in a manner legible for all, and moreover printed on a card in Braille: 'The text describes a method for realizing a non-existent, invisible object. Paradoxically, the invisible object can only be sensed through the touch and the proprioception of the fingers' (2008) (Figure 6.2).

The following chapter discusses the artistic forms and practices of the notation with which aesthetic processes are designed and 'written down', in music, dance and also increasingly in other artistic disciplines. 'Noting down' means, basically speaking, the use of textual and visual signs that – for example in dance – allow for the inclusion of constellations regarding body, time and space into a graphic composition. This composition is then realized within a production or its implementation. Nowadays – ever since the Fluxus movement, Allan Kaprow's happenings, the 'performative turn', also in art-related fields such as architecture, and finally, with the technical notation tools of digital media – notation is actually an almost paradigmatic practice[5] and has become, as for example with Forsythe's *Instructions 2015*, itself the topic of art for some time now. A normative understanding of the relation between score and performance (i.e. the performance as an 'interpretation' of the score and an event which can be reproduced in an identical form), as proposed by Nelson Goodman (1968), is not assumed any more, as this example suggests. Rather, what is explored much more is the potential that the notation provides us with and not focusing on repeating existing models or becoming a model itself. The focus is much more – in a more or less open

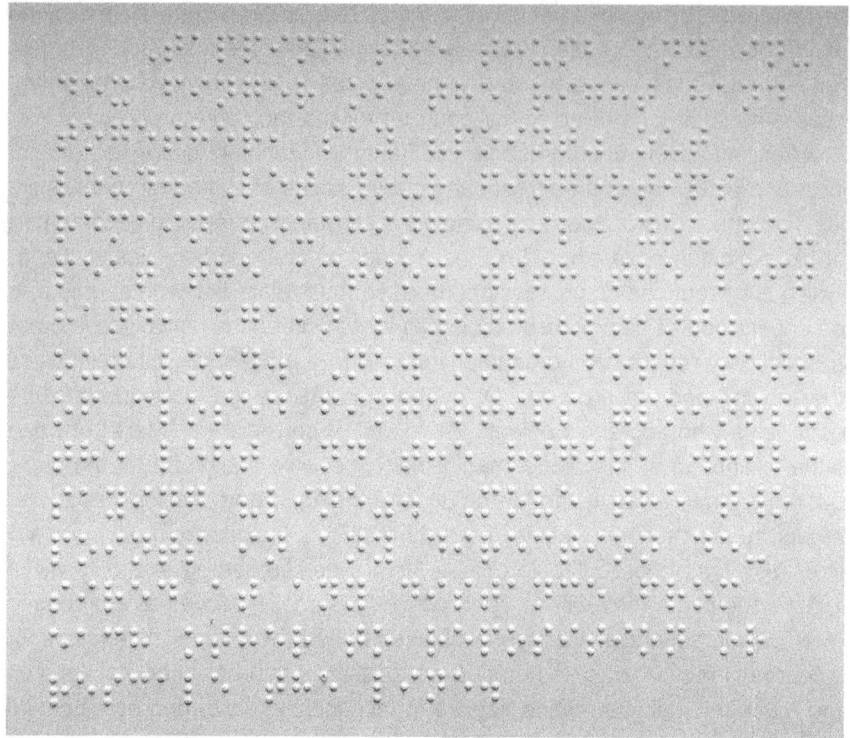

FIGURE 6.2 *William Forsythe,* Instructions 2015. © *Julian Richter / Forsythe Production GmbH.*

manner – on creating constellations between spaces, things, actors and at the same time, both choreographically as well as even scenographically, kick-starting performative processes and actions. Starting with a short review on the history of notation within dance and choreography, this contribution discusses the forms and functions of notation in modern art and its ability to open up the most varied scopes of action and rooms for manoeuvre.

Assigning and arranging as spatio-temporal practices: A few notes on the history of dance notation

Choreography as the art of 'writing space', derived from the Greek words *choros*, which designates the place to dance or a (round) dance with a mostly ritual character, and *graphein,* which means to write, to sketch, to scribble, built the fundament that dance could rely on. The different notational systems were thus the assignments to outline, to sketch out, to prescribe the dance, which itself mostly remained in a secondary position. Historically seen, the relationship between notation and dance always underlay strong hierarchies: Since Raoul Auger Feuillet invented the first systematic dance notation in 1700, choreography was mainly applied as the notation of dance steps. Similar to other manuals such as those focusing on good conduct, dance manuals also held an educational value. Throughout the eighteenth and nineteenth centuries the ways of notation changed in various manners. But only with the beginning of the twentieth century did the accentuation move from the notation of singular steps to the compositional aspects. But also the notion of choreography as 'The Art of Making Dances' (Humphrey 1958) only slightly undermined the hierarchy between choreographer and dancers. And even with the open scores of the 1960s the tension between structuring rules and their execution – or interpretation – still remained.

Not only does the notation guarantee the duration of an ephemeral art form and thereby another kind of relevance (next to the other art forms, which rely on material art objects and as such circulate on the art market), it also allowed for an analysis of dance as Rudolf von Laban stressed with his *Labanotation*, which up to today has been the mostly used notational system. This does not imply that most choreographers would work with it as it is highly abstract and one has to learn it like one learns another language or even having to learn how to program, a very difficult task. Moreover, the question remains as to what goal the notation practice is used for: is it to trace and to record the singular steps in a retrospective manner – and to see it then as a way of remembering and a means for re-creation – or is it in a prescriptive manner, as a kind of assignment to create new choreographies?

Finally, the gap between the conceptual frame and the bodily practice or execution refers to a much broader division in the arts – which in the visual arts goes back to the interplay between *concetto e disegno*, discussed from the days of the Renaissance all the way up to today's conceptualism (albeit in different terminologies): whereas the *disegno* (design) was always conceived as being subordinate to the *concetto* (concept), it allowed at the same time for different kinds of feedback loops (Kemp 1974: 224–30).

Scoring practices

With another definition – choreography as organizing bodies in space and time, as Cunningham and, after him, Forsythe defined it – we get much closer to the aspects of scenography. Especially due to the 1960s and the dissolution of artistic limits as well as the debates on medium specificity, different new genres such as installations, environments, happenings, performances and site-specific works emerged, and the compositional tools within this field were also the subject of several fundamental changes. John Cage's idea of indeterminacy describes the relationship between the score and its interpretation, which helped to gain a more democratic understanding since the interpreters became the co-authors and thus questioned parameters of authorship and virtuosity (Kotz 2007: 59–98). Choreographer Anna Halprin and her husband, the architect and city planner Lawrence Halprin, fostered the idea that everything could serve as a score, which also implied requestioning the status of dance (Halprin 1970). One of their students – Simone Forti – answered this challenge by designing her so-called dance constructions and combining them with short instructions, which are collected in her *Handbook in Motion* (1974). For example, her dance construction *Slant Board*

> requires a wooden ramp eight feet square leaned against a wall so that it forms a surface inclined at about a forty-five-degree angle to the floor. Along the top of the inclined plane five or six holes are drilled and a rope fastened into each. The ropes are knotted at approximately one-foot intervals, and when not in use almost reach to the bottom of the board. The piece begins, when three or possibly four people get on the ramp. They have been instructed to keep moving from top to bottom and from side to side of the board, which can be done only by using the ropes. (Forti 1974: 56)

Only the combination of the objects with the instructions or the tasks noted down actually build the score. This constellation demonstrates the way in which an object unfolds its aesthetic dimension, is generated by the assignment – the partition, the score, the scenario – on the one hand and the arrangement as its spatial constellation on the other. These scores describe scenarios that trigger particular modes of movements and, consequently, also influence the aesthetic experience of the audience. In the co-presence of objects and actors, the space is always negotiated anew and is dependent on the situation; in addition, the context and significance become shifting parameters.

One of La Monte Young's scores, *Draw a Straight Line and Follow it*, which was first intended to be performed by Robert Morris, was later also passed on to several other artists. One of the most famous interpretations is the performance *Zen for Head* (1961) by Nam June Paik. But not only the interpreters became more important – in Kaprow's happenings or George Brecht's Fluxus events the interpreters were not other artists, but the audience members themselves. However, these procedures also changed the behaviour of the performers. The open score allowed for freedom, but at the same time it put them in an extremely precarious situation in which they had to make decisions instantaneously, which in turn fundamentally questioned the status of the subject. All of this demanded different training methods, new techniques, alternative practices etc.

Beyond functionality, identification, representation and reproduction – as reclaimed by Goodman (1968) – notations have a specific logic of operationality and, as such, they become a productive tool within the process of artmaking, and free themselves from being mere reproductive notations.[6] Their different readings open up and can lead to a multiplicity and variety of possible actions. Their potential lies in the transferences of movement. Within the course of these transferences, the differences in the use of media become obvious and productive. Between the latency of the score and its manifestation an in-between space is opened up, which does not rely on the opposition of concept and execution, but rather prolongs the state of making, designing and conceptualizing into the state of aesthetic experience, and to the formerly thought passive beholders. As such, it also undermines the binary opposition between a static oeuvre and its ephemeral performance.

Nevertheless, in the field of performance studies the opposite argument is also quite popular: Peggy Phelan's most famous quote – 'performance's only life is in the present' (Phelan 1993: 146) – has unfolded its own impact and nourishes not only performance artists' practices, as in Marina Abramovic's *The Artist is Present* (2010), but also calls for a more precise analysis of ephemeral dance practices (which, at the same time, visibly materialize in the dancers' bodies). In the many different approaches taken to use scores within the field of choreography and to thereby generate new procedures, the Judson Church choreographers marked a decisive turn. However, there are huge differences between the tables, lists, assignments, complex diagrams and precise geometric drawings, even if all of these approaches work in a rather conceptual-analytical way. Therefore, as Petra Sabisch has pointed out, it seems important to distinguish between different types of notations:

> I distinguish between cues, instructions, scripts, notations and scores: A cue is what determines and disengages a change (in theatre, the conventional example is the technician changing a light according to a prior agreement often related to time, actions or sound). An instruction is a device, that suggests a (way of) doing, moving, thinking (e.g. 'go to centre of the stage'). A script is the often linear description of something realized or to be realized. A notation is an undisclosed system of recording or composing ways of doing, moving or thinking. And a score is a realized composition of articulations that urges for other realizations, interpretations and translations. It is a 'partition' of sensible agencies that communicates and shares modes of perceptibility, close to what Jacques Rancière calls *partage du sensible*. (Sabisch 2005: 31)

These definitions emphasize the commonality between 'partition' and *partage*, as Jacques Rancière puts it in his *Politics of Aesthetics* (2006). It opens up a kind of accessibility and aesthetic experience as well as dealing with a part of choreographic thinking, which questions the conditions of choreographic production, of communication strategies or the negotiation of production within collaborative projects. With the ongoing and increasing debate on discursive, economic and political issues as well as specific artistic techniques, the utopian potentiality of the score is increasingly becoming a field of interest:

> A score is what tends to be exercised and thus waits latently for actualization, for realization. This latent tendency towards a practice is inscribed in the score itself, for it does not have to be realized in order to become a score ... A score is not a genre, but a generator of what escapes from it: its realization. (Sabisch 2005: 30)

Beyond its realization, the score is marked by its potentiality. It gives an assignment, a rule, within which movement can first unfold. Yet it is questionable if this order always unfolds in this linearity, or if there are manifold effects of feedback loops between notation and its performance. These assignments can then be taken as procedures in themselves.

Expanded choreography as scenography

But let us now return to Forsythe's choreographic objects. Presented in the frame of an exhibition, which was curated by the artist-choreographer himself (who included his own works and also works from the collection of the MMK), *The Fact of Matter* not only demonstrated the similarities and differences between performance and exhibition,[7] but, in addition, staged their specific display modes and, as such, the core of each *dispositif*. The character of the singular works and choreographic objects in the exhibition varied from singular pieces of the visual arts from the 1960s all the way up to contemporary works of art, examining the correspondences between these art objects and his own 'choreographic objects' with regard to the aspects of space, body and movement. Next to *City of Abstracts*, *Instructions 2015* and other works by Forsythe, *Nowhere and Everywhere at the Same Time* was one of the most challenging installations for the audience present. First it was presented as variations of a solo piece as well as with the whole Forsythe Company before it became an installation for audience participation. The set seemed quite simple: from the ceiling above, hanging pendulums could be seen that spread over the whole space, swinging lightly in a given rhythm, this rhythm being induced by a computer-programmed score. The task was then to cross the space, having to avoid touching the pendulums. If you touched them, the whole assemblage began to readjust itself, the intervals changed as well as their regularity, new modes of orientation became necessary and the movers had to adapt their rhythm to the new and constantly changing situations. The task of the dancers (even if they were not professionals) in this installation was to synchronize and desynchronize, to heighten perception, and to become aware of the environment and the kinaesthetic sensations, finally having to negotiate the given space in correspondence with this complex setting.

The obvious perspective when looking at this choreographic installation and its performative character comprised challenging the relation to the audience and involving them as participants. In addition, a second aspect became obvious regarding this 'choreographic object'. Freeing choreography from its genuine relationship of moving bodies to 'choreographic objects' and expanding the notion of choreography revealed the agency of things, which, in turn, appeared as actors within these constellations. Similarly, the score here was not a task or a sketch given beforehand that could be defined as the score. According to Forsythe's reinterpretation of scores, it rather consisted of the set of pendulums and their specific arrangement, which, when combined with a computer-generated programme, triggered the rhythm and temporal dimension of the project.

The growing interest in performance and dance within the field of the visual arts has led to various formats for presentation of dance within an exhibition context. Forsythe's exhibition *The Fact of Matter* is one of the starkest examples of this. Another example is the show *Move – Choreographing You!* (2012), which was curated by Stephanie Rosenthal. The presentation of choreographic work was accompanied by a digital archive, set up by dance scholar Andre Lepecki, which contained a canon of the most important works in dance and performance of the past fifty years.[8] The multifaceted project perfectly demonstrated how these participatory exhibitions, which invite the visitors to explore most of the choreographic installations themselves, also serve the modes of spectacle and event. It helped to create a space of experience in the best sense of the so-called relational aesthetics, a term coined by Nicholas Bourriaud. He used this term to describe the development of practices within the visual arts, which mainly focused on social relations, on the (active) participation and the get-together of the visitors. An example here would be artworks such as Rirkrit Tiravanija's soup kitchens, where the artist functions as a catalyst, rather than being at the centre of the action (Bourriaud 2001). The art historian Claire Bishop criticized relational art for its mere self-referentiality as well as the absence of any outside references (Bishop 2004: 5–6) and, moreover, for what Lepecki calls (together with Rancière) 'choreo-politics' (Lepecki 2013: 16–20). Referring to Jacques Rancière's *Disagreement. Politics and Philosophy* (2004), he discusses how choreography can be understood as being an 'art of command', and what kind of artistic decisions could work against or even undermine this authoritarian character.

Within the exhibition space of *Move*, the visitors were assigned to 'move' and to explore the physical and kinaesthetic sensations. They were 'choreographed' by the spatial arrangements of the singular objects – or rather by the assemblage of agents or actors – and had to find their path through the various situations, which gradually also opened up through the contact with the other visitors. The playfulness of these situations is clearly demonstrated, as for example in Forsythe's performative installation *The Fact of Matter*, containing a large field of dangling gymnastic rings, which challenged not only the coordination of body parts with the sensations of weight and gravity. Another example would be Simone Forti's *Slant Board* or her installation *Hangers*, in which the 'performers' had to balance on slopes hanging from the ceiling for the duration of a drone sound sequence composed by La Monte Young. This 'piece', first performed at Yoko Ono's Loft in 1961, also led to questions which often appear within the context of exhibitions: What does it mean to restage, to re-enact performances – and how can the differences in the performance and the interpretation of the scores be interpreted?

Interestingly, these debates can be traced back to the early 1960s.[9] In her essay on 'The Cultural Logic of the Late-Capitalist Museum' (1990), art critic Rosalind Krauss describes the turn from the diachronic to the synchronic museum – from a space for mediating a linear form of knowledge to a space of experience and encounter. She traces back this lineage to minimalist aesthetics and refers to the body perspective these artworks addressed as well as to the reproductive character, which focused the considerations on the conditions and processes of art production, authorship and value. One could also refer to Michael Fried's earlier essay 'Art and Objecthood' (1967) and his invective against minimal art, which in his eyes involves the beholder experiencing a situation in its specific phenomenological condition and for its duration – and clearly shows how an object unfolds its agency. During this era, situational (and not situationist) aesthetics marked a turn in which such presence-related perspectives were favoured over the experiences made with the phenomenological body perspective. The kinaesthetic experience as a fleeting experience marks a crucial point in this constellation, but the immersive character and the effect of feeling overwhelmed does also mark the reverse side of these art forms. What comes to mind at this point of the discussion are the various formats introduced and tried out within the history of theatrical spectacles, as, for instance, the World Fairs that were held from the middle of the nineteenth century. Delightful pleasures and the newest technical devices were used to amuse audiences worldwide.

Comparably, at the beginning of the twentieth century, museums saw themselves competing with the new medium, film, and its institution, the cinema. Since then, mass culture has influenced not only the culture of display but also the involvement of the spectator. Guy Debord's *Societé du Spectacle* (1967) clearly analysed how modes of everyday behaviour and the experience of artworks were changed by the influence of ubiquitous images. Again, with the changes we have faced since the 1960s, our reception habits have also changed, and it no longer seems useful to play off a phenomenological perspective against a reflexive one. Instead, the mingling of different forms of knowledge plays a decisive role for our aesthetic experience. Knowing this and how it works are parts of the experiences we make. In the current dance-related exhibitions, especially, we can explore assemblages of theoretical as well as practical knowledge (and through this, we once again come back to the already discussed dichotomies of the conceptual and the practical, both of which have an impact on the relation between choreography and dance).

It is important to distinguish between several modes regarding the involvement of the spectator – immersive installations on the one hand, as for instance virtual reality surroundings such as the *Limits of Knowing* at the Martin Gropius Bau (2017), or, on the other hand, atmospheric environments such as Olafur Eliasson's *Weather Project* at the Tate Modern's Turbine Hall in 2008 (even if these are set in a scientific context). Relational hospitality, as in Rirkrit Tiravanija's soup kitchens or as in institutional display art, refers to the conditions of artistic production and setting up exhibitions and these are fundamentally different when it comes to how they are re-/presented. Taking these events into account and analysing them with regard to 'the logic of the spectacle', one can and should ask how dance or performance can escape this corset. Resistance in this perspective lies not in the often cited 'presence' or 'authenticity' of the body, and we should be rather sceptical when it comes to taking on a presupposition that actually tries to exclude dance from the art market economy. The argument that there is no object that can be presented or circulated is a very weak one. Nevertheless, the 'immaterial' art form, as it is often called, does not at all escape these effects. Rather, movement here guarantees an ongoing circulation and the body itself is just a tool within it. The phenomenon of curating the performing arts within a service economy has become a critical issue, and therefore it's not for nothing that the concept of 'moving on' perfectly serves (what the art historian Hal Foster in his study on *The Art-Architecture-Complex* describes as a phenomenon of) our neoliberal experience economy (Foster 2011), in which so-called immaterial, communicative or affective labour has partly replaced the work of art as a product.

Scenae: To see and being seen

The crucial aspect of presenting and performing – that is, to demonstrate something and to let it appear in front of the audience's eyes – makes us aware of the mediality of the various individual parameters and aspects of presentation, of the scene staging and the mise-en-scène of the body as being partly semiotic, affective, phenomenological and kinaesthetic. The affective power of these situations opens up what the body can do and, thus, we have to take into consideration the capacities of the body above and beyond the singular body, as a sort of transgression of one's own limits. Dancers often speak about the porosity or permeability of the body, which has to do with the previously mentioned capacities of kinaesthetic awareness. This creates a specific skill that cannot just be trained on its own; it implicates the negotiation of certain assumptions dealing with spacing, timing, touching, feeling, establishing relationships. Here we come full circle back to the first basic definition of choreography: the *choros* as the place designated for dance or even the (often ritualistic) round dance itself. In addition to the function of the *theatron* – the place where the issues of the public could be negotiated (beyond the *agora*), where one could be seen and see the others, and where not only the male citizen but also the excluded ones could take part – the *choros* allowed for the emergence of a (ritualistic) community, whereas the *theatron* served as a venue for negotiating all that is public. Nevertheless, even in this seemingly more archaic grouping, the tension between 'being singular plural' (Nancy 2000) is there and remains a huge task that needs resolving. The relational potential of individuation (as part of a collective) and the emergence of a public sphere only unfolds, when there are specific references present. Rendering visibility to things and aspects, which otherwise cannot be seen, is one of the crucial issues in Rancière's *Politics of Aesthetics* – and here we once again come back to the mingling of the different *dispositifs* of both exhibition and performance as well as their specific tools. A display gives visibility to objects and aspects that otherwise would not be seen or even would be seen differently: it shows; it demonstrates; it exhibits; and in this manner it is simultaneously functional as well as aesthetic. It combines; it unfolds a certain correlation; it refers to a given context; it communicates.

These aspects – including the question of what is shown (or hidden) and how aesthetic processes are structured and organized – are relevant not only with regard to dance and theatre, but have also influenced the development of diverse formats of exhibition since the 1960s as well as the growing interest when it comes to curating. In addition, the debate includes reflections and redefinitions of the architecture of the particular space, the showcase, the pedestal, the lighting, or the colours of the walls – that is, scenography – as well as the arrangement of the art objects, the choreography of the visitors and a specific time regime as well.[10] The display as such has become the medium of the exposition itself – linked to an institutional and discursive situation. It unfolds its potential as a *dispositif* – a net knotted between the singular elements – or it affirms itself within poststructuralist media theory: as an assemblage. Some exhibitions from the 1960s took on the character of a manifesto and remained a point of reference; for instance, Richard Hamilton's *an Exhibit* in 1957, in which the plexiglas display panels and the other displays elements were re-/presenting nothing but themselves and, in this self-referential manner, pointed to the implicit mediality and the politics of the in/visible. Other artists such as Liam Gillick and Heimo Zobernig were in this regard declared as being 'display artists' (McGovern 2016). Zobernig, coming originally from the field of scenography, is an artist who questioned and is still questioning the institutional setting itself and, within the political frame of things, what it actually means to exhibit.

More recent exhibitions, such as *to expose, to show, to demonstrate, to inform, to offer. Artistic Practices around 1990,* presented at mumok Vienna in 2015, reflected on this topic. The focus was on the status of changing exhibition practices. In the 1990s, various artists, such as Félix-González-Torres, Group Material, Zoe Leonhard, Martha Rosler and Louise Lawler, were increasingly discussing the social and contextual issues as a basis for their work. Reflecting on the conditions of artistic production and art's presentation was closely intertwined with work on actual social issues. The status of the object of art and its economic foundation became a subject of ongoing debate as well as an institutional critique that focused on the mechanisms of social exclusion, identity politics and gender issues. An example here is the AIDS crisis, which was reaching a pivotal point during that era. As a case study, Félix Gonzáles-Torres's *Untitled* (a Go-Go Dancing Platform, Museum Ludwig, Cologne 1991) showed a dance platform with neon lighting, where a dancer in a glamorous bathing suit, sneakers and a Walkman performed. Through such projects, González-Torres, who died of AIDS in 1996 and who was a member of Group Material and ACT UP, aimed at 'queering' the abstract art language strategies and, in turn, generated performative narratives of the institutional dialectics of both the private and public, of in- and exclusion as well as the visible and invisible. Other artists, such as Heimo Zobernig, questioned the institutions by the architectural means of works that were installations, choreographing the exhibition space in a particular way, often including minimalist–conceptual displays with contemporary graphic or furniture design (Buchmann 2015: 27). They made visible how certain given rules function and, at the same time, demonstrated the need for change. Practices of using fake identities, playing with fictive labels or switching pseudonyms were crucial to the de- and recoding of the consensual; this remaking of the rules via self-ironic parodies or nonidentitarian appropriations were characteristic of the approaches taken by neo-conceptual art (Buchmann 2015: 24).

Scenography – as has been clearly demonstrated in this article – played and plays a crucial role for these experimental arrangements. One can conclude by saying that scenography and choreographic practices within the contemporary arts are closely related and have even become interdependent if one has a closer look at some of these works. What is significant regarding all of the choreographies and exhibitions that have been cited is the use of notation as well as spatial scores as an artistic device put in place to unfold a plethora of potentialities and to actually open up the scenographic thinking and practices to the audience so that a field of experimentation and shifting repertoires of knowledge are put on display.

Notes

1. Art critic and journalist Susanne Kippenberger (2015), quoted from https://szenografie-kostuem-experimentellegestaltung.de (Website Hochschule Hannover) (accessed 1 October 2018).
2. Forsythe's CD-ROM *Improvision Technologies: A Tool for the Analytical Dance Eye*, CD-ROM (ZKM Karlsruhe Digital Arts Edition), Ostfildern: Hatje-Cantz 1994/1999; see also his research platform 'Synchronous Objects' (2005ff), conceived as an 'interactive archive', https://synchronousobjects.osu.edu/ (accessed 1 May 2018).
3. See also the project description on Forsythe's website, www.williamforsythe.com/installations.html (accessed 1 May 2018)
4. Quoted from www.williamforsythe.com/installations.html (accessed 1 May 2018); see also Gaensheimer and Kramer 2016: 27.
5. John Rajchman, 'Die Kunst der Notation' ('The Art of Notation'), in von Amelunxen, Appelt and Weibel 2008: 68–76.
6. This was perfectly demonstrated in the exhibition *Notation, Form und Kalkül in den Künsten* (Notation, Form and Calculation in the Arts), Academy of Fine Arts, Berlin 2007.
7. In German, the alliteration of *Aufführung* and *Ausstellung* emphasizes this much more.
8. *Move – Choreographing You!* was first shown at the Hayward Gallery London (2010), later at Haus der Kunst Munich (2011) and at Kunstsammlung NRW Düsseldorf (2011).
9. Similar to *Move*, examples are historical exhibitions such as Robert Morris's *Bodyspacemotionthings* (1969) at the Tate Gallery, where he used the dance constructions of his ex-wife Simone Forti to spread them out in a large installation and the visitors had to jump and roll and slide from one object to the next.
10. In this regard, it would be interesting to have a closer look at the utopian scenarios of architect groups such as Archizoom, Superstudio and others, all of which were developed in the 1960s. Their way of designing unfolds a projective thinking-drawing method that opens up in various potential uses. It is significant that most of their ideas did not move on from the status of a project and were not officially produced.

7

One cannot not stage: Scenography – beyond theatre

Scenographic practices in museums, exhibitions and corporate design

Uwe R. Brückner and Linda Greci

The term 'scenography' stands for a discipline explicitly dedicated to space and its presentation in a staged setting. Historically and etymologically, it is closely connected to theatre. In ancient Greek theatre, 'scenography' has been used to describe the paintings of the *skené*; along with masques and costumes, represented the most important visual design element. Conversely, modern and contemporary practices and discourse on scenography range beyond the theatre and across other art and design disciplines. According to these practices, scenography is no longer understood as a mere visual art but instead as a spatial art, which is complex and composite. Prefigured by the 'scenographic turn', which is associated with Adolphe Appia (Pavis 2015 [1996]), as well as, since the 1960s, performance art, Fluxus and Intermedia, the concept has come to include a large range of forms, art practices and design techniques, and since then, scenography has migrated from theatre into various other fields of (re-)presentation (Aronson 2018; McKinney and Palmer 2017). These transgressions have also reached the museum as a context and institution that is no longer understood only an archive of cultural heritage, but as a place that is also designed and perceived as a staged environment with synaesthetic qualities, which presents objects, tells stories and conveys information to offer intellectual and sensual experiences to the visitors. Accordingly to these common roots, the practices of theatre and museum share a lot of parallels and, especially in recent art and design practice, have become similar in the ways things and stories are staged in a narrative, dramatized space and in performative situations (Siepmann 2001; Brückner 2016 [2011]). The transformation and translations of design processes, methods and instruments from the theatre into the contemporary practice of exhibition design and spatial concepts are integral parts of the work of Atelier Brückner. Founded in 1997,[1] the studio realized more than 120 international projects. The selected projects include scenography, set design, spatial installation, narrative architecture and spaces for brands and thus play in the vibrant greyzone of different institutions, production and design formats such as museums, travelling exhibitions and expo pavilions. The wide range of these examples shows that scenography today not only has become an art and design form that operates highly interdisciplinary, but it also operates interculturally in many contexts.

Within this contribution we discuss scenography from the perspective of exhibition design. Our starting point is the shared conviction with other scenographers that scenography is not a built artefact, but a conception that occurs between scenographic production and reception. The aim here is to explore its extensive relation to theatre while answering questions such as: What is contemporary scenography about? Are there scenographic parameters that can be identified? Which scenographic instruments are used in exhibition design? How are they applied, and what kind of impact do they potentially have on the recipients? And finally: Is there a cultural specificity to scenography? Or to what extend has scenography – as an art and design practice that is so deeply rooted in Western theatre and culture – become in its hybridized forms and multifaceted techniques a globalized phenomenon? By discussing these issues from a practitioner's point of view, we will give insights into the work of Atelier Brückner. In our studio, design practice is always connected with research, methodological and theoretical reflection and with that what we call the 'design philosophy' of Atelier Brückner. This practice-based research and 'scenographic thinking' is also documented in various publications[2] and intended as a contribution to the ongoing discourse in this increasingly complex field. As we will point out in this article, scenographic design processes, according to our understanding, can be based on certain parameters. Scenographic design (in the theatre as well as in the museum, exhibitions or in other fields) also makes use of certain media and tools, such as models, scores, sketches and storyboards. At the same time, an ongoing evaluation and revision is happening and a process that can be described, as Susanne Hauser put it, as 'redesigning design'.³ By introducing five exemplary projects by Atelier Brückner (*Expedition Titanic*, Hamburg 1997; *Experiencing Frontiers*, Biel and Switzerland 2002; *GS Caltex Pavilion*, South Korea 2012; *TIM – State Textile and Industry Museum*, Augsburg 2010; and *That's Opera*, Brussels et al. 2008), our aim is to demonstrate the potential of scenography for the design-related tasks of exhibition design and for the requirements of our times. Questions to be posed in this context are: What do the increasing transgression, the dissolution and reshaping of traditional boundaries between different disciplines indicate? As we suggest, scenography (especially in exhibitions and museums) is about creating 'narrative spaces'. But what does that mean? Why do we feel that it is necessary to endow things with a language, what causes us to give stories a stage, and where is the added value in scenographic design for the recipients? As a first step to the impending journey to the heart of scenography, a closer look at its definition – from the perspective of exhibition design – is worthwhile.⁴

Scenography – a universal discipline of spatial design?

From the viewpoint of exhibition design, the primary activity of scenography is the exploration of intangible and tangible subjects (exhibits), and the translation of given conceptual or material content into the three-dimensionality of a spatial narration. The overall composition of a staged setting transfers content into physically accessible displays, charges spaces with meaning, choreographs them dramaturgically and finally involves the visitors. To do so, scenography utilizes a multifaceted set of design instruments borrowed from different creative disciplines, such as architecture and interior design, graphic, light, sound and media design, installation art, performing and fine arts, but also of various genres such as theatre, opera, literature and film. Scenography, as we stated elsewhere, is inherently interdisciplinary, and at the same time potentially part of other artforms: 'Compared to the arts, namely architecture, the fine arts, the dramatic arts, music and literature, scenography is at once a sub-discipline and a discipline that integrates'.⁵ The extent to which traditional borders between the different disciplines are dissolving and reforming is remarkable, and so is how this mutually reinforcing interaction allows for new possibilities and unforeseen results within design. Since scenography is concerned with the interaction of different disciplines, it also involves the use and combination of various design parameters and tools. Due to this interplay and the dynamic treatment of space, scenography is able to create spaces that can generate physical, multisensory experiences. Finally, scenography is not only an aesthetic practice, but an appropriate response to the design requirements of our time and the continually changing way in which our society perceives the world; consequently, scenographic design has also a social and political dimension.

Historic roots and terminology

As a multidisciplinary design discipline, scenography has established itself over the past four decades. The much older roots of scenography can be found in the antique Greek theatre and the *skené*, which means (in ancient Greek) 'shed', 'tent' or 'hut'; *graphein* means 'to write' and refers to the drawings and paintings that where attached to it.[6] Originally, the *skené* was a wooden shed at the edge of the stage in Greek theatre and was used as a screen behind which the players changed clothes (and the appropriate characters). After becoming a hut, it was later changed into a building-high façade that enabled transformations, entrances and exits in ever increasing degrees of complexity. In the history of stage setting, the *skené* would accordingly be the official origin of the off; that is, the zone of the stage that must always remain out of sight. Only here can the actor playing Oedipus change his costume and put on his mask of bleeding eyes; from there, he steps blindly into the view of the public, who respond, accordingly, with tears. The off, as part of this configuration, enables illusion; it facilitates and promotes the seriousness and credibility of a performance. The uninterrupted maintenance of this collectively agreed act of delusion, the unconditional trust in the integrity of the performance, the certainty that what is shown is nothing other than what is perceived – these are essential conditions for the emotion of the addressees and their willing submission to the illusion. It is this primeval human joy that scenography arises from and is dedicated to (Brückner 2016: 12). The term 'staging' (in German *Inszenierung*) was introduced in the theatre in the first half of the nineteenth century. It is derived from the French concept of the *mise-en-scène*; staging was understood as the totality of interpretative means based on the creation of staged 'scenes', such means for example being decoration, lighting and music. Since the 1970s and 1980s, the use of staged settings – not only in theatre, galleries and in public urban spaces, but also in the exhibition space – has seemingly become a ubiquitous social phenomenon.[7] But what does the term 'staging' in the context of museums or exhibitions actually mean?

The practice of presenting objects is as old as the idea of the museum itself (early forms are, for example, royal art and treasure chambers); the idea of collecting, preserving and exhibiting in today's sense began about 1500 (with the so-called cabinets of curiosities). According to Thomas Thiemeyer, the concept of the mise-en-scène and of staging in the museum 'reached museums in Germany in the course of the educational reform in the 1970s when the museums tried to attract generally interested visitors from all social classes and increasingly wanted to tell stories by reference to everyday objects' (Thiemeyer 2012: 199). 'Staging' became a term that curators, but also designers, use frequently to describe the presentation and arrangement of objects in space according to a specific meaning or message. Within these contexts, the term 'scenography' serves as a synonym for 'staging', even though there are subtle differences between them and their embodied potential. Towards the end of the 1990s – significantly in the context of EXPO 2000 in Hannover – another shift happened: exhibition scenography became a widely recognized discipline, which continuously detached itself from the exclusive range of influence and responsibility of museologists, custodians, curators and architects. The term scenography also established itself (in the German-speaking countries) for this new discipline in the context of the expo and, from then on, encompassed the scenic design in addition to the film set and the theatre stage. The scenographer as a designer qualified in a variety of disciplines became known in public discourse.

The art of scenographic design

Since scenography has emerged from the theatre, the scenographic practices in the neighbouring fields of museums and expos have shared a lot of similarities with practices of stage design. As we suggest, the objects of an exhibition can be regarded as 'actors' similar to the actors of the theatre – they are the protagonists and the storytellers. To showcase them and to make them 'perform', the design tools known from the theatre (light, sound, media, projection and graphics) can also be used in the museum to offer them an appropriate stage. Scenography means the translation of the concept and contents into a three-dimensional setting. As we put it elsewhere: 'Scenography creates form from content, endowing the latter with meaning and attitude. It generates narrative spaces from ideas, things and stories and conveys their contents as messages. Scenography re-contextualizes, makes things talk and imbues them with relevance for the presence' (Brückner 2016: 59).

Thus, scenography in museum exhibitions is all about storytelling, narration and dramaturgy. Similar but different to that, exhibitions have brought forth their own, very different narrational formats. The structure of the classical theatre was largely formed by a stage setting that offers a spectacle to be observed frontally and, for the most part, separates the stage from the audience. In contrast to the traditional proscenium stage, contemporary theatre has opened up a wider range of possible constellations, in which the space, actors and audience are not separated but become involved into performative processes; according to Patrice Pavis, this indicates a shift from the mise-en-scène to what he calls *mise-en-performance* (Pavis 2013: 34–47). Inspired by this, exhibition design offers different and alternative ways in which the audience can become engaged; unlike in traditional theatre or film, the visitor can walk around the story. An exhibition is a physically accessible, democratic format in which visitors can only be conditioned and guided to a limited extent; instead, they enjoy their freedom of movement, and their perception experience is to a large part left to their own decisions and self-determined potential. In this sense, scenographic design is an act of staging with its own dramaturgy that guides the perception and experience of the visitor. Connected to this, scenographic design is also about designing processes and dynamics, or as we wrote elsewhere, a scenographed space is also a 'choreographed space or a choreography of sequences of spaces' (Brückner 2007: 126). Dramaturgy and choreography create rhythm and dynamics; they decisively condition the way in which visitors perceive space, exhibits and content. In this field of tension, a multilayered, performative field is created: space becomes a physical, bodily, dynamic and alterable space and, finally, an interpretative, imaginative space. Scenographic design has an impact on the intellectual, and even more on the sensorial, perception. Contemporary exhibition design does not only focus on addressing the visual sense, but tends to synaesthesia by aiming at stimulating almost all of the senses. Moreover, exhibition design provides the visitor with a matrix or navigation system for moving through the space. Consequently, a visit of such exhibition spaces involve simultaneously seeing, moving, hearing, touching, smelling – and also movement and the 'motoric performance' of the visitors. Within such complex, multilayered environments, sensorial and physical levels of perception become addressed.

Parameters of scenography[8]

According to our understanding, scenography is based on five parameters: content (storytelling), object (subject), space (architecture), recipient (addressee), dramaturgy (spatial choreography and choreographed order of perception). At the beginning of each project, these parameters form the basis of and the starting point for the development of any design and conception. The aim is to bring them together in a meaningful relationship and translate

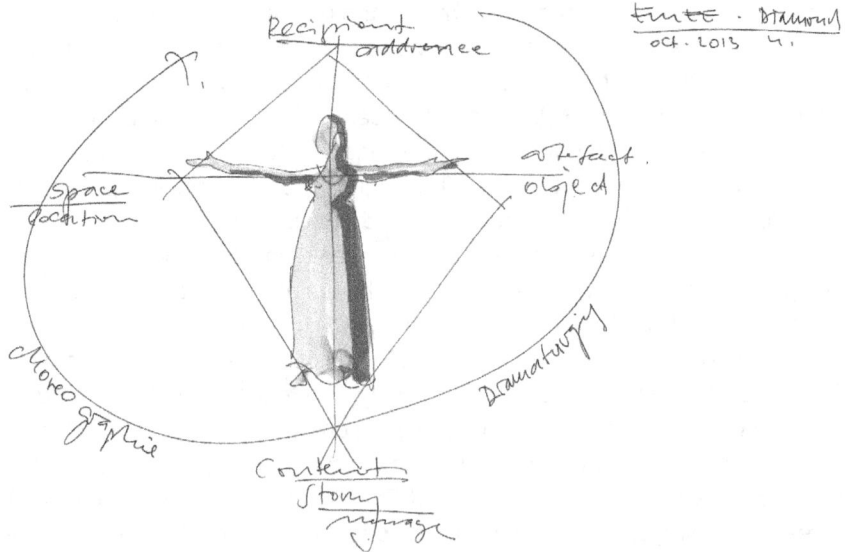

FIGURE 7.1 *Diamond of suspense, EuroVision – Museums Exhibiting Europe, 2013, sketch by Uwe R. Brückner. The diamond of suspense symbolizes the reciprocal relationship between the main parameters: content, object, space, recipient and dramaturgy.* © U.R. Brückner/Atelier Brückner

them into a three-dimensional, narrative configuration. Creating suspense is also an important issue here (what is told/shown/presented when, and in which constellation?). Staging, in this sense, takes place in a dialogue between object, content, space and recipient along a dramaturgical arc of suspense and according to a spatial choreography or choreographed order of perception. The 'diamond of suspense' reflects the context and relation between these parameters, which interact with one another in a reciprocal relationship.

To apply these parameters in a staged setting, a variegated set of design tools such as graphics, light, sound, digital media, projection and film, is used by the designer while endowing them with a certain meaning and dynamic. Various 'tools of scenography' help to implement the key message of objects and the conceptual ideas that are derived from the content. The following sections introduce the five 'parameters of scenography' by describing their potential and impact within the framework of scenographic designs.

Content Parameter. Derived from Louis H. Sullivan's influential phrase 'form follows function' (Sullivan 1896), the maxim 'form follows content' became the guiding principle of the work of Atelier Brückner. According to this principle, the task of design is to translate ideas, content and messages into form, by not only giving them form but also giving them attitude and meaning. Of course, the notion of 'giving content form' gives rise to the question of what content actually is. For us, content means the narrative of an exhibition – the source, the object, the storytelling, the plot and the message. The content is often related to objects that are to be staged, but also to intangible, abstract information that has to be conveyed. The question is, how to use content as a source of creativity and how to translate it into space or a spatial experience: How to approach complex contents? The beginning of a project always involves explorations of the resources, the objects and possible narratives. After that, we work with four requests that have to be answered and described on maximal one page, no matter how large or complex the project is: the title, the subtitle, the content (description) and the message. Which stories and messages are to be conveyed? What is the story that can be condensed to produce a plot? The plot shall follow a narrative structure with a prologue, a middle part and an epilogue (according to the Aristotelian definition). With the help of a 'content matrix', as another methodological instrument that we use, a structure for the plot and the storyline can be developed. The matrix (in the form of a table or spreadsheet) serves as a framework for the concept and incorporates not only the contents and objects, but also the other parameters and scenographic tools. In accordance with these principles and methods, the scenographer translates and transforms the content into a holistic conception.

Object Parameter. The museum is a medium that, on the one hand, collects and preserves historical artefacts in its depository and, on the other, exhibits and interprets a selection of them for the public. Due to the reciprocal relationship between depositing and exhibiting, the museum objects are 'not things that have been "put to one side" but agents of meaning formation that have been kept available' (Korff 2007: XVII). This means that museum objects can be charged with meaning(s) when they are presented in an exhibition. These objects are witnesses and are able to provide information about the past; they actually are able to mediate between the past and the present (Pomian 1988: 49–50). Worthy of mention here is Walter Benjamin's concept of 'aura'. Aura is not tied to beauty but to genuineness and authenticity: It is the authenticity of the object that gives it its actual meaning. Aura does much more than merely reproduce original frames of reference; it enables understanding (Flügel 2005: 29–30).

The object as subject becomes a 'storyteller', a 'protagonist'; it represents the source, the authentic thing and the bearer of meaning. The revelation of an exhibit's potential is not usually enabled by its mere presence but requires a stage setting to sensitize visitors and thus to enable them to perceive its stories and different layers of meaning, and to convey the complex interpretations of the curators. Every selection of an object is a curatorial statement and every spatial arrangement and designed environment is intended to convey particular notions or to communicate a certain point of view. 'The aim of the scenographer is to make the objects talk, to make them engage in a dialogue with the observer' (Brückner 2016: 68). The object and its different layers of meaning – origins, cultural significance, former purpose, societal function and value – become translated into narrative structures, and the staged setting makes them accessible and potentially self-explanatory. Mediated through scenography, the objects become endowed with meaning and purpose.

Space Parameter. Designing space, stage settings, scenes and narration is the central task of scenography; space can even become a medium itself that integrates other media, design elements and instruments, in the sense of a *Gesamtkunstwerk*, a 'total work of art' (Wagner 1850: 32). The 'space parameter' consists of four categories, which are basic to all staged spaces: the physical, the atmospheric, the narrative and the dramatized space. Seen from the perspective of scenography, space has also different dimensions – architectonic, media-relevant, sculptural and performative. The physical space is a constructed or existing building or architecture. It can be analysed according to its physical conditions such as dimension, entrance, exit, light conditions, climate conditions, materials and physical surfaces such as floor, walls and ceiling. A narrative space is an overall composition that uses and orchestrates diverse design tools to create spatial subjects that are poignant and meaningful. Their spatial qualities appeal to the non-cognitive, to the deeper layers of consciousness, potentially with a sustained and lasting effect. In this way, 'spatial images' (*Raumbilder*) can emerge. Narrative spaces potentially also convey knowledge and, in turn, offer authentic experiences. And finally, a well-composed, content-generated narrative space has the capacity to (re-)contextualize objects and convey their hidden stories – immediately or associatively; it involves the visitors and makes them part of the staged setting. Narrative spaces also indicate time: they stage the past, interpret the present and point to the future. Beyond its physical function, the exhibition space turns into a stage that communicates and becomes a speaking medium in its own right.

Recipient as Parameter: The recipient plays a central role in a contemporary understanding of scenography and is on how staged settings are designed. In the 1970s, the linear and one-sided model of communication, namely 'from the curator to the recipient via the object' (Flügel 2005: 98) was superseded by a new model. Since then, communication in museums has been understood as a 'dialogue-based relationship' (Flügel 2005: 98), in which the visitor is not a passive recipient but actively takes part in the processes of assigning meaning. Yet our contemporary understanding from the perspective of exhibition design goes far beyond this; today the recipient is regarded as a 'parameter of scenography'. As a visitor of an exhibition, he/she becomes involved in the staged setting and enters into a reciprocal relationship with the other parameters – space, object and content – while his or her experience is triggered by dramaturgical and spatially choreographed structures. According to this new understanding, the recipient has become the essential starting point for all considerations regarding the conceptualization and design of exhibitions. The recipient is the addressee (and potential co-player) of all efforts; during the design process, therefore, the curator and the designer attempt to see things from the recipients' perspective. Following the maxim 'start thinking from the end' (Uwe R. Brückner), they try to anticipate how the recipient will perceive the intended message or the exhibited object, and therefore they have to change their vantage point. However, the designer's conception on the one hand, and the audience's reception or perception on the other hand, are not necessarily congruent – there is always scope for differences and interpretation. Also the visitors, by bringing in their different national, cultural, social or demographic backgrounds,[9] will differ in their experiences while being immersed in a dramaturgically organized, scenographed and choreographed spatial configuration of meanings.

Dramaturgy as Parameter. Dramaturgy structures an exhibition parcours by generating a certain narrative, a distinguished routing and a path of perception. During the design phase, an overall storyline, which creates connectivity between all spaces and all objects, has to be developed; as a narrative route offered to the visitors it will allow them explore all contents in a concerted order. To create a curve of suspense, it might be helpful to think of the dramaturgy of an antique drama, an opera, a movie's dramaturgy or a novel's structure, which takes the form of prologue, the main part with single acts and an epilogue. As an act of stage setting, it very often operates in an interdisciplinary way by referring to theatre, film or performance art. Scenographic design in museums is not only about narration but also about choreographed movement in space and about creating 'choreographed sequences of spaces' (Brückner 2007: 126). Moreover, scenography is always concerned with the current snapshot of reality, in which the visitor is located at a particular moment in time – knowing that for the presence there is a relevant 'before' and also an 'after'. By using means of dramaturgy, a coherent curve of suspense can be achieved, thus inviting visitors to experience content and messages physically and emotionally, cognitively and associatively, actively and passively. Dramaturgy operates as the guiding thread through the exhibition and structures the visitors' experience along a spatial structure and routing (exhibition parcours). The routing can be a so-called 'free flow routing', a 'proposed or an optional route' or a 'defined or linear routing' (Brückner 2016: 117). The routing prescribes possible or ideal pathways for the visitor through an exhibition.

Methods – the score as design instrument

Scenography as a design approach is a powerful strategy for elaborating holistic concepts. Still the question arises how to move from an idea to a concept, and from a concept to a conception? Using what we outline here as the design approach, the methodology and 'scenographic thinking' of Atelier Brückner, we believe in the power of storytelling and we therefore write storyboards to create dynamic settings. We also believe in spatial choreography, in the choreographed order of spaces and in the dramaturgy of perception depicted in a score.

During the design process, storyboards are created to convey the dramaturgy of the exhibition. The storyboard, namely the story as a series of drawings, includes sketches of the plot's individual scenes and sequences. Storyboards can also be used to make the dynamic or performative aspects of a subject comprehensible, through means such as light, sound and media choreographies. In the score, storyboard and content matrix[10] fuse with each other to form the blueprint of the entire project. The score (Ital. *partitura*, meaning 'division') in music refers to the method of writing instrumental parts and vocal parts on different lines (layering) (Michels 2001: 69). In a *partitura*, all the parts of a composition are recorded and written underneath one another so that their interrelationship bar by bar becomes clear horizontally and vertically (Ziegenrücker 1997: 228). In exhibition design, we use the *partitura* method to orchestrate different instruments of design. This makes it possible to legibly illustrate carefully thought-out dramaturgies and complex spatial installations or spatial choreographies. In the simultaneity of all processes, elements, sequences and stage directions, the score, despite its complexity, is also comprehensible to non-professionals. This is where messages in respect of content and form come together, where things, information, perception and the staged environment become orchestrated. The score encompasses all the contents as well as all the scenographic means and instruments, processes and sequences – including the narrative spaces. The score is a medium and tool for composing, integrating and orchestrating heterogeneous design elements into a holistic design, a performable matrix, in which dramaturgies and spatial conceptions become comprehensible.

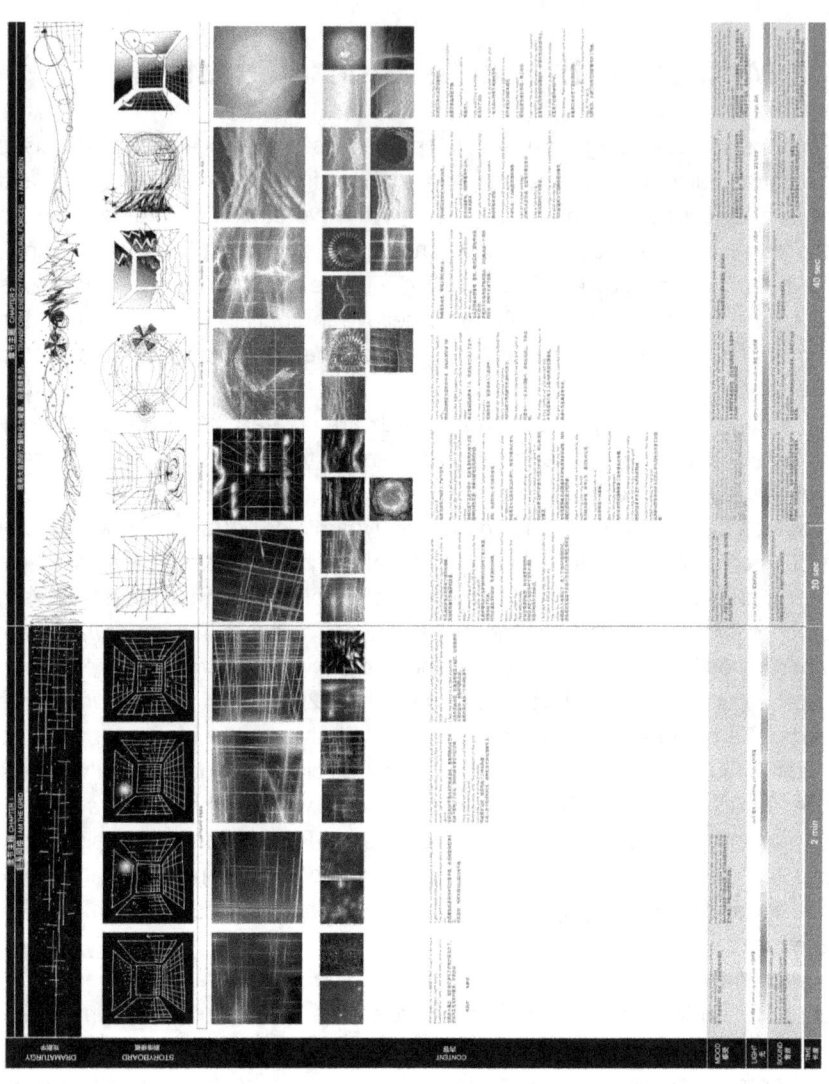

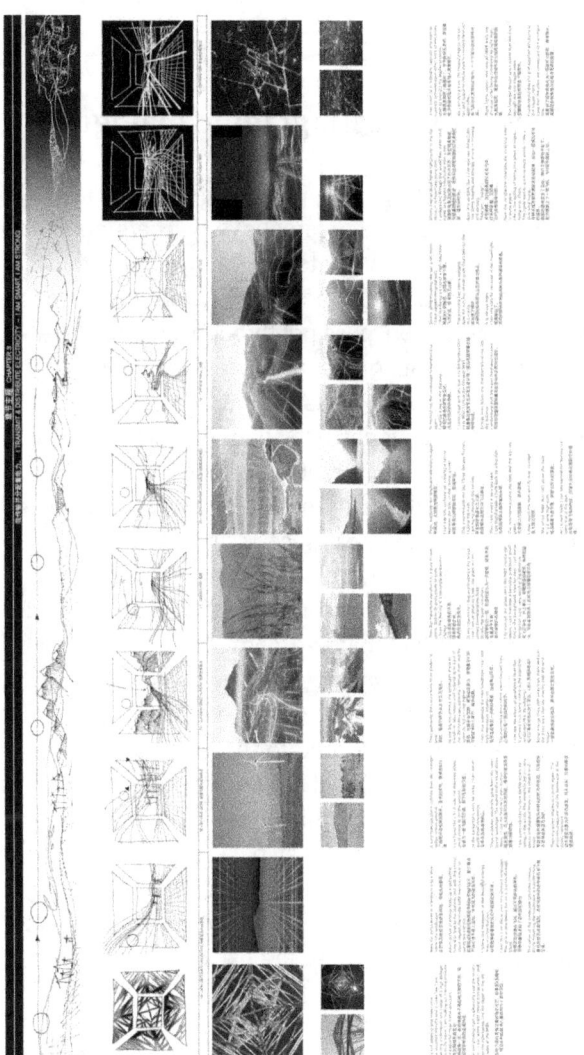

FIGURE 7.2 Notation/Design Partitur, State Grid Pavilion, Expo Shanghai 2010. Partitura for the first cubic cinema showing the orchestration of all design elements. © Atelier Brückner.

Scenographic designs by Atelier Brückner – selected projects

Following this discussion of Atelier Brückner's holistic approach to scenographic design, we would like to give some examples from our design practice and projects.[11]

Expedition Titanic: The art of scenographic dialogue

One of our earliest works was the scenography for an exhibition entitled *Expedition Titanic* (1997). It took place in the famous 'Speicherstadt' in Hamburg and is one of the early exhibitions staged with dramaturgical means. Five protagonists, either survivors or contemporary witnesses, guide visitors episodically through the exhibition passing through an imaginary ship's corridor and chronologically narrating the fate of the *Titanic*. The contradictory statements of the survivors served as the starting point for the concept. The exhibits as well as the tragic stories behind them were the focal point. Inherent in them were the emotional occasions of contact between the staged setting and the recipients. Within the overall exhibition concept there were spaces dedicated to specific themes, such as the 'Silent Space' or a room dedicated to the ship's bell. In addition, there were spaces that were interposed as interludes, as intermezzos dealing with the phenomenon of the *Titanic* on a meta-level. In the 'Champagne Room', for example, six champagne bottles from the first-class section that were rescued from the sea were dialectically juxtaposed with a worker's shoe from third class without comment. A separate space was dedicated to these few exhibits – a quasi-associative space that offered access to the aura and eloquence of the objects and served as a subtle reminder that the *Titanic* set out to sea not only as a luxury liner but also and primarily as a ship carrying emigrants. This kind of staging, which challenges observers to come up with their own interpretation, was still unusual at the time. Our task here was to achieve a sustained and dialogue-based relationship between the exhibits themselves but also between the exhibits and their observers.

Grenzen (er)leben (Experiencing Frontiers): Narration as spatial experience

When the eight cantons located at the Swiss border chose the title *Experiencing Frontiers* for their pavilion at the Arteplage Bielin 2002, they envisioned – on a metaphorical level – the problems of the individual and collective experiences with limits and boundaries. Placed in a 900 sq m (about 9,700 sq ft) exhibition space, the aim of the project was to evoke a strong sense of limits and taboos and enable visitors to emotionally experience the phenomenon of restrictions. Social, psychological, cultural and ethnic issues such as domestic violence, transsexuality, cloning or assisted suicide had to be handled sensitively with regard to the diversity of the Expo audience. Hence, we designed a space that would provide the opportunity for individual as well as collective participation on the part of the visitors. Concealed in a forest of rods, which served as a load-bearing structure and could be interpreted symbolically as toll barriers, a shiny silver cube supplied the architectural framework for the staged film setting. Twenty-eight cabinets grouped around a central interior space were accessible through a membrane-like translucent foil-screen. Inside the cabinets, the visitors were invited to listen to audio plays and watch film projections, thus taking part in the personal border-related experience of seven different protagonists. In the central interior space of the pavilion, these individually shared stories were condensed in a 360-degree film projection to create a collective experience, a choir of collective border violations (Brückner 2016: 36). The effects of personal action on other people and on the community were brought up, for example, by the real story of an attempted suicide who inadvertently killed another person instead of himself. The visitor became involved in this moving film and experienced it from two perspectives: he/she either identified with the individual person or, as soon as he/she crossed the border, was part of the collective. By crossing this border, the visitor became part of the subject. It would have hardly been possible to present the theme with conventional means, but due to the staged setting an access to such an abstract, problematic issue could be opened up; the real act of undergoing complex border experiences was demonstrated and made tangible within a narrative space (Brückner 2016: 37).

GS Caltex Pavilion: The art of dynamic space

The CS Caltex Pavilion is an example for corporate design. At the Expo Yeosu, in South Korea (2012), the pavilion of GS Caltex, a Korean oil corporation established in 1967, illustrated the company's mission. It offered a three-dimensional expression to the idea of energy in harmony with nature. The pavilion architecture was presented as a dynamic ensemble, which, at first glance, was reminiscent of an outsized rice field. Eighteen metres (59 feet) high, so-called blades swayed like grass in the wind; their continuous motion symbolized the never-ending flow of energy in nature. When darkness fell, the 380 coloured blades shined brightly into the night. Touching activated individual sensitive blades and initiated pulses that spread out in the shape of waves over the entire 'energy field'. The blades were designed to change intensity and colour of the light in two different modes. The fifteen-minute light choreography in the active mode was preprogrammed. During the five-minute interactive mode, people could activate different light impulses by touching the blades. One person could only trigger a small light effect, whereas two people or more could illuminate the whole field. A centrally located star-shaped pavilion building was optically withdrawn in its entirety. Its mirrored facades made the energy field appear to stretch into infinity. Via raised corners of the star, the visitors gained access to the also mirrored entrance area on the ground floor. Prismatic reflections encouraged a collective spatial experience of social networking – without any hint of scale whatsoever. In the centre of the pavilion was a seven-metre-high (twenty-three feet) round room with panoramic projection. Poetic, light-line shaped images in a reduced black-and-white aesthetic conveyed the company's will to assume responsibility with regard to sustainable energy concepts and for a life in harmony with nature. The visitor also became involved: in the last chapter of the film, the shadow he/she threw became a surface for a back projection. In this way, the message of sustainability was directly aimed at the individual; the circle of interaction between the recipient and the staged setting was closed.[12] Especially with digital media, spaces can become dynamic narrative spaces that develop enormous immersive power; real-time tracking and synchronization as well as the choreographed use of different technological means turn the recipient into a participant of the media environment.

TIM – State Textile and Industry Museum: Transformations on stage

Opened in Augsburg in 2010, the State Textile and Industry Museum (TIM) presents the history of Bavarian textile production and its socio-historic context. The worldwide unique collection of pattern books of the former New Augsburg Cotton Factory is the core treasure of the museum. This unique selection comprises more than 600 books with about one million patterns from over three centuries. Here, the task for scenographic design was to make the pattern books and their contents accessible to visitors in an attractive and interesting manner. The goal was not only to present such a book with an opened double page but to make the entire fascinating content visible. This was achieved by means of a digital, interactive pattern book that, as a real-time instrument, invites the visitors to immerse themselves in the fascinating world of historic fabric patterns. From a selection of digitalized patterns, the visitor can pick out one and design a dress from it, which is then projected onto one of the three 4.5-metre-high (about fifteen feet), slowly rotating so-called graces in real time. It causes a jump in scale and alters the aggregate state – from the physical, two-dimensional pattern book, via the interactive medium, to three-dimensional projections onto larger-than-life graces in a walk-in environment that can be directly experienced.

That's Opera: Opera as a model for integrative design

Atelier Brückner has created scenographic designs for exhibitions since 1997. However, when we were asked to create an exhibition about 200 years of Italian opera, we asked ourselves if opera as a performing format would be displayable at all and if so, how opera could be transferred into an exhibition. Soon we realized that the way opera is composed is rather the key to structure the exhibition, and it is the multidisciplinarity that is their shared characteristic. The staging of an opera integrates several disciplines, such as concept, design and performance. Similar to the opera houses that do not only employ singers or musicians, but also tailors, carpenters and many other craftsmen, we do not only employ architects or interior designers, but also other professionals such as graphic artists, light designers, communication designers or art historians. But what does opera mean to us today? Is there any desire or relevance for a contemporary interpretation of a 200-year-old composition? And even more important: Does the format of a museum exhibition match the subject of the opera, whose key feature lies in the liveness of the performance and its real-time experience? Is it possible to achieve a translation of its dynamics and dramaturgy into the more-or-less static format that exhibitions traditionally pretend to be? These are all questions that the scenographer must consider when addressing the general public with something that seems, at first sight, as austere as dry archival documents. But at second sight, we noticed that these documents are the signposts of a complex and passionate process from the original idea of an opera, to its scenographic, musical and performative realization, and this is what the exhibition attempts to share. Both formats – theatre and exhibition – use the same resources by organizing them within a composed and choreographed space of light, sound, time-based media (motion pictures) and setting. Scenography means having an 'orchestra' of media, which are ultimately arranged and defined in a kind of score *(partitura)*. These media are comparable with musical instruments, each playing a major part in a specific area or time frame. Together, they form a body composed of space, sound, narrative and emotion. In the prevailing perception of opera, we generally think of it as an event, in which the audience faces a raising curtain that reveals a stage representing the world of music and performance and offering only a fixed viewpoint. In an exhibition, by contrast, the visitors can stroll around; by this, they constitute an anarchical and independent parameter, which must be taken into account (and might be used as a choreographic advantage).[13] But we also think of red carpets, evening dresses, chandeliers, singers in costumes, the silence before the overture starts and the frenetic applause at the end of an evening full of emotion. However, the most exciting part of an opera is the world behind the curtain. Opening opera to a wide audience means giving access to the backstage world both physically (in the scenography) and conceptually (in the storytelling). The exhibition intends not only to satisfy experts, but also to reach those who never thought that they would ever be interested in opera at all.

When Ricordi[14] celebrated its 200th anniversary, Bertelsmann decided to make Archivio Ricordi's rich collection of Italian opera – original exhibits, handwritten scores, drawings, sketches and letters – accessible to the general public. The dramaturgical structure and the choreography that we developed for this exhibition followed the successive creative process of composing an opera from the script till the rise of the curtain: the creation of the libretto and the score (*partitura*), development of the stage setting (*scenografia*), voices and costumes (*voci e costumi*) including the final performance on stage (*rappresentazione*). In this order, visitors were invited to experience the fascinating world of the opera in spatial installations and at interactive media stations. As an example, one of the key parts was the 'accessible orchestra pit' (Figure 7.3) that introduced the complexity of a composition by means of an interactive score, inspiring the viewer's admiration for the conductor's ability to form an orchestra. Experts, as well as interested amateurs in particular, were invited to acoustically and visually relate to five opera excerpts shown on media as parts of partitures. The opera excerpts chosen by the visitors were played via an interactive conductor's rostrum and showed the instruments and voices that could be heard. The visitors followed the score in its original handwritten form and in its printed version and, when walking through the room, were able to acoustically pick out the individual instrumental parts as separate, concentrated components of the music from the overall sound via directional loudspeakers. In the end, it was indeed the accessible orchestra pit that bridged the distance between the exhibit and recipient by allowing the visitors to read and receive the original exhibits on show. Paper begins to speak, the scores whisper melodies, and the word is given to the protagonists. In this kind of scenography, the visitors become involved in an installation, what Richard Wagner would call a *'Gesamtkunstwerk'* according to his conception of the music drama. In the figurative sense, this backstage environment also plays with the metaphor of the Ricordi family's engagement and carefully balanced relationship with all their singers, composers and clients. The scenography of the exhibition echoes this constellation by creating a sort of corporate relationship between the world of opera and the visitors, just like the Ricordis achieved through their entrepreneurial spirit and unconditional passion for opera.

FIGURE 7.3 That's Opera, *Exhibition Project, Brussels 2008/9, walkable orchestra pit. Accessible orchestra pit making the object talk – or even sound.* Photo: A.T. Schaefer, © Atelier Brückner.

Epilogue – scenography beyond theatre

Contemporary scenography moves beyond the theatre and also operates in museums and other cultural venues as well as in public spaces and in various media. According to our understanding and with regard to our specialization on exhibition design, the term 'scenography' stands for a dynamic, narrative spatial design staging objects, stories and protagonists in an thematically consistent, physically accessible setting. As we hoped to demonstrate, ongoing research and (self-)reflection on the design processes, its parameters, means and methodologies, is an integral part of this art and design practice. Nevertheless, each staged setting of a museum exhibition or installation is to be created individually and uniquely and, each time, it becomes a challenge for scientists, curators and designers. In this regard, exhibition making and curating is always an act of staging, and staging is an act of curating. 'Choose an ordinary rice corn, place it in a showcase, light it smartly and let it tell the recipient that this one was recovered from Mao's table': this utterance is a curatorial statement, and it is also an act of staging. Therefore, 'one cannot not stage' (Uwe R. Brückner). You may call it 'exhibiting' to differentiate it from the practices in theatre, opera or cinema, but still it follows similar rules of staging, dramaturgy and storytelling. And that's what it is all about – to make things talk and to share insights, empathy and emotions.

Notes

1 Atelier Brückner, based in Stuttgart (south Germany), was founded by Uwe R. Brückner and Shirin Frangoul-Brückner in 1997 and has received numerous national and international design awards (European Museum of the Year award 2017, red dot prize et al.). Today the studio employs 108 team members who speak twenty-one languages and come from twenty-seven nations, www.atelier-brueckner.com/en/
2 See Atelier Brückner 2016 [2011] and 2019. Throughout this chapter, these publications are referred to as 'Brückner 2016' and 'Brückner 2019'.
3 Susanne Hauser, 'Spaces in Process: Designs', conference paper presentation at *The Art of Scenography: Epistemes and Aesthetics*, International Conference, Munich, 17–18 November 2016.
4 This article provides insights into the definition of scenography according to Atelier Brückner, its terminology and historic roots, the five parameters of scenography: content, object, space, recipient and dramaturgy, Uwe R. Brückner's design philosophy 'form follows content' as well as on his methodology 'creative structure'. For an in-depth discussion see Brückner and Greci (2016), and Brückner and Greci, 'Scenography. The Art of Holistic Design', in Atelier Brückner 2019: 143–287.
5 Quoted from the book section 'Scenography – Universal discipline of spatial design', in Atelier Brückner 2016: 12.
6 For a short history of the *skené* see Trüby 2010.
7 See Scholze 2004: 148. Some exhibition examples are: Francois Confino's *Ciné-Cité* (1984), Hans-Dieter Schaal's *Berlin Berlin* (1987), Bodo Baumunk's *Sieben Hügel* (2000) and Peter Greenaways *Hel en Hemel* (2001).
8 See also 'The Five Parameters of Scenography: Content, Object, Space, Recipient and Dramaturgy', in Brückner and Greci (2016: 25–79).
9 The globalization on scenography needs further discussion; cf. McKenzie 2008.
10 See section Content Parameter.
11 For detailed descriptions of these projects see also Brückner 2016 and 2019.
12 http://www.atelier-brueckner.com/de/projekte/gs-caltex-pavilion
13 See also Kirsten Maar's chapter in this book.
14 Casa Ricordi is an Italian publishing house, founded by Giovanni Ricordi in 1808 in Milano; its archive contains works by famous composers such as Verdi, Puccini, Rossini, Nono and Varèse, among others.

8

The art of thinking and designing space

Notes from the studio

Annett Zinsmeister

Contemporary debates on scenography are obviously in flux, as can be seen from the fact that numerous publications (McKinney and Palmer 2017; Aronson 2018) include a discussion of the term, its etymology and its diverse definitions within the various artistic genres and design cultures within their introductions. In the German-speaking countries scenography is above all the application-specific design of theatre and film spaces as well as of exhibitions in museums and even trade fairs. The dictionary *Duden* (Germany's equivalent of the OED) confirms this very limited perspective – that is, clear demarcation between various disciplines.[1] Today, there seems to be consensus that 'scenography' can be understood as a further development of the classical stage set or scenery, and has, by also going beyond that, developed into its very own and very dynamic discipline in recent decades. As this book project shows, scenographic concepts are realized in the most varied of formats and with the aid of different media. They draw their purpose, their identification and their content-based orientation from the respective contexts and their conditions. Still, it is quite difficult to grasp it as an art and design practice, as well as a discourse that has its own knowledge repertoire. In the field of scenography, some set designers work for both theatre and film, while others move beyond the stages and film sets to experimentally implement scenographic concepts, within the public sphere and various urban contexts (environmental scenography). Architects, often in collaboration with artists, develop 'performative architectures', relational art projects, scenographic interventions and participatory formats. Finally, design studios, who work for profit, specialize in exhibition design, corporate scenography, cross-media advertising and staged commercial events.

So one could question whether the term 'scenography' can also be helpful as a tentative, open search or work term in this multifaceted field to understand spatial design and contemporary work on space as interdisciplinary artistic and cultural practice. It is noticeable that the term has so far primarily been used by practitioners – mostly to describe different inter- or transdisciplinary, often innovative or experimental practices. Based on this question, I will discuss the borderlines and shifts between 'fine arts' and 'applied art' and between 'art' and 'design' in the first section of this chapter. In the second section, I will introduce my own multidisciplinary perspective as a trained architect, artist, author and professor for experimental design and interdisciplinary theory – who is working between the different disciplines. The principles and parameters that are implied in scenography as art and/or design will be discussed therein.[2]

Art or design? 'Free' or 'applied'?

In an era in which artists and designers are increasingly poaching audaciously from other disciplines, and the markets for fine and applied arts are converging, the question arises whether and how disciplinary distinctions and dividing lines can still be drawn nowadays. Despite many similarities and overlaps between art and design, there are differences specific to each discipline, which are initially noticeable when it comes to specialist knowledge and competence. Thus, the drawing of boundaries in creative training is a basic prerequisite to delineate specialist knowledge and define teaching content. This explains the division into disciplinary departments in art schools and academies, which, in turn, are split into individual directions and subjects of study, so that in teamwork we can convey the necessary spectrum of creative competence for the relevant discipline.

This is true of fine as well as applied arts and the comparatively young discipline of design[3] has expanded over the course of the twentieth century into the study subjects of product and industrial design, communication and graphic design, fashion, textiles and so on, which all call for different competencies regarding individual techniques. Things are similar in the case of scenography. As a subject in German universities, scenography also covers spatial productions beyond stage design in the theatre such as exhibition design for museums, set design for film and other media productions.[4] Scenography and architecture are the most complex of all design disciplines and both require a very broad as well as a clearly defined spectrum of competencies. There is more freedom within the fine arts: today the traditional division of the departments or subject classes is primarily still oriented on technical knowledge, dependent on material and media – such as sculpture, painting, drawing, ceramics and glass – but this division is becoming increasingly problematic, especially as many contemporary artists no longer orient their work by having knowledge of one specific medium. Often, therefore, they do not have such pertinent knowledge and cannot teach it. Therefore, what benefit or value do artistic classes have beyond a technical, subject-based knowledge and what kind of knowledge is still being conveyed?

Certainly, in German, the word '*Kunst*' is derived historically and etymologically from the Old High German word *'kunnan'*, which means something approximating knowledge, skill or mastery. It is widely known, however, and has been described often enough, that twentieth-century art has departed from a traditional understanding of the work as such. At the latest since Marcel Duchamp presented a urinal entitled *Fountain* at the art exhibition of the Society of Independent Artists in New York in 1917, the link between skilled craftsmanship, specific disciplinary knowledge and the work concept in art has been gradually disappearing. Around fifty years later, concept art completely departed from the traditional idea of the work: art is the formulated concept, which no longer requires any realization or materialization.

In art, today it is common practice to delegate the production of objects and installations to specialist companies as commissioned work. This means that the development and the actual production processes in the fine arts are rapidly approaching those in the applied arts – the artist is evolving from a producer into a designer, a planner, a commissioning client. Accordingly, only time will tell whether and how the traditional range of artistic knowledge can survive: it may become outdated or gradually disappear. The question is: How willing are we to rethink the content of teaching – do we wish to make new, up-to-date specialist insights available in the free arts as well? So once again the question is raised: What is the current position regarding disciplinary distinctions and dividing lines as many 'undisciplined' artists and designers operate on the margins of an established yet porous structure, which in turn is maintained by others with power?

In the light of these observations, it is obvious that the interrelations of free and applied art are not easy to survey, and one could ask: To what extent (if at all) are the distinctions between *free* (= independent, wild, untrammelled) and *applied* (= serviceable, conforming, purposeful) still plausible today? In the following, the attempt will be made to highlight the emergence of boundary lines and boundary shifts as well as the beginning of spatial representation and production as a prerequisite for scenography. Here one should first of all note that the so-called free art of former times has little in common with what we understand it as today.

From antiquity to the modern age, the term 'free art' (*artes liberales*) referred to the capacity of a free man (*homo liber*) to work creatively, which meant that intellectual and linguistic skills, as well as scientific skills such as grammar, dialectics and rhetoric, geometry and arithmetic, astronomy and music were considered to be free art. Painting and sculpture, as well as a large number of manual skills in the fields of textiles, metal-working, agriculture, building and so on were categorized as being mechanical or practical arts (*artes mechanicae*), based on technical, artisanal knowledge (*technē*) and not serving science, but rather the more profane need to earn a living.[5] Also, an evaluating line had already been drawn between high art and low art, with which intellectual abilities were placed above artisanal skills but not fine art above applied art. In other words, the distinction was made between intellectual knowledge and artisanal skills; the fine artist was regarded as a *bánausos*, as an uneducated manual labourer or artisan. His core task was the realistic reproduction of nature (*mimesis*), that is, *imitatio*, but not artistic invention. Later on, in the medieval period, crafts and guilds regulated procedures for artistic training, trade and competition, and defined the qualitative standards; the artist, as a person, did not play any part in the matter at that stage.

Since the beginning of the modern era, much of this changed and scientific research became part of artistic practice. For instance, Filippo Brunelleschi's discovery of the central perspective introduced scientific methods into the arts, and the method of perspective construction not only made the correct representation of space possible but also linked the scientific activity of *artes liberales* to the artisanal ones of *artes mechanicae*. Here, for the first time, *technē* became an instrument of science, and therefore social recognition was given to the fine arts. Particularly relevant here is the work of Leonardo da Vinci, which is not only characterized by his artisanal abilities in painting and sculpture, but also by his research in various disciplines of medicine, mechanics, architectural construction and so on which he, in addition, documented in a most impressive manner. As an autodidact, he taught himself how to work both empirically and scientifically, covering a broad knowledge spectrum, and all this elevated da Vinci to the status of *uomo universale*, a leading representative of court society, a status that was also transferred to the fine artist from that point onwards. Moreover, one could also describe him as being one of the first scenographers who worked artistically as he was responsible for the organization and design of the court ceremonies and festivities at the ducal court of Sforza in Milan between 1482 and 1499. He took on, among others, the role of painter, stage and costume designer, engineer, architect and mechanic. To present the court events in a spectacular manner, he developed diverse lighting and projection devices (including the first stage lights). Less well known is that he also invented a revolving stage, a hall of mirrors and automated instruments (e.g. the drum machine).[6] He therefore already anticipated in the fifteenth century the art of spatial design and production, which goes above and beyond the theatre and stage set.

The historical discourse of the boundary settings between free and applied art can, at this point in time, not be discussed in depth (see Zinsmeister 2013: 9–40). Therefore, we now take a large step in time and space from Italy to Germany, and from the early modern period into the twentieth century to have a look at the noticeable coincidence of disciplinary delimitation and experimental production of event and space that, just like the example given here of 430 years ago, took place in an era of radical cultural changes and technical revolution. When founding the Bauhaus school in Germany, during the time of the so-called Weimar Republic, in 1919, Walter Gropius proclaimed in his 'Bauhaus Manifesto' the abolition of the distinction between free and applied arts: 'art and technology as a new unity' was the hypothesis put forth[7] at the birth stage of modern design practice, which then would fan out into different design disciplines (such as graphics, furniture, product design and stage design).

Oskar Schlemmer, one of the first masters that Gropius appointed at the Bauhaus, conducted the Bauhaus stage and workshop from 1923 on. In his courses he taught the mechanical and kinetic laws of the body and staged with the students in Dessau the so-called Bauhaus Dances, which, among other things, addressed the exploration of movement in space as well as geometric and modular principles.[8] In the attribution of colours and forms to temperaments and speeds of movement, Schlemmer endeavoured to create a certain type of *Gesamtkunstwerk* that unifies all art forms: painting, sculpture, architecture and dance. Oskar Schlemmer was likewise committed to abstraction, just as the Swiss architect and stage designer Adolphe Appia was with his 'rhythmic spaces' (*rhythmische Räume*) (1911–14), which he staged in Hellerau,[9] and he considered the stage to be less of an illusory than a compositional pictorial space. As a visual artist, in the Bauhaus Dances, he choreographed sequences of physical movement through the modularization of the body. With the development of sculptural costumes, the movements of the dancers were dominated and defined. It was not space and dancers, but forms and colours that governed the dynamics of events. The restriction of the physical range of motion was to geometrize movement and transform it into an abstract composition. The dancers were moved like marionettes with a modularized body within the artwork and – as in a modular construction system – directed to specific places within the composition.

The limitation of the radius of bodily movements would lead to the geometrization of the movements and transfer these into a superordinate, abstract composition. In addition, in the Bauhaus, the staging of movement and event was not just limited to the stage area but actually extended all the way to the legendary Bauhaus festivities, whose very deliberate production left the stage behind them – just as the festivities that da Vinci organized at the court of Sforza did in their time. However, Schlemmer and his concept of the 'mechanical Bauhaus stage' went far beyond this as there were considerations to stage productions without any human actors at all. These aimed to put the mechanization as well as the abstraction into the focus of the production. For example, the piece *The Mechanical Ballet* (*Das mechanische Ballet*) by the Bauhaus student Kurt Schmidt was produced in Dessau in 1923; the piece *The Mechanical Eccentric* (*Die mechanische Exzentrik*) of the Bauhaus master Laszlo Moholy-Nagy remained only a concept, as it was technically far too elaborate and complex. In contrast to his student's choreography of abstract forms and figures, Moholy-Nagy designed various moveable levels and objects as well as grids and backdrops, which he in addition wanted to interlace with cinematic recordings. Helpful here are Fernand Léger's notes (published in 1924):

> If he does not want to be upstaged by the gigantic staging of modern life, then there is nothing else left for the artist of today, who would like to create his own audience for these stagings, but to behold – from his aesthetic point of view – everything that surrounds him as raw material and to choose the corresponding artistic and stage-related values from the colourful storm of everyday life that surrounds one, and to then redesign these into a production and to uplift these under a sceptre to a higher, scenographic whole.[10]

Léger's thoughts on the matter also aimed to overcome the boundary between the stage area and the audience area – in the sense of an extended concept of scenography with which this extends itself and both uses and plays in/with other spaces and contexts.

Scenography, in a modern and contemporary sense, cannot be considered without content-related and spatial transgressions of boundaries or without the usage of technology. As the examples mentioned have shown, there are historical precedents for an extended scenography definition and, since the turn of the millennium, it is again obvious that new technologies and the 'digital turn' are having an effect on the scenographic discourse and practice. Nowadays scenography does not necessarily have to be connected to a specific genre or medium; rather, it has established itself beyond its medium of origin – the theatre – and can be seen as design practice in museums and within the commercial spaces of companies and trade fairs. As a rule, it is connected to a specific event and therefore earmarked for a – more or less – specific purpose. This also explains why the term 'scenography' is usually not applied within free art, as here we have a fine but clear dividing line towards installations and performance as well. Art is only then really 'free' if it is not hierarchically subordinated and dependent (as, for example, in the theatre) or if it remains as unaffected as possible by the laws of the art market as well as art funding and project tenders. It is much more an independence of thinking and acting that, within art, is ideally stipulated but – as already pointed out – is often undermined in reality.

Notes from the studio

My artistic work with space is also based on spatial transgressions of boundaries and is questioning the 'digital turn' of technologies in space production and perception of space. In contrast to the common scenographic practice, as mentioned above, my artistic work is independent, driven by and based on a theoretical interest and research in space-shaping parameters and cultural techniques: the cultural meaning, production, design and perception of space is one of the focal topics in my own art projects and publications, intertwining art, architecture and cultural and media studies. Scientific research and studies of the environment as mapping, photography, recording etc. mark the first step in my artistic investigations of space.

My artistic approach when dealing with the perception in architecture can best be described as follows: I introduce a few selected experimental projects in which, in particular, the façade plays a central role. Façades define spatial and visual boundaries; they are the most memorable elements of architecture within public space. In modern times, the façade has lost its importance as an independent, artistic building component and became an equivalent or subordinate part of a functional whole. Concise structural evidence for this can be found in the concrete slab or so-called *Plattenbau* buildings, a mass socialist architecture that can be found in all former Eastern Bloc countries in various types of design. These buildings frame the urban space in huge housing areas – not as a result of design considerations, but by reason of industrial production technology. The *Plattenbau* façade is constructive and decorative at the same time. In its endless repetition, the calculus of efficiency becomes evident: it oscillates between deterrence and fascination. Through my research, I explore the possibilities and limits of image construction in relation to our visual perception.

At the beginning photography was a documentary research tool, and then became an artistic medium of representation and expression. In a second step I interpret – in the spirit of modular mass architecture – the documentary photographs of the *Plattenbau* as *medial modules* and assemble them into large façade images and wallpapers to cover existing interiors. The very strong spatial effects of these experimental installations lead to a borderline experience for visitors in the confrontation with two extreme effects: the brutality of endless repetition and the fascinating aesthetics of both structural and serial patterns. These architectural invaginations of facades into interior spaces are contradictory to our use and knowledge of architecture and offer new spaces of perceptual experience.

With this approach I try to ascertain and unsheathe structures and patterns, so to say: spatial codes, as well as their beginnings, meanings and functions. Akin to Roland Barthes' definition of 'structural practice',[11] I disassemble the detected urban codes and spatial elements and rebuild or sample them in different creative ways, in order to find out more about the relevance of the combination system, the composition model and the complexity of the complete texture and structure of the investigated architecture, city or space. The search for evidence in different cities and studies about spatial urban change is an attempt to get on the track of the particular, the specific, the identity of spaces, places, cities – even though these may at first glance seem so forbidding or unspecific.

FIGURE 8.1 *Annett Zinsmeister,* virtual interior *(2007/15), commissioned installation for the MoMA Collection, Museum of Modern Art, New York, USA. Photo: Pippa Drummond.*

FIGURE 8.2 *Interaction of a visitor with* virtual interior, *installation by Annett Zinsmeister at* Endless House. Intersection of Art & Architecture *(exhibition, 2015/16)*, MoMA – Museum of Modern Art, USA. Photo: A. Zinsmeister.

In the installation series called *virtual interiors*, the prefabricated façade becomes a descriptive spatial element of an absolute space, in which a top and a bottom, an interior and an exterior can no longer be distinguished. The result is a double intersection of the outside and the inside: a rolled-back inside of the outer space without an interior; interestingly, this is less a spatial installation than a visual construction. In the first realized installation it was the opposite side of the street, from where the central perspective illusion was perfect. As a (re-)construction of façade elements, the simulated hybrid of in- and exterior became part of the building façade as well as a temporary event in urban space. Through these invaginations of exteriors in interiors, specific effects of mass architecture were scaled, condensed and put to extremes. New perspectives, surreal spatial impressions and spatial irritations emerge and blur the boundary between the outside and the inside, between private and public. The installations oscillate between photographic document and artistic artefact, between authenticity and deception. Here architecture occurs ambiguously as real and virtual at the same time.

The visualization of distant, real and fictitious events by means of representation technique in the medium of photography prevent us from mapping images and leaves the viewer uncertain concerning the boundaries between documentation, simulation and fiction. The development of new technologies broaches the issue of how urban space constitutes virtual space and how virtual spatial elements transform real spaces. Installations such as *outside_in* and *virtual interiors* represent this engagement: one could say that this is a strategy of urban hacking that stacks real and virtual space or simply conjoins them. These works address less the practical tweaking of structural substance or the illegal appropriation of spaces, but rather alludes to the question of how to identify urban as well as architectural structures and codes.[12]

Conceptual enquiries, theoretic assumptions and the design process are for me basic artistic aspects. As opposed to purely conceptual art, my works function or – perhaps it is more accurate to say – operate on an aesthetic level as well. The art historian Beat Wyss called my installations 'sublime' in Edmund Burke's sense, since it has a powerful effect (*Wirkungsmacht*) on the viewer. At first glimpse, the intellectual and conceptual background of the work does not play a large role. The work takes effect – it stands for itself. On closer inspection or study, a density of content is revealed, which conditions the work, and in which the viewer can get involved and become engrossed and sink into – but does not have to.

As with my theoretical work, I regard my artistic work as being research: it serves the aim of acquiring knowledge about the cultural techniques with which we create and perceive space. In and with the creation of my installations, I thematize historical and contemporary developments of perception and the design of space, especially in connection with new technologies. In the form of installations, I call habits of seeing into question and open up new and surprising approaches to supposedly familiar themes. It is an artistic, sensory game with the perception, technologies and tools of rendering and design, and I scrutinize their potential as well as limits. My works aim to reveal unexpected contexts, intersections and parallels within the perception, depiction and experience of space, thus raising questions and opening up new perspectives. Despite spatial interventions and settings, they often point to the presence of unusual, overlooked details, or contradictions and unappreciated beauty, whether in the random, the serial, the ornamental, or the cliché.

The creative process: Tools and strategies

At the start of every one of my works, there is an observation, an idea or a question that at first is purely virtual and mainly quite vague. Normally, I search for evidence in different places and cities and deal with the spatial changes especially in those contexts as well as with the changes in our perception. Thereby, my focus is on problematic urban areas, places that are conflict-loaded: war-torn cities, architecture that is to be demolished and politically controversial megastructures; therefore, places of transition or those with a special past or even with an unknown future. The first step includes the recording, documenting and saving of impressions and moments as well as of one's own thoughts and associations. The photo camera and writing equipment are my constant companions on this quest. They help to collect these fragments of the real and virtual, of my observations and thinking at the time.

Creative processes are primarily intuitive. Especially in art, it is mostly emotional decisions that lead to the creation of a work of art and much less the rational ones. With this comes the gesture, the gesturing of the design/the 'throw' comes into play. As a conscious or a spontaneously made movement of the body or a body part, it is a component of every creative act. It can be sympathetic or provocative respectively depreciative, interesting or even pragmatically indifferent. A next step in the creative process is the integration and contextualization of my worked out image and topic archive in which the saved fragments help form a project.

This process can best be understood using a concrete example. In 1990 I moved to Berlin after the fall of the wall to study at the University of the Arts (Hochschule der Künste). I came to a still divided Berlin where the historically and politically shaped cultural borderline crossed through the middle of the city. It was a personal new start in a city that had to find and invent its identity after reunification, respectively.[13] I documented the urban redevelopment and the disappearance of GDR culture. Through this, a pool of photographic documents on places and architecture was created, which were either demolished (e.g. the former seat of the GDR government, the Palace of the Republic/Palast der Republik) or restored (old Berlin tenements, various types of *Plattenbau* buildings) or even completely new-built (e.g. the former wasteland of Potsdamer Platz). These were locations that were historically as well as politically loaded and that, due to the destruction, decay or violence inflicted upon them, were in a desolate, contourless state and even had a deterring effect. For me, they had a powerful appeal, for example regarding the monotony of *Plattenbau* developments that seemed to provide a very high level of anonymity but actually were able to provide a neighbourhood feeling in which the people knew each other and gave them a sense of home. I travelled to Sarajevo, the capital of Bosnia-Herzegovina, right after the war that took place in the former Yugoslavia in order to document the situation after a three-and-a-half-year siege. My guiding principles were shock and wanting to understand, looking at, not looking away and drawing consequences, where possible with the means of art as well as architecture. Years went by until, from these observations, works of art such as work series, spatial installations and publications came about and the respective projects were realized.

How, though, is this process designed and the artistic works created, aside from the technical know-how and the prescribed processes within material or technical planning and production processes? How does an idea materialize? What role do gestures play here and what is its meaning with a view to photographic and digital tools? Friedrich Nietzsche's media-related theoretic insights that the writing equipment helps to work on and shape our thoughts is a fundamental enquiry of my work.[14] What influence can we assume that the writing utensils as well as analogue and digital media have? They force the creation of new language forms as well as forms of thought, the results being text messages and the Twitter format that require an economization of gesturing movements as well as communication due to their limited number of characters and typing movements. That these sorts of reductions can be inevitably found in everyday communication can be seen in our day-to-day mail and text communication. Even within the creative arts it is clear that the choice of artistic techniques to a large degree defines the form and, occasionally, even the contents of the works of art. As an example, just compare the traditional techniques of painting with printing technology, photography and video that either promote, support, infringe upon or even inhibit certain forms of portrayal as well as content. Media, that is, devices of all kinds used to represent something, going from the writing equipment, pens and pencils, paint brushes and utensils all the way to the computer and specific software, determine how our thoughts and ideas are technologically transported – and this either on a 2D or a 3D level.[15]

My projects and the corresponding formats are therefore created through conceptual thought as well as through media, materials and their possibilities. The *Plattenbau* project, for instance, encompasses several groups of works. Every single group has a certain format to it: from documentary photographs I extracted excerpts as so-called medial modules having the measurements of 40 x 40 cm (about 16 in. x 16 in.) as a material work or as a playful element within a digital memory (*Memodul*, 2002). The first image montages were created as additions at 80 x 80 cm and as a rapport for wallpaper with which I could cover entire rooms. The group of works created within this context, *virtual_interiors* (since 2005), has moved on from the Plattenbau topic. The artistic process, though, has remained the same: At the start, there are documentary photos that are transformed into image modules, which in turn become basic elements of virtual façades that are then invaginated as fictional image spaces into existing spaces. So my installations always relate to the given space that makes up the starting point for the new work of art; the design tools are either projections (*outside_in / virtual interior*, presented at *Paraflow – Festival for Digital Arts and Cultures*, Vienna 2009) or even the lining of the artistic space itself (*virtual interior*, 2007/15, MoMA collection New York, since 2015).[16] The use of various media is always justified in an immersive sense, but also technically as well as conceptually. The completion of the process is represented by backlit images of these temporary installations. The project ends just as it began: with a documentation. With the documentation of the installation, the process of a work or of the respective project is concluded.

Notes

1 See *Duden. Deutsches Universalwörterbuch*, Berlin: Dudenverlag 2015 and www.duden.de/rechtschreibung/szenografie (accessed 1 May 2018).

2 In parts, this chapter builds on my edited volume *Kunst und / oder Design. Ein Grenzgang. Art and / or Design? Crossing Borders* (2013).

3 As a comparison: The visual arts and architecture have been taught as a course of studies at a university since the founding of the first academy of drawing in 1563 in Florence; only since the second half of the nineteenth century have schools of arts and crafts been around.

4 See Thea Hoffmann-Axthelm and Robert Kraatz's chapter in this volume.

5 Accordingly, painters and sculptors were not to enter Plato's ideal state, as they are not creatively active but merely copy and reproduce nature, that is, something that already exists, and so they do not create anything new – quite by contrast to philosophers, poets and musicians; Zinsmeister 2013: 12.

6 See University of Applied Sciences Bielefeld (2012).

7   Walter Gropius, *Staatliches Bauhaus in Weimar 1919–1923*. (Ed. Staatliches Bauhaus, Weimar and Karl Nierendorf in Cologne, Bauhaus Publishing House, Weimar and Munich 1923).
8   See Annett Zinsmeister, 'Modularisierung von Raum und Bewegung als ästhetisches Programm' (Modularization of space and motion as an aesthetic programme), in Brandstetter and Wiens 2010: 76–102.
9   See Beacham 1994 and Brandstetter and Wiens 2010.
10 Fernand Léger, 'Das Schauspiel: Licht, Farbe, bewegliches Bild und Gegenstandsszene' (The Spectacle: Light, Colour, Moving Image and Object-Spectacle) (1924), in Léger n.d.: 151ff, quoted from Simhandl 1993: 72f.
11 Barthes 1966: 190–6.
12 For more information, see Hemken, Pias and Schimpf 2012.
13 Also see the video documentation: Annett Zinsmeister, 'Dialogues I: Art and Technology', a conversation with Manfred Mohr, New York, 2011, www.youtube.com/watch?v=XgTQb53TLgw
14 On these aspects, see also Zinsmeister 2005: 95–109.
15 This is discussed in more detail in Zinsmeister 2003 and 2005.
16 See the website of the MoMA – Museum of Modern Art, New York, www.moma.org/collection/works/188450

9

Don't be afraid of the art of *parCITYpation*

Scenographic intervention as social design

Benjamin Foerster-Baldenius

This chapter is about collaborative design practice, participation and negotiation within processes of art-making and design. The design approach of raumlaborberlin, a Berlin-based network collective run by nine partners – all of them trained architects – working in experimental architecture, art, urban planning and artistic intervention can best be described as radical social design that also involves the audience with regard to the design process. Characteristically, our projects emerge through a design practice that goes far beyond what, for a long time, has been defined as 'participation' or 'involvement' in the arts; thus, we not only seek to actively integrate audiences into actual performances, exhibitions and other artistic events but above all into the processes of design, construction and production. Architecture and scenographic design have become tools for social interaction, public discourse and a context-driven, critical reflection on spatial design. To explain this approach, this chapter provides insights into the making-of process of projects such as *Eichbaumoper/Eichbaum Countdown* (Mülheim an der Ruhr, 2009, 2010, 2011), *Hotel Shabbyshabby* (Mannheim, 2014)/*Shabbyshabby Apartments* (Munich, 2015), *Rush Hour Rest Stop* (Durban, South Africa 2014), *Le Théâtre des Negociations* (Nanterre, France 2015), as well as *Forms of Turmoil* (Milan, Italy 2017).

Performative architecture and scenographic design as an artistic practice of invention and intervention

Henri Lefebvre, in his landmark study *The Production of Space* (1991 [1974]), raised awareness of the inherent sociality of space as it exists in human society, involving the association of appropriated places and social relations. As a social product, space, understood thus, becomes representative of social life. Accordingly, we also believe that art should not be merely based on aesthetic parameters but should be created through a code of representation that is constantly renegotiated, in this way reflecting and interacting with space as well as cultural contexts. Our understanding of space, and therefore art, carries a significant relational dimension: it is defined by 'obligations, duties, entitlements, prohibitions, debts, affections, insults, allies, contracts, enemies, infatuations, compromises, mutual love, legitimate expectations and collective ideals'.[1] The wordplay in this chapter's title – *parCITYpation* – is meant to highlight this approach.[2]

raumlaborberlin works within the public realm and its urban territories and our approach owes a lot to the likes of Cedric Price and Archigram, an avant-garde architectural group formed in the 1960s. As proponents of 'paper architecture', the Archigram team primarily worked through hypothetical architectural drawing, exploring alternative realities and inspiring new forms of discourse in the world of architecture, which they circulated through their own magazine, *Archigram*. Archigram's *Instant City,* for example, had been conceived as a mobile technological event that drifts into underdeveloped, drab towns with provisional structures, or performance spaces, in tow. The process was thought to proceed as follows: a funny circle appears in the sky – an airship – and, upon closer inspection, it can be seen to be carrying infrastructure and technical equipment. An event becomes established in the previously dead city, and the performance, engagement and chaos gradually intensify, becoming stronger and stronger, louder and louder. Through this infiltration, stimulation and activation of the public space, life and culture are conceived and become recomposed. During these moments, the network takes over, introducing a new kind of urban practice into the city.

In a sense, this is where raumlaborberlin is heading. We think of architecture as an experimental laboratory: not merely an object and built-up artefact, but rather and perhaps more so a layer of a place's history, a platform where one can ask questions and a performative practice space in the urban realm. Thus, we do not think of the city as a 'stage' or as a decor or backdrop for urban life, but – by also referring to an extended notion of scenography – we see and explore space as being part of a dynamic 'actor constellation'.

As architects, artists as well as through our educational formats (which include workshops, excursions, open discussions, improvisation and collective experimentation), we often act as activists, using architecture as a tool in search of a city's potentialities.[3] In all our projects, we operate at the intersection of architecture, city planning, art and everyday life, addressing city and urban renewal as a process. When deciding on the context, we are quite often attracted to locations with difficult urban conditions: places torn between different systems, time periods or planning ideologies; places that fail to adapt are abandoned, left over or in transition, containing some relevance for the processes of urban transformation. These places are our experimentation sites – they offer untapped potential, which we try to activate to develop new perspectives for alternative usage patterns, collective ideals, urban diversity and different approaches that can be taken.

Expanding participation: Spatial design as a collaborative practice

For each of our projects, we take great care in forming teams of interdisciplinary experts. City residents are also specialists for their particular contexts: no one knows better about living conditions and the respective local situation than those who have to deal with a place daily. By starting up a dialogue within the neighbourhood, we gain valuable insights into the history, fears, desires, existential needs and deficits that form, as it were, an invisible network over the spatial situation. However, we are aware that intimacy and familiarity can often hinder the vision people have for the future, and specifically how far reality can be radically changed.

To trigger this awareness and to bring an outside perspective into the process, we forge active alliances between local and external experts and, thus, we discover new areas of action and open up new fields of experimentation by testing and examining their possibilities on a collective basis. These practices that can be called 'performing architecture' (or, in some cases, can be described as being 'environmental scenography at work'[4]) and they allow the merging of space with individual experiences and social relations; potentially, they make room for the revelation of hitherto unseen possibilities and to let the city become reinvented in the minds of its users: a new horizon appears where before nothing seemed possible. With our work, we cross artistic formats and boundaries, in both commissioned and independently run projects. The following is a selection of projects that illustrate our approach to spatial design as a product of social interaction, always including the sharing of design knowledge and collectively reflecting on the cultural production of space.

No spectators, only actors: Eichbaumoper (Mülheim an der Ruhr, 2008/9)

This project was kick-started through a joint initiative by the Grillo Theatre/ Schauspiel Essen, Ringlokschuppen Mülheim and Musiktheater im Revier Gelsenkirchen. The chosen context for this project was a neglected metro station on the urban periphery of Mülheim a.d. Ruhr. The project aimed to artistically appropriate and recapture this abandoned place. The task was to temporarily transform this location into a venue for opera productions, with performances taking place in June and July 2009. The station, Eichbaum, is located at a crossing point between the cities of Essen and Mülheim, situated at the centre of the highway intersection between the A40 motorway and the B1 national road; as a 'fit-for-the-future' infrastructure project it was built in the 1970s, using a lot of concrete. Once considered a place of aspiration and hope, it became plagued by vandalism, fear and foreboding. Nevertheless, up to today, it has remained an important junction within an urban landscape that is dissected by highways and metro lines. The site can be viewed as being a model for the current situation of this former industrial region which today is facing quite a number of urban and social challenges.

Eichbaum, with its conditions and requisitions, became the starting point for the topics of an opera project. The newly built *Opernbauhütte* (opera building hut) in the square – once a small market for potato farmers and the local 'egg granny' – stood out as an architectural symbol of reactivation and transformation, offering space for workshops, conferences, a bar, a cinema, an art gallery, meeting places, a reading café and so on. The opera was run by invited composers, librettists and local residents. Taking account of their fears, hopes, dreams and memories, the real world of everyday life started to merge with the artificial world of our production. In addition to the local people's stories, the noise of the highway, the rhythm of the passing metro and the surrounding bleak and dreary spaces all became the 'scenographic' components and a formative part of the *Eichbaumoper*, blurring the distinction between theatre and urban life. Eichbaum, a neglected metro station, became a theatre without spectators, having only actors present.

The second part of the project was entitled *Eichbaum Countdown* (Mülheim an der Ruhr 2010, 2011, in cooperation with Ringlokschuppen Mülheim) and conceived as a further intervention at the station. It addressed young people in the catchment area of Eichbaum. We wanted to understand how they used the site and what they hoped it could become. raumlaborberlin realized, in collaboration with the youths – our local experts – and various external experts, the best ideas that came out of the workshop: *Eichbaumboxer*, a regional boxing championship, *Eichbaumbauer*, a participative building workshop,

FIGURE 9.1 *raumlaborberlin*, Eichbaumboxer, *Mülheim an der Ruhr 2008–11*. © *raumlaborberlin*.

a *Wall of Fame* and a local *Rap Battle*. As a result of these events, we proposed a permanent transformation plan in which the cities of Mülheim and Essen, the public transportation company and the motorway administration would have to work together to design a spatial project called *Eichbaumpark*. The target group is teenagers and this plan is still being discussed.

Provisionary architectures – developing and testing spatial designs: Hotel Shabbyshabby *(Mannheim, 2014) and* Shabbyshabby Apartments *(Munich, 2015)*

raumlaborberlin's approach is to use and to redefine architectural and scenographic design as cultural techniques. These tools are primarily used within the framework of art projects which, in turn, often lead to more sustainable developments. Therefore, the second task is to establish these practices of discourse and spatial design, also going beyond the artistic context as a social practice. Several of our projects have their starting point in theatres and international festivals, supported by the fact that some of our team members and close collaborators have a professional theatrical background. These projects that become performatively implemented in public spaces, for example on the occasion of a festival, serve as an experimentation phase (or, as it were, as a public 'rehearsal') that point – beyond conventional city planning and commercial space usage – to future potentials of community-driven design.

A case in point here is the project *Hotel Shabbyshabby*, which we developed and conducted in Mannheim in 2014 in cooperation with the *Theater der Welt* festival. The project's topic and starting idea was the observation that hotel rooms – in general – are rarely pleasant places to fall asleep or wake up in. Very often, they present their visitors with ghastly carpets, antiseptic surfaces, perfidious artworks and dreadfully decorated walls, not to mention a disappointing view as well as a catastrophic hotel bar. Is it so difficult to design a room where one would enjoy spending a night? A room that offers a unique view, a divine bed and is as snug as a beaver's den?

Several months before the festival, we tendered an architectural competition and invited design students and professionals to build the hotel room of their dreams. After an international jury made up of renowned architects and artists had picked a choice of winning designs, twenty-two single hotel cabins with 'individual comfort', made from the city's actual construction waste, were created by 120 individuals from France, Belgium, Switzerland, Portugal, Poland, England, Austria and Germany. This was all undertaken in the purpose-built construction camp next to the national theatre in the city of Mannheim. From this central hub – the open workshop and camp area – the construction teams fanned out into the city where each group set up and installed one hotel cabin in a selected location: in parks, next to statues, along the banks of the rivers Rhine and the Neckar, on the site of a former US army barracks, and on the roofs of houses. From 22 May to 8 June, the duration of the *Theater der Welt 2014* festival, the hotel cabins could be rented for one night by the festival visitors and by anyone who had always dreamt of spending 'Holidays in Mannheim'.[5]

With this approach, the processes of spatial design and construction were performed collectively and made public; therefore, Heike Schuppelius, who is a scenographer and a teacher at an art school, described the process as a *Bauprobe* (build-up rehearsal) for the city:

> In a theatre context, this process is comparable to the customary 'set design mock-up': fixed at the beginning of a production, on which the set design is built in a simulated form using the simplest, most inexpensive materials possible. ... It's the day when brainstorming and conception come together in a model, and the set size is checked for feasibility. Set designers, directors, costume designers, actors and workshop

managers are present to get an idea of the planned space, think it through and make corrections. It is a unique experience, and has resulted in some set designs that were more beautiful, playful and experimental than the real thing. But the special quality of the set design mock-up is the real-life experience of putting an idea into practice as a full-scale model – a virtual idea, up until this point, which has matured as a 3D miniature form. Seen this way, *Hotel Shabbyshabby* was also an ideal counterpart to and continuation of teaching practices in universities and colleges.[6]

One year later, we took up this approach again and conducted the project, in an altered version, in Munich, again in collaboration with a theatre, the Münchner Kammerspiele. Again, we invited students and professionals, this time twenty-four teams from Germany and abroad, to realize an experiment in Munich, proposing different views of the city. Munich is one of the top ten cities in Europe when it comes to paying rents for living spaces so the question posed was: What would happen if everyone leaves their homes and builds booths at the most unlikely places within the city? Might it create a whole new kind of bonfire society? A society in which opinions and information are exchanged while roasting marshmallows over an open fire and drinking cowboy coffee? These were the questions the project started with. The *Shabbyshabby Camp* was set up at Marstallplatz in the very centre of the city. From 3 September

FIGURE 9.2 *raumlaborberlin*, Hotel Shabbyshabby, *Mannheim 2014. Photo:* Arthur Bauer, © *raumlaborberlin.*

to 13 September, the teams lived and worked in the camp and spread out into Munich to build their *Shabbyshabby Apartments*. Each of these apartments could be rented between 12 September and 13 October by anyone for one night. The aim of the project was to offer a different view on the city, a city where people have to pay rents that are among Europe's most expensive. At about the same time, thousands of refugees from Syria and other countries arrived at the train station in Munich as part of the massive migration wave into Europe that took place since the autumn of 2015. The project was discussed quite controversially by both audiences and art critics for not having reflected on this very special situation.[7] The topic of migration also became the central focal point of several other raumlabor projects that followed in the wake of the project.[8]

Changing the hidden 'scripts' of public space: Rush Hour Rest Stop *(Durban, South Africa, 2014)*

raumlaborberlin's artistic approach and socio-spatial thinking aims at exploring the performative dimensions of space, that is, the ways in which people and things become organized in manifold constellations. The term 'performative', coined by the renowned philosopher John L. Austin in his lectures *How to Do Things With Words* (1955), defines the speech acts of language as being 'performative'. By adopting this term, Judith Butler has argued that gestures and human behaviour are performative in that they generate identity by inscribing culturally predefined features and behaviour patterns into one's body (Butler 1990). But what does it precisely mean to say that space is performative or, as Erika Fischer-Lichte has asked, 'What do we do to spaces and what do spaces do to us?'[9] For some of our projects, for example *Rush Hour Rest Stop*, a project we conducted in Durban, South Africa (by invitation of the Goethe Institute, South Africa), this even became the initial question. When visiting Durban for the first time, we met Doung, a Durban-based artist and architect who focuses on post-apartheid spatial practices. He took us on a walk through Durban, which brought us to the highway, the main entrance point into the city. Running parallel to the highway is a pedestrian path connecting the townships in the west to Warwick Junction, a knot of underpasses and overpasses, tunnels and transit stations, where a massive and bustling informal market lives and breathes, the quintessence of the African city. Durban is a city on the move. Congested with cars, pedestrians, taxis; people here don't stop – there are few places to rest and it's rarely safe to do so. Despite, or perhaps due to the nature of all of the movement taking place, Durban appears fractured and disconnected: twenty years after the end of apartheid, the spatial separation of the city is still very intense. Thousands of people walk up and down this pedestrian path into and from the city: a dirt path that meanders along the highway, between lanes, through green patches, under bridges, to the overwhelming sound of moving cars.

The site we chose for further exploration was one of these green patches, a leftover triangle between the highway and exit roads; a very busy place, a convergence point for the numerous flows of movement that exist within this urban environment. There is an informal stop for taxis on one side, the pedestrian path on the other, and further down, a meeting point at the highway level for hitchhikers heading west. The basic idea of the project then, developed in collaboration with the local artist group Dala Collective, was to acknowledge all of these forms of informal transport and to transpose them into a physical manifestation; to create a station for informal traffic, a hub, a rest stop and a shelter. The crown of the simple roof-and-beam structure was sourced from the city's many scrapyards and resembles a five-lane traffic jam. At the same time, the roof we built is extremely practical – the car shells protect pedestrians against the sun and rain and the benches offer a place of rest. Rather than addressing the problem of traffic in a way that further fragments the city, this intervention – which is, in a wider sense, scenographic – provided a piece of infrastructure embracing Durban's motion, allowing this unchoreographed, improvised urban dance to thrive.

FIGURE 9.3 *raumaborberlin*, Rush Hour Rest Stop, *Durban, South Africa 2014.* Photo: Roger Jardine, © *raumlaborberlin.*

Le Théâtre des Negotiations (Nanterre-Amandiers, France, 2015): A political, scientific, pedagogical and artistic experiment

Can the space in which an important meeting occurs influence its result? And if so, is it actually the case that we as architects and scenographers can (potentially) change the world? These questions were the starting point for an experiment that we conceived in conjunction with SPEAP (Programme d'expérimentation en arts politiques de Sciences Po) and Bruno Latour, and in collaboration with Philippe Quesne at the Théâtre Nanterre-Amandier. Two hundred students from all over the world took part in a simulation of the international conference of parties on climate change, the COP21, in front of an audience for five days. The real COP21 took place in Paris in December 2015; it was a significant point in time with regard to our race against the increasingly rapid changes that our planet is now facing. Policy changes regarding climate change have encountered countless delays for the past twenty years as the need to address global warming becomes ever more urgent. So far the lethal ineffectiveness of any political efforts is a consequence of the enormous

FIGURE 9.4 *raumlaborberlin*, Théâtre des Négociations, *Nanterre, France 2015*. *Photo © raumlaborberlin.*

complexity of issues in play as well as the formats and processes of such international negotiations.

The initiator of this event, Bruno Latour, believed that the failure of past conferences was caused by a crisis of representation: Who represents the problems at stake, and who are the different communities of people affected? Who represents the oceans and forests, the polar regions, climate refugees and (soon to be) extinct animals in a conference of nations? What if the atmosphere, the soil and the cities all had their own vote during the negotiations on a reduction of CO_2 emissions? raumlaborberlin created a space for the conference in which it could take place – a non-hierarchical and flexible structure that supported a positive outcome. Of course it may be difficult to say how space influences the flow of negotiations – but by letting the climate play an active role, by giving each member, each delegation and each thematic discussion the chance to change the space for the best outcome possible, definitely helped as much as our tables did; these could be easily transformed into flipcharts.

Scenographic interventions into the urban space: Forms of Turmoil *(Milan, Italy, 2017)*

As was clearly demonstrated in the previous sections, using concrete examples, the projects by raumlabor are in principle context-related and, in addition to this, defined in a participatory sense in a very wide scope. This is especially true for how the projects already integrate the audience during the creative formation process and invite them to actively participate in the design and production processes. To kick-start such processes with the participants, the projects propose design practices and design modules, as well as possible approaches to how to go about implementing the projects. These can all be seen as being counterstrategies to conventional urban planning methods and standardized architectural and commercial design, which in turn need to be tested and tried out. As has become clear, architecture and scenography not only serve as an artistic tool, but are simultaneously becoming vehicles for experimenting with alternative social practices or even political activism. A further example of this approach which especially highlights its political dimension is the project *Forms of Turmoil*, which reflected on forms and manifestations of protest and discourse within the public realm.

During the first week of April 2017, in the framework of the *Fuorisalone* in Milan, an annual festival dedicated to contemporary design, we set up a laboratory for designing, experimenting with and producing pneumatic microarchitectures. The base element is a dunnage bag, a commercially

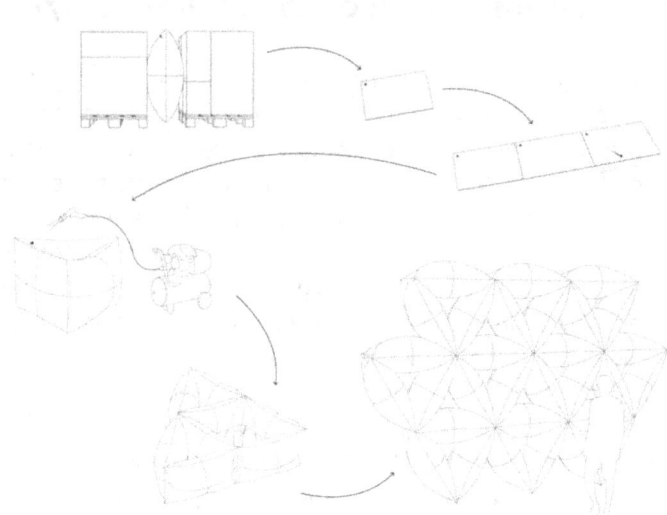

FIGURE 9.5 *raumlaborberlin,* Forms of Turmoil, *Milan 2017, preparatory design work (drawing and collage)* © *raumlaborberlin. Drawing for the production of the air cushions which were deployed during the event/artistic intervention; the collage is referring to the painting* Il Quarto Stato *(The Fourth Estate) by Giuseppe Pellizza da Volpedo (1901), Museo del Novecento, Milan, Italy.*

available air cushion, used for securing cargo in industrial containers. We developed a system for the aggregation of these single modules: different 'microarchitectures' tuned to carry the individual expressions of several local activist groups in public spaces throughout the city. During a time when crowds of design-savvy tourists invade Milan looking for trends and innovation, our pneumatic structures, developed to act as canvases, banners and protest signs, drew their attention to more meaningful topics. We invited groups of activists to create a dramaturgy within this public space, using banner objects to express their desires with regard to the city. A performative discourse involving citizens ensued, transforming and opening up spaces in Milan, both for discussion and an exchange of ideas. The individual portable architectures were assembled, becoming inhabitable structures, thus creating a new prototype for spaces of urban political discourse.

raumlaborberlin's scenographic work is driven by the belief that public spaces are spaces where one can meet and interact. Our scenographies and provisional architectures intervene, inhabit and enhance existing public spaces in museums, at festivals, theatres and fairs; thus, we aim to extend the inherent potentials of the public sphere. In other words, we do not want to remain within the comfort zone of artistic productions, but we rather want to influence urban contexts as well as current social processes and debates. With some of these projects we even manage to make a lasting impact on and change the 'cultural script' of public spaces that go above and beyond the project event itself and its actual duration. Here we see, according to our understanding of it, a huge potential for scenography, now and in the future.

Notes

1 This quote has been taken from Peter Danielson's chapter on 'Social Space', in Danielson 1998: 236–8: 236.
2 See also Beyes, Deuflhard and Krempl 2009.
3 For a more extensive discussion of this approach see Foerster-Baldenius and Liesegang 2013; cf. also our ongoing documentation and publication on raumlaborberlin's multi-faceted projects, http://raumlabor.net/publications. What we call the 'open raumlabor university' is a virtual institution: for more information on raumlaborberlin's various departments, including the dept. for 'real utopia', 'participative building', 'scenography', and others, see http://raumlabor.net/category/3-departments/.
4 With this term we refer to Arnold Aronson and his study on 'environmental scenography' (2018 [1981]); our approach is similar but different, particularly with regard to the ways in which our audiences become involved not only in performance events but also in design and production processes that are inherently part of each project.

5 See also the project description in raumlaborberlin and Theater der Welt 2014: 3.
6 Heike Schuppelius, 'The Set Design Mock-up', in raumlaborberlin and Theater der Welt 2014: 110f.
7 Parts of the discussion can be found at www.nachtkritik.de/index.php?option=com_content&view=article&id=11478:shabby-shabby-appartments-muenchner-kammerspiele&catid=38:die-nachtkritik-k&Itemid=40 (accessed 10 May 2018)
8 For example, raumlabor's involvement in the planning process for the conversion of the former 'Haus der Statistik' at Berlin's Alexanderplatz as living spaces for refugees as well as working and event rooms for art, culture and education.
9 Erika Fischer-Lichte, 'Performativity and Space', in Wolfrum and von Brandis 2015: 31–38: 31.

PART THREE

Rethinking scenography

10

The ungovernableness of the scene

Dieter Mersch

The term 'scenography' can hardly be defined; instead, scenographic work encompasses the ephemeral and fragile production or performance of spaces and their transition. Since spaces are manifestations within the perceivable and the physical world and not just manipulable tools, their scenographic handling involves practices of assembly, collection, montage and installation by combining and contrasting things, actions and the play of light and shadow in the broadest sense of material as well as immaterial matter and relations. They always transcend our ability to close them into a complete and controllable image. Therefore, scenographic staging is associated with experiments or discourses which account for certain choices and aesthetic positions, including a variety of impacts and agencies that at the same time unwillingly produce side-effects, impediments and blind spots. Every technique is bound to the ambiguity between intended and unintended consequences. Thus, through the creation of new, unexpected and overwhelming experiences, it produces its very opposition, its backlashes, dark sides and resistances. By definition, their making suffers from its interior finitude and 'non-totalizability', from contingency and incompleteness; hence, scenography turns out to be a complex practice that exists between openness and closure, between composition and collapse or between mastery and opacity. Partly an art, partly a science, it refers to the old meaning of 'Art' (with a capital letter), which derives from the Latin word *'Artes'*, in the sense of what the Greeks called *technē*, based in method and tacit knowledge that attempt to master different objects or proportions and figures to establish both spatial and temporal situations of 'narrative environments' that at the same time cannot but fail. In this respect, one can even say that scenography, both as a theoretical and practical discipline linked to architecture as well as to visual arts, music, and performance (to name but a few fields), is one of the daughters of the Wagnerian *Gesamtkunstwerk* and its hypotrophy. It is composed of the 'construction' of events and atmosphere through the collection of an 'ecological' entirety of human and non-human elements that act and 'react' in their unpredictable entanglements, building up modelled 'worlds', which decompose and decay the very next moment. Here one might take Heiner Goebbels' *Stifters Dinge* (Stifter's Things; 2007) as an example. This theatrical post-human opera – centred around things mentioned in Adalbert Stifter's novel *Nachsommer*, such as water, salt, wood, metal or stones and their unique noise or sound, which were confronted with voices of Indians and speeches given by Malcolm X and Claude Lévi-Strauss – creates a complex pastiche that never allows the listener and observer to synthesize it into a single interpretation and meaning.[1]

The following remarks attempt to explore at least some aspects of the intricate and confusing relationship between scenography and art – scenography as an art and the art of scenography as choreography – by considering their impact from the perspective of philosophy and aesthetics, to illuminate the genuine 'ungovernableness' of the scene. These remarks also give some glimpses into the strange and chronic impossibility to master art with regard to its teleology of completeness and finitude. In addition, the goal is to clarify their interconnection with knowledge – that is, scenography and art as a kind of research or recognition (see Badura et al. 2015) that at the same time destabilizes both, making them more uncertain than they normally appear to be. They also draw some distinctions between art and technology to reveal the potentiality of the first against the mere illusion-machinery of the second, and thereby to distinguish aesthetic experience as well as insight from the incessant proliferation of spectacular images and their surprising effects aimed at impressing an audience. Beginning with this question, we are immediately confronted with the inherent contradiction between – on the one hand – the necessity to construct or sketch and design a scenery in order to make a narrative plausible or a drama run, and – on the other – the immanent unruliness of what we have created, which tends to produce a life of its own and to develop in a direction we never intended. There is an unavoidable gap or disruption in any creative result, a withdrawal of elements, their materiality or modalities of relations. Nothing seems to be simply ready to hand, made for our application and availability; rather it turns in our hands and through our work into something different and alien, making a mockery of our will and intentions and independent of our imagination as soon as we usher it into reality.

However, to be precise in wording and denomination, we have to divide negative notions such as 'withdrawal', or 'recalcitrance', from positive ones such as 'agency', 'power' or 'affordance', as widely used in *Actor-Network Theory* or *Object-Oriented Ontology* and *New Realism* (Byant, Harman and Srnicek 2011; Harman 2011; Ferraris 2014). These pertain to things or matter and are themselves highly strange and inconsistent. Objects, matter or things are generally opaque; they do not react or answer because 'responding' and 'acting' or 'reacting' as actions depend on choice: the ability to select different possibilities from the vague and indefinite field of chances, causes or effects. Thus the term 'agency' also makes sense only as a 'negative' term, that is to say, as something that remains unhuman and can only be spelled out as a form of resistance. In opposition to this, we have to consider the besetting differences between the scenographic composition on the one hand – which always already requires our observation from the outside, or a meta-position that allows us to keep a distance to posit and manipulate constellations of diverse elements, effects and material that might be referred to as the scenographic ecology – and, on the other, its chronic uncontrollability. And although the notion of ecology seems to be awkward in this context, and is used mainly due to a certain theoretical fashion rather than to provide a new approach, it, at the same time, serves as a proper metaphor for the unwieldy entirety of the scene, its 'given-ness', literally a 'gift', something which we receive without being able to capture or 'objectify' it. The starting point of our consideration is then the essential non-calculability of the human situation and its so-called mastery, and if we specifically speak of the *epistēmē* of art and scenography and their unique epistemological impact, their way of revealing new insights, then we also have to take into account the impertinent non-knowledge or counterfinality immanent to human construction, which usually remains beyond our awareness and accessibility.

Symbolon and *diabolon*

We should add that there is no need to be afraid of this 'negative' result, because negativity does not necessarily mean 'negation' or 'rejection', but rather refers to looking at things from their 'dark' angle.[2] Learning requires addressing such weird or strange aspects, the persistent ruptures, fissures and breakdowns of our products, their almost inevitable release into blind alleys and abysses. Demolitions, unfulfillment or mistakes can reveal a lot more about the hubris and vulnerability of human effort, and allow for a better understanding of the insurmountable incompleteness of any mastery of the real. Elsewhere, we have called this oblique 'view from the side' an 'anamorphotic methodology', referring to the technique of anamorphosis in baroque painting, which renders an image discernible only from an extreme angle of 180 degrees, an angle from which one normally sees nothing. Anamorphosis unfolds odd and irresolvable life-and-death-plays in order to show the true image by concealing it (which is normally the mystical image of our vanity) (Mersch 2008). Hence, scepticism with respect to scenographic success does not mean a fatal resignation pertaining to its work, but rather the opposite. Instead, an anamorphic critique reveals the relentless disturbance of our intentions in design practices, aesthetic production and technology. Or, to put it more paradoxically, there is no command or control of a dramatic situation and its *symbolon* without a *diabolon*, a 'throwing-apart' of its collection of condensed signs and things, a literal disturbance that carries the processes to their very 'catastrophe' (in the literal sense of a twisting or turning point). Thus, the art of scenography is truly founded on the non-mastery of mastery, its deconstruction through construction; that is, it is at once a practice of production and its critique. And this in particular holds true for the increasing significance of scenography today, which is due to the seemingly intriguing and fascinating possibilities that have become available as a result of digitalization and its exploding fetishism.

However, the work of art in general is linked to 'composition', which, as an imaginary act, serves as a key notion for artistic construction and design, not only in music, but also in architecture, film, theatre, painting or literature, as well as scenography and scenic urbanism. In opposition to the dialectic between *symbolon* and *diabolon* that we are emphasizing here, composition can be seen as the intentional 'language of art', the most fundamental and elementary means of creation, be it in the realm of presentation or representation or of embodiment and play. This is because it seems to be the very model of 'expression', the turning inside-out or rather showing by positing phenomena, things or 'percepts' (Deleuze) together to make things or symbols or to produce perceivable meanings. In opposition, I would like to point out that the notion of 'language' generates nothing but vague metaphors, misleading us in their connotations. Rather we should remember here Adorno's *Fragment on Music and Language*, which signifies music only as similar to language and not as a language, because those who take it literally would be trapped by it, ensnared and led astray. Instead of referring to words, propositions or rhetoric, we therefore prefer the term 'com-position' with a hyphen; a term that designates both an orderly structure or alleged syntax and a synthesis, a collection or a combination. It literally means a 'togetherness' that produces an event, a significance or 'work' and its performance. The hyphen does not only alienate the word, but demonstrates its own 'com-position' out of the two particles 'com', literally 'together-with', and 'position', the act of setting, of positing something. 'Com-position' as the so-called language of art thus means – in contrast to verbal language – to pose things, materials or actions by tying them together, joining them, not necessarily into one unit or identity but into a certain interrelation or cohesion, which unfolds its own strength and power. Hence, by 'positing' we mean in the first place to associate different phenomena together, that is, staging materials, or objects and so on, and to put them into places or into a series, which, at the same time, means relating them to each other and separating them, collecting and juxtaposing them, to reveal their inner tensions, strains or forces as well as their disorder, antagonisms, hostilities or conflicts. 'Com-position' thus implies the creation of a 'constellation', which again means literally a 'con' or a 'putting together' of *stellae*, stars, which happen to be there by pure contingency, a mean variation or dispersion without any essential or interior interconnection, rather which are, at the same time, included and excluded, thrown apart and, however, inclined to be seen together and to relate to each other by the act of figuration.

Figuration of the non-figurative

Hence, 'com-position' – as the basic operation of art and therefore also of scenography, which is, again, literally, a *graphein*, a scripture or score or notation – is then grounded in the conjunction of at least two different elements that were not connected with one another beforehand. Conjunctions, also connections, collections and congregations, are in this respect the basic operation of artistic production. And if we compare this operation – the 'com-position' as conjunction – with language, or rather with discourse, we see that, instead of being based on propositions and the *copula*, the form that is 'A is b' with the determination of the 'A' (as the subject) *as* 'b' (as the predication that is responsible for its specific signification), the arts instead are grounded – grammatically speaking – in conjunctional functions and their different forms – such as 'and', 'or', 'either ... or' or 'neither ... nor', both ... and' or 'not only ... but' and so on. Conjunctions are interesting elements, because they are immediately dialectical: they connect as they separate and separate by connection (Mersch 2015). This means: conjunctions include disjunctions; they connect or combine even as they simultaneously break apart and reveal their differences through identification. And since the basic mode of aesthetics is showing (which includes plural acts of presenting, manifesting, exhibiting or exposing, etc.), and also since showing always answers in the affirmative, the positive and the negative are both revealed together in one metastable combination, like figure and ground in the image or 'changing aspects' (Wittgenstein) or vexations, and so on. This also implies that both the separation of elements and their interconnection are always already visible, side-by-side, in every work of art, precisely because they operate in the realm of the perceivable. One cannot but work aesthetically without immediately falling into this dialectic of simultaneous approval and negation. Instead of the propositional *copula* and its identifying logic of determination in discourse, the so-called language of art is based on series of 'dis-tinctions' or cut-offs – and here we should put a hyphen between the two particles of the words to destabilize and also multiply their meanings. Hence, art always already presents itself in differences rather than identifications; its way of production is, so to speak, based in a difference-engine, a strange mechanism of doubling and multiplying contrast and discrimination. This is why – to extend our analogy with language – what we might name an 'artistic proposition' never shows itself to be unambiguous. It plays with the openness and ambiguity of the conjunction/disjunction in such a way that the connection of elements produces, paradoxically speaking, an irresolvable solution. To make the point clear here, from now on, we will make the two words conjunction and disjunction into one word by using a slash. This also means that the simplicity and complexity (at the same time) of the artistic 'statement' and its 'wit' in the form of 'wittiness' or cleverness are defined by the 'cut' of assemblages or montages, founded in contrasts, in opposition to discursive contradictions and their logical consequences. Even more so, the montage's glue of contrasts coordinates the contrasted elements alongside one another, presenting them in perpetual suspension, or imbalance. Hence, if there is a 'language of art' or a scripture of scenography, then it would be, rather than a *graphein*, a writing of differences. If art thinks, then it thinks through the medium of 'com-position' and 'contra-position', again with a hyphen between them, which emphasizes their fracturing, their simultaneous non-identity.

And yet, simply putting things together or separating whatever happens to be lying around and showing it are not enough. It is necessary to transcend banalities. Thus, to make scenography an artwork requires more than just tying contingent things, objects, materials or actions together and making a meaningful entity out of them. Certainly, in every aesthetic creation, the 'com-position' as conjunction/disjunction serves as a basic operation. And certainly, every random series of things or actions forms some aesthetic arrangement, as a collection of tones creates a melody or playful effects of space, shadow and light a distinct atmosphere, but sometimes also mere confusion. Exceptionally, they might be productive, but in general they will confront us with 'non-mysterious riddles' (Ernst Bloch), which induce nothing. As such, not all arrangements necessarily produce a meaningful work or an epistemic surplus or stake out an artistic position. To produce something relevant through constellation and its differential modes, the art's conjunctionality/disjunctionality must transcend the sum of the arrangement's parts, must refer to something that goes above or beyond the arrangement itself, must stage an inversion in the 'And' or the 'Or' or 'Neither … nor' and so on, that reveals an Other or alterity, or gives rise to a sudden leap in insight. In the intriguing words of Rainer Maria Rilke's *Fifth Duino Elegy*, the artwork's conjunctionality/disjunctionality forms such a non-discursive nexus in which, as he puts it, the mere constellation 'leaps around and changes' 'from the pure Too-little … / into that empty Too-much; / where the difficult calculation / becomes numberless and resolved' (quoted from Vilain 2011: 150f). The series of poetic associations constantly follows one paradox after the other. Wittgenstein referred similarly to the shift as a 'change of aspects' (Wittgenstein 1958: 193–229), which gives figure to a non-figure (*Ungestalt*). In contrast to discursive propositions, which always either express a judgement, invent a metaphor, produce an allegoric network, construct fictional narratives or draw a logical conclusion, the juncture (and interstice) in question here marks that part of the 'aesthetic proposition' or 'language' where what we can call an 'epistemological leap' takes place. It is the site of a non-subjective reflexivity, a reflexivity in mediation that plays with perception, its materials or its interconnections with actions, their disruptions and conflicts. And if we want to understand the specificity of art and its challenging impact, we have to take a closer look at this 'epistemological leap' and its peculiar functionality.

My thesis here is: only at moments when such leaps happen, does art occur, and thus, only at such moments does the peculiarity of the artistic *epistēmē* and its unique form of knowledge come into being. Or to put it another way: the capacity of an artwork's joints and assemblages to provoke reflection and produce knowledge stands in direct correlation to the degree to which these joints and assemblages are constructed in – what I call – a 'catachrestic' way. Here, the term 'catachresis' is used as a metaphor for the various figurations of 'thing-languages' in which Walter Benjamin saw the language of art itself (Benjamin 1974: 140–57). These 'thing-languages' act or argue on the basis of chiasms and juxtapositions in order to open up distances or interspaces which let us see or perceive the 'thingness of the thing' (Brown 2016), as well as unexpected eventful situations, or the drama of the human condition in its ecological milieu in a new and unforeseen way. The 'catachresis' is indeed a rhetorical figure in which an expression wholly divergent from conventional use is forged to say something inexpressible or as yet unsaid. For this reason, catachreses are not normally included in the classic canon of rhetorical devices, even if they are sometimes listed in its series of figurations. In truth, however, they are impossible figures that exceed the limits of rhetoric. Like the 'joke', they are 'non-figures'. Therefore, catachreses are often viewed as transgressions or abuses of language, because they go beyond established meanings and disrupt the distinction between rhetorical registers to say something at the margins of the expressible. The same holds true for scenography. It should become catachretic to create an artistic knowledge, to be productive in the sense of presenting a unique insight. More than that, catachreses enable the speaker to make use of different or even strange modes of speaking and of the sorts of inversions manifest in enigmas, dissonances and contradictions, thus allowing him or her to constructively shape their oppositions and tensions into a third that can only be hinted at.[3] Specifically, the art of scenography is devoted to this third. Like the semiosis of a non-semiotic, or an 'a-semiosis' of the semiotic, it crystallizes into a 'non-sense' which does make sense without any expression or explicit meaning. This is also why its epistemic impact is experienceable, but not entirely controllable or governable.

Unexpected leaps and the creative event of artistic knowledge

The art of scenography then deals with this impossibility, although it tends to form or construct a totality – and yet miscarries. But it is its collapse that makes it great, because it finally discloses the scene – understood as situating a complexity of world – as ineffable. Its artistic knowledge, besides all tacit, technical and practical knowledge, which is undoubtedly included in all artistic practice, aims exactly at this: the opposition between the aesthetic production of a scene and the construction of its entireness on the one hand and its concurrent impossibility on the other, its non-closure, which is related to openness; and it is precisely the depth of this opposition that in turn induces the epistemic power of the scenic. Hence, artistic knowledge is, at the same time, always linked to the critique of knowledge; it reflects its limitations and is, as knowledge, by heart a self-reflexive knowledge. It happens in those moments when art's catachrestic figurations produce ruptures and fissures that give rise to irresolvable vexations. The vexation, therefore, is the emblematic figure of aesthetic knowledge. As a pointed remark: artistic cognition only happens in the moment of vexation, that is the neither/nor or in-between, where both sides are at the same time in balance and in movement. Vexation then means the eventfulness of reflexivity that, by definition, cannot be mastered; instead it occurs so to speak in the middle of its incessant alteration – and it only comes to pass if we, simultaneously, try to grasp it to accept its chronically incomplete attempts. And by this, of course, we propagate a certain concept of art as well as a certain concept of artistic knowledge, which doubtless can be rejected, but I am convinced that – in opposition to science – the goal of art is not success or the achievement of a positive result or progress in truth, but, literally, a constant crisis in itself.

The indeterminate, ambiguous and conflicting constellation thus creates in itself an openness, in which art and the event of artistic knowledge can take place. This means that art comes primarily into play when control and construction are interrupted, and when contradictions or chiasms and paradoxical figuration reveal the inexpressible, or that which can neither be presented nor represented in symbolic language. It is the moment of in-betweenness, of indecision and swinging oscillation, a third place that allows for reflection, which cannot come into being otherwise. Art then confronts us with the experience of an alterity – and artful scenography comes correspondingly into being when it restricts itself from mere technology and strategies of attacking or provoking the beholder with miracles and wonders. That is, it is most effective when it withholds unfolding the full power of images or, as it were, oversensualizing our senses, overloading them and adding more fuel to their fire to accelerate their explosions of effects. Instead, the work of art argues more gently and cautiously. Its process demands subtle shifts and unexpected leaps in attention and cognition, in which something happens with us rather than the opposite, when we are replaced in our experience and find ourselves in moments of confusion: 'for here there is no place that does not see you', Rainer Maria Rilke concludes his description of the *Archaic Torso of Apollo*: 'You must change your life' (quoted from Vilain 2011: 80f).

These moments might be fragile, but they are always striking because inherent to them is a demand for self-recognition and reflection. Here we might consider that Joseph Beuys declared the 'hare' to be his heraldic animal, his personal emblem for art, because the hare resembles the wit, the ruse or artifice in that it possesses the ability to leap aside suddenly and to spring in another direction. It is as if it is not even the hare itself that jumps, rather it seems to be rapt and torn away by its own leaps, which it must unwillingly follow. Something alien, like a spasmodic tic, appears in the hare, which at the same time seems to surprise it, and allows for a new direction of escape. Something quite similar happens to us when artistic wit (*ingenium*) offers us a different trajectory in thinking. Art in this respect allows for new ways of seeing and hearing, of perceiving the perceivable and its limitations, and thus reveals the unperceivable conditions of the visible and audible. Artistic statements are 'witty jumps'; they dislocate or displace our way of living and our behaviour; they alienate the 'given' and install dysfunctional interruptions into the expected, to open up new perspectives of awareness and attention. The head is round, as Francis Picabia states, so that it can constantly turn in different directions. Marcel Duchamp named these tiny, microscopic cuts and holes *inframinces*, shifting our alertness or affectivity into different understandings of the real and increasing our sensibility for the *presque-rien*, the almost-nothingness. There is another association we can draw on here, relating to one of the most ingenious propositions Heidegger made in his later work: '*Der Satz macht einen Satz*' (Heidegger 1978 [1957]: 96 and 151), literally: 'A sentence makes a "*sentenz*"' (in the Latin sense of 'sententia'), and, at the same time, a pun: 'A proposition makes a leap'. The German meaning allows for the double sense, because on the one hand it reads the mere tautology that a sentence is nothing but a sentence with the slide transition that it also hints at the famous, also almost tautological phrase that only those differences are relevant that 'make differences' (Bateson 2013). On the other hand, it contains the twofold meaning that first a sentence produces insofar a '*sentenz*' (in its Latin meaning), in that it offers us a short and dense insight, and second, by doing so, the sentence requires a leap in understanding. Again we are confronted with the important notion of the 'leap'. Heidegger addressed the 'event of thinking', which requires passivity rather than active search, because we must leave ourselves open to its unpredictable transformation, rather than creating it. The same holds true for both the 'anamorphic view', or 'oblique critique from the side', which I mentioned at the beginning of the text, and the artistic statement that jolts perception into movement and forces it into conversion by creating contrasts or contradictory constellations. The art of scenography, its artistic way – beyond any sensual barrage of attraction – is related to this.

Performing art statements

There is more to say, because it is of particular interest in what way and based on what practices art is able to install its 'sentences', not only because they confuse our senses but also because they compel us to reflect upon our sensual and practical conditions to develop their capacity. However, to speak about 'sentences', even in terms of 'jumps' and 'transitions', seems to privilege a structural view and a perspective on correlation, order and sequence. Instead, looking at practices that combine, or 'com-pose' things, matters or actions together requires a different approach, specifically an understanding of execution through performative acts. Hence, rather than looking at 'structures', 'grammatical aspects' or 'score', we should also take the notion of performativity and its relation to an event into account. Limiting ourselves to the artistic 'language' of 'com-position' and its conjunctional/ disjunctional constellation also means that we will tend to fixate on networks of 'relations' and their agencies only, and indeed, most scenographers try to manage them like a large machine by investing an entire assembly of technological devices that assault our senses without allowing us any escape or exit from their violence. In contrast, drawing on performance and practice channels, our focus is more on dynamics and energy, on movement and transition and their unexpected effects or random changeability, and thus on certain oscillations between governability and unavailability or the loss of control. Every assemblage of phenomena, things, materials or agents has to be instantiated, realized or spatially manifested, which, at the same time, resolves them into something different. Using things or objects includes the possibility of misusing them, turning them against their capacities, their aims and ends. Therefore, the 'language of art' or of 'scenographic writing' as a differential scripture, even as a loose association of combined and juxtaposed elements, resembles more a cloze text that allows for the rearrangement, disruption or non-use of lacunas and clefts. Hence, every scenographic score or manipulation remains, even when nothing is left to chance, incomplete and fragmented. The performative – which, rather than a staging, is an act of instantiation, setting or realization – embeds the scenographic script into an unstable space or situation, so that the shift of perspective from 'structure' to 'performance' causes its own, unpredictable consequences.

However, first and foremost it is important to clarify what we mean by 'the performative' with respect to scenography and how performances produce unintended alterations and events. In fact, performativity is an ambiguous term and is used differently depending on context. However, pertaining to the so-called languages of art with respect to conjunctional/disjunctional assemblies, it seems obvious to refer both in contrast *and* analogy to the paradigm of 'performative acts', applied to proposition and discourse, as it was introduced by Austin and Searle in linguistics. We should keep in mind the similarities and differences, because rather than simply following their model, we also intentionally misuse the concept to shift it from identity to difference, and from intentionality to non-intentionality. As is well known, Austin based his investigations on the distinction between constative and performative acts, to destroy the common language-theoretical focus on statements and meaning as representation. He asserted that all utterances are genuinely performative – which, as a thesis, holds true quite similarly for artistic expressions and work (Austin 1975 [1963]). The clue in Austin and Searle was that language does not only speak *about* the real, expressing or signifying something; rather, it creates practically what it says and is therefore actively involved in the way of our 'being-in-the-world'. In analogy to this, we can claim a similar reality effect for art. The social would not exist if we did not perform language – or art – to create both the real and a communication about it, as well as social relationships and discussions which tie us together in various ways (Searle 1996 [1995]). Hence, in both cases, the power of the performative has its peculiar relevance regarding the constitution of the social and social understandings, which, as Jean-Luc Nancy rightly points out, is always in the becoming and is 'unattainable' (*désœuvrée*), and therefore a never-ending task, a process without a clear goal or arrival (Nancy 1991). The same holds, as we strongly assert, for concepts of performativity in art.

It is precisely this characteristic of an always unfinished process of the human condition that is of interest here and – pertaining to the art of scenography – makes it clear that by no means does it produce a complete work or result, but remains, so to speak, chronically 'unworkable' (Mersch 2018). Austin and Searle never considered these consequences of their approach. So we must explain them by taking a detour that reverses some of the main distinctions and insights of speech-act theory to adapt them to cultural phenomena, including, in particular, scenographic practices. My starting point therefore is the distinction between 'illocutionary' and 'perlocutionary acts'. Austin introduced these concepts in the second part of his lecture *How to Do Things With Words*, to distinguish something we do in saying, and by saying, something (Austin 1975 [1963]: 114–17). Both mark disparate modalities of performative forces, whereby the latter addresses the unmeasurable extra-linguistic causalities – unmeasurable because we can neither control nor anticipate what an act does or, literally, 'causes'. Hence, in the case of illocution, saying is the reality that it signifies: sense and reality are directly related to each other, because the promise means itself as content only to the extent that it is simultaneously an obligation. The practical and the hermeneutic are immediately intertwined: we are dealing with the figure of identity, whereas perlocutions stand for those effects which may detach themselves from what is meant and abruptly invert the practical situation. Therefore, a promise can become disdainful, for instance, when it is clear that it will not be kept; it can also be a lie, an offence, a humiliation and the like. Consequently, perlocutions induce differences, and it is telling that Searle believed, as Austin did, that it is possible to deduce general rules of intelligibility only from the figure of illocutionary identification, which are subsequently condensed by Habermas into parameters of rationality, while perlocutions, to the extent that they alienate the accomplishment of linguistic meaning, transform it into something else, have been neglected, to thenceforward languish in subcutaneous shadows.

Difference and withdrawal

We should also keep in mind, that in this context here the term 'perlocution' serves as a metaphor, a model for uncontrollability or a 'systematic' non-fulfilment of scenographic calculations. It hints at the recalcitrance of practices and its materials. In a broader sense, thus, the illocutionary and the perlocutionary reflect divergent formats of the 'performative'; however, by privileging illocutions and hence identity-figured speech acts, the theory of performance retracts the radical nature of its approach. Instead, the decidedly performative effects emerge out of 'perlocutions', which stand for differential results in the practical because each performative 'performance', as it were, sets something in motion, causes a caesura and fundamentally alters the conditions of what follows. Not only is the concept of the 'performative' therefore relevant for the analysis of communications, but also for the study of life forms, artistic processes, political demonstrations, organizational forms, economic transactions, and the design of architectural spaces or the construction of atmospheres and scenic 'graphs'. It indicates that scenographic processes – like all art and most cultural processes beyond algorithmic calculation – cannot be fully mastered because there is always already the intervening face of alterity, leaping all of a sudden out of the picture. In consequence, nothing seems to be completely controllable or ready to hand. Even the most artful and sophisticated techniques tend to produce dysfunctional effects or unpredictable consequences. Rather, we are constrained to deal with a chronic lack or surplus, an indeterminacy or unaccomplishability, each expressible only in a negative manner, inasmuch as a moment of fragility befalls each practice, which makes it uncertain and unstable in relation to itself. Each time it turns out to be furnished with the possibility of accident or failure, even more, each act is intrinsically entangled with collapses, while in turn no act is immune to them – the shift from the illocutionary to the perlocutionary makes this clear in a particular way. For with the illocution, a rational dimension appears, to the extent that the principles of intentionality and regularity are constitutive; with the perlocution, an incalculable or 'tragic' element comes 'in between', insofar as the consequences that our actions induce allow neither complete control nor recovery. No practice can be sure of its implications. This also means that there is no escaping its principal irrationality in the human register. It remains, by the power of the performative, irreconcilable.

The systematic basis of this irreconcilability is that practices are subject to their inevitable contingency: they tend, so to speak, to fall out of the frame or to modify the situation they derive from and to which they relate. At every moment, they are therefore already another, stolen at the location of their engagement, every bit as timid as 'beside themselves' – and this applies to perlocutions to a far greater extent than to illocutions, inasmuch as only the latter appear normatively bound while the former have a transgressive character.[4] Thus the concept of performativity tends to remain inexpressible, with the consequence that performances and practices refuse any reasonable theoretical modelling. My thesis is that scenography also remains always provisional, incomplete and not conferrable. One can demonstrate this again pertaining to speech acts: what we say, according to Austin, is neither limited to the statements that we make nor to the importance that we give expression. On the contrary, we engage in the world with our utterances and transform it to the extent that we are a part of it, with the 'gravity' of our 'weight' – and yet we do not know what effects our engagements cause. To speak as to act then is to be purloined by the performativity of our practices, or to be subject to a frightening dispersion and decontrol, so that the performative at every moment contains the possibility of a rupture or dislocation. Then to 'turn out' a sentence means already to have 'turned' it and to have exposed it to its 'alienation'. And this is also true for the exposition of things or objects with their own agency, or actions that at the very moment of their execution are transformed into something other. Hence, in the performative, we are unprotected and confronted with a chronic incompleteness, an irretrievable unavailability.[5] We can therefore designate the performative as the unlawful, ungovernable or unpredictable. It is the power that includes the power of otherness. Once performed, it not only refers to an unrevisability, but also forces us to something that is beyond our intentions and breaks with our sovereignty.

Notes

[1] See Goebbels 2015: 25–32, and Mersch 2018: 40–55. For a discussion of the scenographic concept of *Stifters Dinge*, see also David Roesner and Klaus Grünberg's chapter in this book.

[2] For the same reason, Timothy Morton named his investigations in non-naturalistic ecology, *Dark Ecology* (2016); the ecological as 'weird weirdness', 2016: 4–7.

[3] On catachresis and its non-figural use, see Mersch 2002: esp. 28–43.

[4] This thought is systematically developed from the triplicity of establishment, exposure and transposition in Mersch 2004.

[5] Related thoughts are evoked in Mersch 2009: 21–37.

11

Scenography and actor–network theory

Analytical approaches

Wolf-Dieter Ernst

While the impact of actor–network theory (ANT) on cultural and media studies is great, its dissemination in the field of performance and theatre studies is still rather limited. This chapter introduces some of the key considerations of ANT and examines a possible transfer to the scenography and performative constellation of Rimini Protokoll's *Situation Rooms*. It aims at a more detailed investigation of how we can think of scenography as an active part of theatre as well as an understanding of the power of objects, which is, of course, beyond the common notion of set design illustrating a dramatic scene. How can we better understand scenography in performance when using ANT?

To meet this aim, it is helpful to consider scenography less as a product but more as a production process unfolding before the spectators' eyes or even immersing them physically. Admittedly, most of the time, this process remains invisible to the audience. Yet in Rimini Protokoll's multiplayer video piece *Situation Rooms*, scenography is directly connected with its reception, as spectators and scenographic objects re-enact past performances simultaneously. This kind of interaction is definitely of interest, as it indicates a symmetrical agency in Latour's understanding. To unfold this agency, the following analysis will investigate more closely the interaction with scenography and how it is related to its construction, the design, the staging and the rehearsal process.

The art of scenography gained autonomy during the theatre reforms around 1900, and it is evident that theatre theory should consider it in its own right. In her study *Das Drama des Sehens* (The Drama of Seeing; 2005), German theatre scholar Ulrike Hass has convincingly shown that the proscenium stage only gradually, and never fully, became the symbolic form which theatre and art historians considered it to be. Already Adolphe Appia's idea to arrange the theatrical space in Dresden-Hellerau is known for a radical turn away from the proscenium stage towards a renewed connection of the auditorium with the architectural and organized space of the stage (Beacham 2006). In fact, the separation between stage and auditorium, perfected in Wagner's music drama with the orchestra becoming invisible and the darkening of the auditorium, was called into question. In the light of these findings, Patrice Pavis defines scenography more as the arrangement and conception of a specific venue, rather than the visual design of a stage in accordance with the idea and perspective of a *trompe de l'œil* (Pavis 2015 [1996]) and, similar to that, Joslin McKinney and Philip Butterworth have suggested that scenography should be (re-)defined as the 'manipulation and orchestration of the performance environment' (McKinney and Butterworth 2009). Finally, Birgit E. Wiens in her essay 'Scenography as Dispositif' proposes that, 'in performative processes, the presence of media, things and (human) performers shall be investigated in the sense of "symmetric relations" (also akin to B. Latour), and as a consequence – at the level of design, project development and rehearsal – scenographic design and concepts of movement should be analysed as interdependent concepts' (Wiens 2016: 225).

The starting point

This article focuses on some methodological issues which occur in applying the Latourian approach to the study of scenography. It is intended to test the ANT perspective, yet without embarking into another 'Latour de force' as concerns the sociological terminology. Rather, the focus will be on one particular case, *Situation Rooms*, and three implications ANT may have on the analysis of scenography in performance: the starting point of analysis, the symmetrical agency of human and non-human actors and the question, whether or not a given entity is part of the network.

My analysis starts with a few remarks on *Situation Rooms*. This 2013 production by the Berlin team Rimini Protokoll, that is, Helgard Haug, Stefan Kaegi and Daniel Wetzel, is the object of study, simply because we can take advantage of one of its particular features: the scenography, designed by *Blendwerk*/Dominic Huber, is special, insofar as it unfolds in real time in interaction with the audience. In other words, the spectators replace the actors and enter the scene itself, and in doing so they are traversing and experiencing it like a *parcour*. Rimini Protokoll emphasizes this special feature with the subtitle 'multiplayer video piece'. So we have to imagine about twenty spectators at a time who walk through and explore the installation – one by one, and on different routes – guided by a voice and by moving images that come from portable tablet computers and headphones.[1]

In addition to these introductory remarks, one should briefly sketch out the content. The research material (which can also be found in the programme booklet) includes a prominent press photograph: it depicts the then US president Barack Obama and secretary of state Hillary Clinton among their staff in the White House during the military operation that was carried out to kill Osama bin Laden in Pakistan. They assembled in the Situation Room, a sort of information centre, and followed live images on a screen. With this press image a rather complex and informal war against terrorism suddenly seemed graspable. Against the pictures' alleged clarity, Rimini Protokoll set a multi-perspective concept: twenty people – all of them, biographically

FIGURE 11.1 *Rimini Protokoll,* Situation Rooms, *remake of the White House Situation Room. Scenography: Dominic Huber/Blendwerk. Photo © Jörg Baumann, Ruhrtriennale 2013.*

or because of their occupation, involved in the war in different ways – were invited to tell their life stories (in seven-minute videos). The rooms in the installation were modelled in accordance with their living and working spaces, and the audience, equipped with iPad and headphones, are then asked to re-enact their part.

The production's plot deals with the international arms trade, a dramatic subject whose dramatis personae, however, often act anonymously or – in the case of the victims – fall into oblivion. *Situation Rooms* conveys this content in a montage of different characters' voices and perspectives, in a style reminiscent of documentary theatre. During the staging, the spectator/user is then asked to take on these different roles and perspectives of the characters involved in the arms trade: producers, traders, politicians, perpetrators, victims and so on.

After having sketched out form and content of the production, let's start with the analysis of scenography in performance. But what is the starting point of this analysis? The desire is obvious. First of all, one should give the reader an overview of the staged world. Especially the fact that *Situation Rooms* uses the idea of a multiplayer game makes the spectator/analyst want to zoom out and see the whole game architecture before he or she embarks on the theatrical voyage. Yet it is only the program booklet that provides this overview of the individual characters, their rooms and the corridors of the installation. The programme note says:

> [The audience] ensnare themselves in a network of incidents, slipping into the perspectives of the protagonists, whose traces are followed by other spectators. One spectator sits at the desk of a production manager for air defence systems. At the same time, another follows the film of a Pakistani lawyer representing victims of American drone attacks in a cramped room with surveillance monitors. On her way there, she sees a third spectator who follows his film into the shooting range of a Berlin gun club, listening to Germany's shooting champion. Around the corner stands another spectator in the role of a doctor carrying out amputations in Sierra Leone, while in the room next door a press photographer sorts pictures of German army missions in Afghanistan, only a little later he will be right there in the shooting range himself and do exactly the same actions he observed a few moments before, thereby becoming a subject for observation himself. Thus, the audience gradually becomes entangled in the film set's spatial and material labyrinth; each individual re-enacting one part in a very complex multi-perspective film shoot.[2]

A quote of this length requires some explanation. This apt description of a possible aesthetic experience of *Situation Rooms'* scenography, that the 'audience is becoming entangled in the film's spatial and material labyrinth', is *not* what one should interpret as an adequate description of the scenography in performance. Certainly, the description is related to our subject as it convincingly summarizes the effect of scenography in performance, but the question of scenography in performance is much more complex than this and it just can't be adequately addressed by the reference to a 'spatial and material labyrinth'.

After all, one can confidently view the programme note as the starting point of this actor network. We have already begun to trace it. It is important to determine the starting point carefully. ANT aims to avoid the premature reduction of the object of study and to allow for more complexity in demanding a 'strong theory for the recording frame and no middle range theory for the description'[3]. So, basically ANT scholars should bid farewell to the idea that methods would not have an effect on the object of study in one way or the other. Thus, they are asked to find the right balance between theoretical and empirical approaches for themselves. Therefore, it would be inadequate to start the analysis of scenography with, say, the beginning of the video piece or with too familiar elements such as the story, the characters and the rooms, which all tend to be improper generalizations. What is required is the careful selection of a particular starting point similar to that of a particular moment of disturbance within phenomenology and performance analysis. Thus, the starting point for this actor–network analysis is a text, a programme note that has presumably been read through quickly just before visiting the performance, only to become the first document used as the written analysis unfolds.

But should one not start with the issue itself, with the scenography? Unfortunately, to understand scenography in performance, ANT provides only a 'negative argument'; 'It does not say anything positive about any matter' (Latour 2005: 142). Hence, this method does not say anything positive about scenography in its essence and consequently it makes the distinction between built scenography and perceived or experienced scenography less central. As Latour points out, ontological categories are not very helpful for the analysis of a social world, which cannot easily be grasped in terms of its appearance, its complexity and its transformation. So, too, the scenography in *Situation Rooms* is not a given product. That is to say, an analysis cannot simply be based on it without losing sight of the performative aspect.

Other theories 'are good at saying *substantive* things about what the social world is made of. In most cases, that's fine: the ingredients are known, their repertoire should be kept short. But that doesn't work, when things are changing fast' (Latour 2005: 142). As far as theatre is concerned, as long as it is possible to clearly distinguish stage construction from its use, it is possible to operate with strong theories of illusion, aesthetics, form, content and so on.

But in contemporary theatre, as in *Situation Rooms*, things change quickly, its forms tend to be self-reflexive so that they undergo inversions and ultimately appear as well on the content level. The arms trade as a form of related individual actions finds a substantive equivalent in the dramaturgy of the multiplayer video piece, which in turn is formally transferred in the game architecture with a first-person shooter perspective and so on. The levels of illusion and reality reflect each other. This shift towards self-reflection and the hybridization of theatre elements calls for altered theories and methods of investigation.

Anti-hierarchy between social and technical aspects

Surely, one of the certainties in theatre studies is the consideration of the planning, organization and material composition of a stage set subordinate to its symbolic and aesthetic dimension. The former fall into the field of technical trades and administration, the latter into the field of artistic design, and usually these distinct disciplines relate in a strict hierarchy to each other. Indeed, most of the time the theatre industry is actually stratified in this manner. This distinction between art and technology cannot be upheld with regard to *Situation Rooms*. If you closely observe how scenography unfolds in this case, what follows, after the program note has been read, is a rather crude, technical impression – and not art. Upon entering the performance space, you don't start the game immediately. First, you are standing in front of a long table in an empty theatre space with the installation awaiting you in the background.

    This is the moment when you spot it as a whole for the first of a total of three times (second is a view from the roof and third the exit from the building). This sight is not irrelevant to our question about scenography in performance as all of the spectators, before entering the installation, receive a longer briefing – at least on the occasion that I was witness to the piece staged in the Spielhalle of the Münchner Kammerspiele in 2014. Part of the explanation of necessary rules of conduct inevitably is to constantly refer to the construction in the background.[4] So while the audience learns what to do in case they have lost track, trying to navigate with the handheld tablets and headphones, the bungalow-sized installation is waiting for them in the spotlight.[5] One can see the individual elements, built from plywood, and a large screen on which images of an urban landscape are projected. As on a film set, some areas are flooded in limelight and heat radiates from the units in the otherwise rather cold space. One can observe how individual parts of the installation are attached to the rigging pipes above, how the top and side lights are positioned and how various cables and water pipes connect the building to the house's supply systems. The confusing thing is that you do not get a picture or a look inside. Rather, the outer walls of the building reflect the techno-material atmosphere of the bare theatre space, with which they maintain a very functional connection.

The onlooker gains the impression of a backstage atmosphere, which at the same time suggests the pleasure of entering the lit stage, the rooms. A clear contrast emerges: on the outside, the open design of the installation, inside the brightly lit, staged world. It must be part of the concept, otherwise it would have been easier to position the introduction in an adjoining room.

At this point, the ANT analysis of the scenography in performance already deviates from conventional performance analysis with its focus on the reception process of the here and now. Materials assembled by scenographer Dominic Huber now fade into the analysis, and give an impression of the technical and organizational effort taken to mount the installation: as Huber describes it in an interview, 'At the end, we had around 45 people employed by Rimini Protokoll in Berlin, alone for technical purposes ... we outsourced the scenery building and worked extremely tightly for three and a half months' (Kedves 2014). This information is woven into the memory of the – doubtless fleeting – impression when I first saw the installation at the Münchner Kammerspiele: Its size and design reminded me of Günther Anders' observation that man, being confronted with manufactured goods, tends to feel ashamed about their embarrassingly high quality. Anders has coined this feeling using the term 'Promethean Shame', caused by the insight that man is only born and not manufactured to higher standards, and thus will always lack perfection (Anders 2002 [1956]). Anyone who has ever seen backdrops on the theatre stage from behind knows about their nature, being usually supported by timber beams and sandbags. They never hide their design as a provisional and sometimes tentative solution. Simple supports with steel hinges are attached, which are fixed with archaic-seeming iron 'stage stones'. Their crude construction reveals a risk of injury, and suggests access only for experts.

Situation Rooms is different in this respect as we are dealing with a high-quality, self-supporting construction. All walls are stiffened in small sections, corrugated iron edges sit on top of it awaiting the rain. Some walls have windows, which are covered with theatrical foil and illuminated by bright lights. You see an overall design, in the technical and aesthetic sense, which reveals the handwriting of an architect. The design is more reminiscent of a trade fair design or a film set – both industries with a higher budget for set design than the contemporary experimental theatre has available to it. All the more, it is astonishing that all of the scientific articles on *Situation Rooms* which I have consulted do not contain a detailed description of the construction and organization (Schwanecke 2017; Lavender 2014; Wihstutz 2015).

Before we continue with the internal scenography, it might be helpful to consider where we are at. So far the analysis of scenography in performance has taken a significant deviation. We followed the contention that scenography in performance is more than a means, and thus we have looked at the outer appearance in relation to the usual set design. Accordingly, the analysis has neglected the chronological order of the performance and followed a paper trail documenting the production of *Situation Rooms*.[6] We took the deviation because we assumed that the discourse about scenography is not as familiar to scholars from the humanities as, say, the discourse on the international arms trade. The first we can easily follow by carefully consulting the news regularly; the latter, in comparison, asks us to read through crude to-do lists, setup and strike plans, photographs and technical drawings.

According to Latour, such deviations in the analysis are typical of an ANT approach and usually focus on the issue of technology. In his reflection on the question of technology, as raised by Martin Heidegger in the wake of the atomic age, he notices the tendency towards subordinating technology, among other main goals. According to Latour, this subordination takes place in four successive steps. He illustrates this process of subordination by considering the case of a technical malfunction.

As Latour points out, the sentence 'This is a technical point' triggers, first, a subordinate action program, which suspends the actual action and the main objective pursued. Second, the phrase defines technology as an area of subordinate competencies, people, and objects that do not really matter and have not made any difference so far. Third and consequently, the sentence defines the role of a specialist, the technician, who is situated and brought in and out of the area, what is referred to as 'reversible blackboxing', and fourth, technology from now on will be delegated and inevitably creates a mandatory 'passage point' for the pursuit of future main goals. The characteristic feature of technology, according to Latour, is thus to make a necessary deviation, a translation in the sense of Michel Serres, where things change their nature as they are being translated. We state here that taking such deviations is what the analysis of scenography in performance is all about. It is the effort to unpack and reflect possible as well as likely subordinations. Therefore, the exterior view of the installation *Situation Rooms* and its staging within the theatre space Spielhalle was given much more space in the analysis than one would expect in the first place.

Scenography as an actor

Probably the most difficult point to transfer ANT to theatrical performances is the sociological approach to grant symmetrical agency to human and

SCENOGRAPHY AND ACTOR–NETWORK THEORY

non-human actors alike. After all, scenographers build sets, but sets do not create scenographers. The ANT perspective asks us to consider carefully the decentring of the subject. This surely cut through the paradigm that within theatrical communication primarily people, and not things, perform in front of other people watching them.

However, Latour insists on the idea that specific actions also emanate from things. One can recognize such a reified agency if one asks less about their ontology but more about the socio-technical actions inscribed into them. He makes this point of inscription clear by taking the simple example of a speed bump. In a metonymic shift, this object represents a 'sleeping policeman', who/which, by his/its mere presence and material quality, teaches the motorist to slow down. While many people would possibly only recognize a threshold of concrete, the sociologist Latour sees the object of study as one of those blind spots where 'society and matter exchange properties' (Latour 1994: 41).

Interesting for the subject matter is the temporal dimension of this exchange between human actor (policeman) and non-human actor (threshold). 'The threshold is there day and night, but the spokesman for this technical act has disappeared from the scene – where are the engineers, where is the policeman? – while somebody, something, acting as deputy, holds the speaker's seat' (Latour 1994: 39f).

There is a striking parallel to the installation and its somewhat ghostly atmosphere of absent voices. In the moment the spectator enters the room, all have gone. The 'performers', the Rimini Protokoll directorial team, the planners, the scenographer Dominic Huber, the technical director and numerous helpers – they have all disappeared from the scene and are now acting through their representatives. These are primarily and in equal proportions the spectators with their tablets, the rooms and props to which the characters are assigned, the hallways and walls that ensure that the actions remain distinct from each other, the narratives and procedures that are in turn a timeline for the interaction, as well as numerous visual and aural cues that orient the audience. These entities all act and amalgamate into a socio-technical chain of actions. They all make the possible multiplayer video piece a real one, because they act as representatives of aspects of human actors elsewhere. Backdrops do not build scenographers, but scenographers send plans to workshops, which in turn produce walls that steadily and staunchly choreograph the users' movements anywhere – wherever in the world the production is shown. The analysis of scenography in performance must trace these chains of action more closely as it approaches the ability of scenography to act as a representative for human actors, and sometimes – as in the case of the 'silent policeman' – the analysis might find out that things convey their respective inscriptions much more clearly than their human comrades.

Indeed, this translation and inscription between human and non-human actors can give more of an insight into scenography, and in what follows I will demonstrate this by looking at just one of the rooms more closely. Within the folder provided by *Blendwerk*/Dominic Huber, one room is documented in detail, the military hospital. It is the situation where the performer Volker Herzog, one of the Doctors Without Borders, and Abu Abdu Al Homssi, who fled Syria, meet. The program mentions the following action script, lasting a full five minutes:

0–1:30 Al Homssi is lying on the patient table

1:30–2 Herzog enters the hospital

2:30–3 Interaction at the patient table

3–3:30 Stick stickers on hand / Point to Geilkowski in the next room, who peeks through the tent's entrance

3:30–4 Herzog ignores Geilkowski / Al Homssi sets off for the shooting range

4–4:30 Herzog at the surgical plan / mirror, Al Homssi exits

4:30–5 Herzog at the surgical instruments[7]

Not all details of the schedule shall be discussed here. It is important that two spectators meet at the surgery table for 30 seconds at 2:30. The one who represents the physician Volker Herzog briefly approaches the spectator, who has taken the position of the refugee Al Homssi on the patient table. Each of them listens to a different story and accordingly interprets the situation very differently. About Al Homssi the viewer learns the following:

I was involved in a peaceful demonstration when I was shot in the leg by a policeman in June 2011. It changed my whole life; I had to hide because wounded people are being hunted as rebels and often tortured or killed. I had to flee to Jordan, after another three months I made it to Hannover with the aid of the German Foreign Ministry. In Germany, my gunshot injury was operated on but my leg remained paralyzed (Protokoll 2013: 56).

The person who embodies Volker Gerlach learns that he is in the Connaught Hospital in Sierra Leone. He says, 'Here's a patient with a typical injury from the war: both hands were cut off' (Protokoll 2013: 53).

A simple choreography matches both storylines: enter the room, go to the patient table, take the hand or, on the receiving end, lie down on the patient table, let your hand be taken and scrutinized and so on. At the centre of this encounter, of course, is the patient table itself, a commodity, which

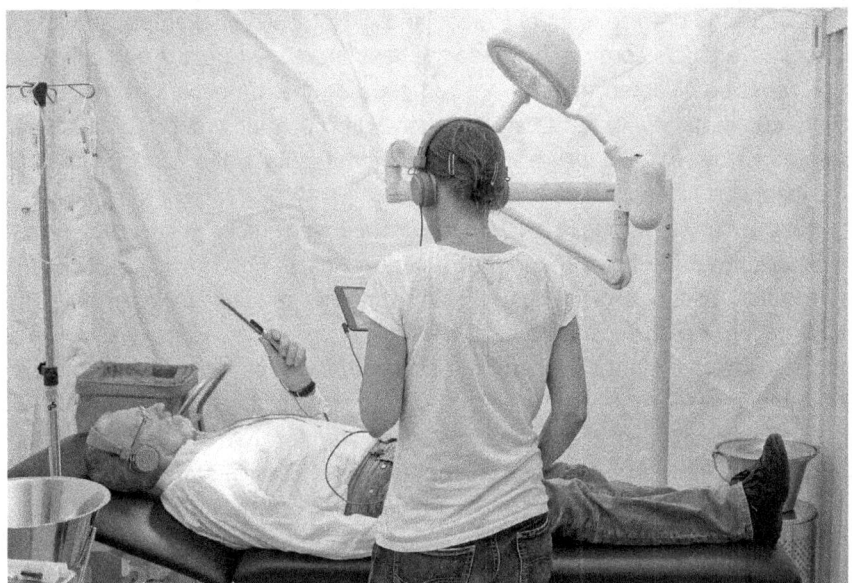

FIGURE 11.2 *Rimini Protokoll:* Situation Rooms, *Patient table in Room 'Military Hospital'*. Photo © Jörg Baumann, Ruhrtriennale 2013.

I remember as having had a very everyday, common look, built from spray-painted square steel tubes and using artificial leather, covered with some kind of paper or cloth, if at all.

For scenography in performance, however, the object makes the difference, so that we can reflect the encounter between doctor and patient as an aesthetic experience in its own right. The dramatic scene has to be arranged in a tight-knit manner around the table, as the rehearsal time for the actors is of course limited and so is the ability to emotionally identify with the characters. It is clear that the table itself has to make sure that any given spectator will find the proper position to meet other spectators. And this task is fully delegated to the object in question.

It is helpful in this respect that the production team can assume a patient table as being both: a physically and culturally well-known object. In a physical respect, it invites the user to rest the body on it or to approach the object in a certain way. Culturally, the object cites the special situation of patient communication, in which a doctor is usually authorized to look down on a person, to touch a person, and to handle the very personal matters of one's own health and well-being.

In *Situation Rooms*, this patient table has a slightly diverging inscription, adding some special agency to it, as it serves the theatre industry and allows for entertainment as well as instruction. It proves to be fully functional regarding the theatrical aspect in that it provides a foolproof way for amateur actors to take on the desired roles of Herzog and Al Homssi. For example, the spectators have to feel comfortable to do the handshake gesture, the vertical direction must be clear, so that the desired coup de theatre occurs. If the object were completely new to the audience or built much too wobbly, or if it were tainted with the stains or scratches of a dramatic past, the gameplay would inevitably be different, if not disturbed.

One can ask at this point: How many similar meaningful and effective alternatives are there for the scene in the military hospital? How many scenes were formulated, built or only thought of? What specific contribution, what dramatic advantages does the scene 'hospital' have to offer for the topic 'international arms trade'? From the point of view of the scenography in performance, the simple object thus poses far-reaching questions to the staging, if one only lets it speak.

As a staged object that is inscribed with the plot 'two actors meet at the bed', the patient table does not act. However, we still cling to the assumption that, according to Aristotle, an acting object would at least have to move. It would have to strive for a subject status, be autonomous and changeable in time, but from an ANT perspective, this subject–object separation is not at stake. Instead, there is talk of a circulating agency. This concept tries to grasp the fact that the spectators act in a rather passive way, that is, they cite their roles more than emphatically asserting their characters. It is very true that the audience actively decide to immerse and embody these characters and to follow the rules of the game. However, this decision is made once at the beginning of the piece, and in ignorance of what is to be expected, of course. In addition, the decision is not an individual one alone, but is based on the theatrical contract, which keeps the audience aware of the fictitious nature of the action at all times. Last but not least, the decision is based on a perfidious staging, to produce gestures in real time by using tablet and headphones as prompters. If users do not follow the instructions, they are at risk of falling out of the game.

Thus, to lie down on the patient table is in itself a weak action from the perspective of the subject. It only draws its strength from the concatenation of various entities, which allows the scenography to make a difference and thereby gain actor status. It is in this sense the patient table that leads to the fact that two volunteers are playing 'doctor', which is actually performed against the probability of Aristotelian physics.

The ends of the network

Frequently, critics of the ANT method have complained about its relativity. If everything is networked with everything, they maintain, then, in particular, power relations and hierarchies tend to be neglected. Latour responds that relationality should not be confused with relativity (Latour 1996: 371). If we are to transfer ANT to performance theory, one can suggest that a certain threshold moment should be implied and we should prevent linking entities randomly to each other. After all, it should make sense to speak of performance in a specific way and even if (or more precisely, just because) performance is a necessarily contested concept, performance scholars have productively used it and still develop it further. Latour, in his later writings, suggests the idea of composition instead, which seems more apt to his interest in natural science and engineering. In his attempt to 'regroup in one term those many bubbles, spheres, networks, and snippets',[8] which an actor–network analysis traces, he might as well have termed it a performance, thus highlighting that the concept 'performance', of course, also has a strong technical and scientific connotation, meaning the 'effectiveness and efficiency' of an effort or event resulting from strict rules and scripted proceedings. Whatever the conceptual choice might be, one of the main characteristics in performance (and of a composition in performance) is the transgression of a threshold, that is, the moment where one accepts a performance as taking command or considers oneself as being part of a performance situation. Not everything people do is quite a performance, as Goffman's very broad definition envisages. Added to this is an observer who considers or endures a situation as if it were a performance, which is John Cage's take on the matter.[9]

So the analyst has to actively determine what is part of the respective actor network. One has to stay focused, similar to a performance, to maintain this perspective, at times against phases of seemingly trivial, boring, overstrained or unwillingly perceived moments. And that also means that one has to decide what is not part of the network and when that performance shall end. This is what happened in the case of the hospital and is finally demonstrated.

In fact, quite a few other objects in the military hospital are centred on the patient table. On the side of the bed's head, for example, is a trash can, a mobile infusion holder and a stainless steel washbasin on a tripod stand. An operating light coming from above sets the stage. At showtime it should be switched on, according to the reset list, and so should the ventilator under the ceiling. Also, there is the instruction '1–2x daily: inject disinfectant onto the fleece cloth in trashcan', so that visitors of the very narrow space have the sterilized smell of a clinic in their noses. Certainly, all of these elements surrounding the bedside can be seen as part of an actor network, because they more or less add to the particular scenography during the performance. That is to say, without their presence one can argue that the scene would significantly change its characteristics. Likewise, the remaining elements, such as the green consumables trolley and the anaesthesia unit, may be considered being part of another actor network in which the spectator, re-enacting the physicist Volker Herzog, is confronted with photos of injured people which are in the upper drawer. However, there are also small details, which ask us to test the limitations of the unfolding actor network and, in particular, to resist the tendency to see significant actors in all objects and details alike. We can even protocol some irritation here which occurs when flipping through the documents and we can allow the actors to 'do their work'[10] – as Latour puts it. These actors include a .pdf file, which meticulously documents the equipment and props used to set up and reset the said room while touring the piece. A total of fifteen photographs precisely define the arrangement of, for example, the numerous surgical instruments and some important props, such as the stickers for marking certain patient's urgency levels. The fourteenth photograph depicts a drip bottle in close-up. It contains a liquid that, as the label reads, is 'Stereofundin ISO', manufactured by Braun Melsungen. According to the package leaflet available online, the drug is given intravenously and replaces 'fluid lost from the circulatory system'.[11]

Its expiration date is imprinted on the bottom and, of course, it has expired at the time of the analysis. One would expect nothing else as the whole installation deals with traces rather than actual events. All characters are absent and reading through their CVs in the booklet soon informs you that most of them were already retired when Rimini Protokoll worked with them. *Situation Rooms*' scenography is also a materialized narrative written in the past tense. Given all that, however, the question arises as to whether the expiry date is of scenographic valence. To clarify this, I consulted the setup list again. Yet any hint how to properly refill or replace the liquid itself is missing. At this point, one loses track, because the more one reads into the document and compares it with the photographic documentation, the more it seems that the dripping bottle is not clearly recorded. There is the information that one should open the upper sterilization bottle before the actual showtime. Yet the drip bottle contains no sterilization liquid, and the liquid would only run up the tube, anyway. The kind of liquid used makes no difference. So does 'sterilization bottle' refer to another object with which one ought to moisten the fleece cloth in the trashcan? It seems that the document decomposes its own status as an actant, especially since, at one point, the disinfectant even becomes an 'infection medium'.[12] Such deviations lead to nothingness. This is not a shortcoming of the ANT method, but simply a heuristic point, at which one receives the clear feedback to rethink the path taken and, if necessary, to let things rest on their own.

Notes

1. See also Dorita Hannah's discussion on Rimini Protokoll's *Situation Rooms* in McKinney and Palmer's *Scenography Expanded*, analysing the spatial constellation and intermedial scenography of this project (2017: 48–50).
2. Protokoll (2013: 4–5).
3. Latour 1996: 375.
4. The setup in Munich follows the description in the technical rider, and other reports about the visit of the installation as well as photos of the structure indicate a consistent implementation. See 'SR_TechRider_130926', internal document of Blendwerk/Rimini Apparat. The author thanks Dominic Huber for providing this and other documents; see also Protokoll (2013: 2 and 8).
5. As the technical rider explicates, the space must be at least 16 metres (about 52 feet) wide, 18 metres (about 59 feet) deep and 6 metres (about 20 feet) in height to accommodate the installation. Headphones and tablets are handed out on a 1 m x 6 m (about 3 ft x 20 ft) table. In addition, mechanical and electrical equipment is required for the room: Several rigging points for partition walls, numerous weights and screw connections on the wooden floor provide for the stability of the temporary architecture. Independent circuits for sound, light and video ensure the function of technical devices. See 'SR_TechRider_130926'.
6. See 'SR_TechRider_130926'.
7. Protokoll (2013: 92).
8. Latour 2013: 93.
9. Erving Goffman and John Cage paraphrased in Schechner (2003: 22).
10. Latour 2005: 143. 'It depends entirely on what you yourself allow your actors (or rather, your actants) to do'; see also his reference to semiotics in this respect in Latour 1996: 7: 'An "actor" in ANT is a semiotic definition – an actant –, that is, something that acts or to which activity is granted by others' and more rigorously put on p. 374: 'Finally, from semiotics is kept the crucial practice to grant texts and discourses the ability define also their context, their authors – in the text –, their readers – in fabula – and even their own demarcation and meta-language. All the problems of the analyst are shifted to the "text itself" without ever being allowed to escape into the context. Down with interpretation! Down with the context! The slogans of the 60s and 70s "everything is a text", "there is only discourse", "narratives exist by themselves", "we have no access to anything but accounts" are kept in ANT but saved from their ontological consequences.'
11. See Braun Melsungen (2018): 0085-PL-Sterofundin-ISO-DE-MRP-d.pdf, available online: https://aspregister.basg.gv.at/document/servlet?action=show&zulnr=1-26228&type=DOTC_GEBR_INFO, 1 (accessed 30 December 2018).
12. See Blendwerk and Dominic Huber (2013), 14_surgery_sep13_komp.pdf: 1.

12

Scenography

Research, education and training in the German-speaking countries – some observations

Thea Hoffmann-Axthelm and Robert Kraatz

Many of the artists and designers who work as stage and costume designers at theatres in German-speaking countries (and beyond), or those who appear as scenographers in adjacent artistic and cultural fields are often also involved in academic teaching. Prominent representatives, for example Katrin Brack, Barbara Ehnes, Anna Viebrock, Michael Simon and Uwe R. Brückner, hold professorial chairs at art academies, universities or colleges in Germany, Austria and Switzerland. Others teach in German-speaking countries or even internationally as guest lecturers or workshop leaders in the most varied of contexts. In recent years, in addition to this institutionally centred teaching, several independent initiatives have taken place as those by (third party-funded) artistic groups, for example, raumlaborberlin, who are involved in research projects and education programs.[1] The question we are now faced with is: How are stage design and scenography taught today and how are 'scenographic knowledge' and 'scenographic competence' actually understood to transfer, pass on and discuss possible artistic processes, tools, techniques and methods to future scenographers, that is, the students?

The spectrum of scenographic practice, which covers several disciplines, has, for a few decades, been articulating itself as a certain contrast and friction to the historic formation of scenic design as a subject of study and a training discipline. Today, the theatre-related field of stage and costume design is usually still taught at (mostly state-run) art universities, that is, at academies for the fine arts. From the end of the nineteenth century, 'theatre painting' or 'decorative theatre painting' was offered at the so-called schools of the fine arts and crafts, for example, at the Königliche Kunstgewerbeschule (Royal Academy of Fine Arts and Crafts) in Dresden (later on the Staatliche Akademie für Kunstgewerbe Dresden – the National Academy for Fine Arts and Crafts Dresden).[2] In 1950, it was finally incorporated by the University of Fine Arts Dresden. In contrast to the so-called 'free arts' (such as painting, graphic art, sculpturing), stage and costume design were for a long time, and are partly still today, defined as 'applied art'. An important impulse for the reassessment of stage and costume design as a – potentially independent – 'art form' came in German-speaking countries from Oskar Schlemmer's teachings at the Bauhaus Dessau (1925–9) and in Breslau (1932), which, however, only came to their fore with the later reception of his work after the end of the Hitler regime. Even Bertolt Brecht's 'model productions', developed together with his 'stage builder' Caspar Neher, and his work principles, which interconnected stage and costume design with dramaturgic thinking, were relevant. In the following decades in both the FRG and GDR, this was taken up and reinterpreted in theatres and universities as well. In general, and this is well known, the common theme that runs through the entire European theatre discourse of the twentieth century is the renunciation of using the stage set as a 'decoration' or 'backdrop' (Eckert 2006 [1998]; McKinney and Butterworth 2009). This also became a challenge for artistic research and teaching: with various approaches, it has been the case ever since then to understand and conceive scenic design as an integral element of productions and staging. In addition, today we also have to include the challenges that we have stated since the start of the twenty-first century: 'the delimitation of art' and the digital turn have clearly led to an ever-widening spectrum of scenography, ranging from stage sets and theatre scenography, performance design and 'environmental scenography' through exhibition scenography, film and media scenography to urban environments, spatial design and staged commercial events. The definitions of what we currently understand 'scenography' to be are in motion and, in addition to this, they are crossing genres nowadays. That is why there is a continuous discussion at universities about what is taught there, what we call 'stage design', 'set design', 'scenography' or 'spatial design'.

So what is 'scenographic knowledge', what is actually taught and dealt with if the field has in fact become so wide today and is constantly in motion? Clues can be given by artists or designers when they make statements on their works of art – be it in catalogues, their own publications or articles in books, interviews or workshop discussions like the ones in this book. Here scenic design articulates itself – and the reflection on it – most of the time in relationship to individual projects connected with insights into the 'making-of' process, into contexts as well as with far-reaching artistic thoughts. Implied therein, even if it hasn't necessarily been formulated, is also what we describe as 'tacit knowledge' within the 'art as research' debate; that is, an artistic doing and thinking which is, as the Finnish scenographer, design theorist and lecturer Laura Groendahl puts it, 'embedded in performance strategies, technologies and habitual work methods' (Groendahl 2016). Systematic descriptions of how 'scenographic knowledge' is produced and amended are currently not available and are, based on the manifold artistic and design approaches, maybe not even doable at all. However, so postulates Groendahl, one can assume that there is a certain 'repertoire of techniques and practices; scenographers, like all artists, have shared beliefs as to what a good working process is like, and what tools and methods are better than others: how an artwork can be done, what it consists of, how it is structured, how it works and how it should be evaluated' (Groendahl 2016).

Teaching – that is, the courses of study and training programmes at universities of art and other universities where, with the profile setting of the respective programmes as well as the daily knowledge transfer and work with the students, these questions are focused on – in a certain sense particularly condenses the scenographic discourse. As such, they are even the 'initial forerunners' of the artistic discourse and reflection as well as scenographic knowledge production. Based on these thoughts, this article provides insights into the stage design and scenography training courses in the German-speaking countries: How is teaching and studying scenography being practised, what has changed during recent years, were there or are there certain traditions and which approaches are currently being tested? How, for example, is the relationship between the sometimes conflicting fields of theory and practice? We, the authors of this article, both work as stage set designers. In addition, we are editors of and authors for an online platform on scenography and stage design, www.ueberbuehne.de, which we launched in 2014. We studied in Vienna and Berlin not that long ago so we remember quite well, almost vividly, our scenography studies. In the following, we will not and we cannot give a complete outline of the German-speaking academic landscape. Instead, we offer our very personal 'expertise', obtained from talks with students and colleagues, visiting different universities and conducting interviews with professors, which we have also published on our online platform.

Expanded scenography: Concepts and shifts in contemporary teaching, artistic research and education

The very first question that came to our mind is one of a rather philosophical nature: Can art be taught, and if so, how? Is scenography considered an art form at all and what are the valid definitions? Let's start with the theatre. The conception of what 'scenic designers' are actually doing at the theatre seems to have notably changed in the past few years: in their self-understanding as well as their reception throughout the theatre world, a stage designer is no longer primarily male (Behr 2013) nor works *for* a director, but rather is an independent artist who has individually developed concepts, manuscripts and aesthetics. The scenographer collaborates with directors and actors, dramatists, musicians and so on as a part of the directing team to shape the overall artistic concept. Considering the shift that is taking place in the German-speaking theatre scene – away from the classical theatrical structure with its associated functions and hierarchies – it goes without saying that this also affects the education and profession of the scenographer. Postmodern and poststructural aesthetics inspired scenographers to go beyond the theatre space and to use non-theatre spaces as scenic locations. Whether it be industrialized warehouses, former supermarkets and office tracts or urban areas, whether it be creating performative and integrative or immersive exhibitions, children's books or films – scenographers today work in a much wider field than that what was originally defined for their profession, this still being regarded so by some of the educational and artistic institutions.

Taking account of the shifting artistic image of what scenographers in and beyond the theatre space actually do, we asked ourselves:

1. How can artistic authorship and scenography be taught? What do students learn and how do they learn? What will be practised and rehearsed during studies (sketching, drawing, working on the model, designing, using digital media, etc.)?

2. How much theory, research and possibilities of theoretical reflection will be given to the soon-to-be self-employed artists? How do the schools incorporate theory and when does art practice become 'artistic research'? What concept of stage design or scenography is represented?

3. When is a student ready for the theatre or art world? How much does practice affect their studies (for either better or worse) and how do

you prepare students for finding their way regarding, on the one hand, the aspiration for artistic independence and, on the other hand, the wish or even need for a professional and social perspective – in a job that sometimes makes it rather difficult to live in just one place, not to speak of planning or caring for a family?

In the German-speaking world, 'stage and costume design', 'scenography' or 'scenic space' are mainly taught at art schools and in classes generally assigned to one professor. Depending on the individual content, size and financial resources, these courses may differ considerably. In the following, we will try to sum up and label the variety of positions by identifying four basic approaches, and then use examples to show how the given questions are dealt with within the educational practice of each programme and school.

The first approach is that of a 'classical', crafts-oriented education as we experienced it at the Kunsthochschule Berlin Weißensee (Weißensee Academy of Art) and, comparably, it can also be found at the Mozarteum in Salzburg. The second approach is a rather interdisciplinary, more curricula-free education – including performative or intermediary aesthetics, focusing the artistic development of the students. Examples here are the classes of Katrin Brack at the Kunstakademie München (Art Academy Munich) or of Raimund Bauer at the Hochschule für Bildende Künste (University of Fine Arts) in Hamburg. A third approach is characterized by a focus on a close connection to the practical theatre world through cooperation, which can be of substantial importance for the stage designer's artistic development and career. We found an emphasis on these tendencies in the very active MA training programme 'Bühnenbild und Szenischer Raum' (stage design and scenic space) at the Technical University of Berlin, as well as the masters programme 'Bühnenbild' (stage design) at the Zurich University of the Arts (ZHdK). The fourth approach is an education that includes theory as a fundamental part of the curricula. The course 'Ausstellungsdesign und Szenografie' (Exhibition Design and Scenography) at the Hochschule für Gestaltung (Academy of Design) in Karlsruhe is a good example for this approach. Also, the MA programme 'Scenographic Design and Communication' at the University of Applied Sciences and Arts, Dortmund (bilingual, conducted in English and German) can be mentioned here. Obviously, these are very coarse classifications. The extensive freedom given to each professor leads to very individual ways on how content, techniques, collaborations, project-driven work and so on are balanced. The teaching at the Hochschule der Bildenden Künste (University of Fine Arts) in Dresden by Barbara Ehnes is different from that of Johannes Schütz at the Kunstakademie Düsseldorf (Art Academy Düsseldorf), Martin Zehetgruber at the Akademie der Bildenden Künste (Academy of Fine Arts) Stuttgart, Hartmut Meyer at the University of the Arts (UdK) Berlin, Anna Viebrock at the

Academy of Fine Arts Vienna or Bernhard Kleber at the University of Applied Arts in Vienna, to name a few. None of the above can be restricted exclusively to one of the categories that we have defined. We will focus on the partial aspects regarding the subject we are discussing in this article.

'You can have 100 ideas per minute': Scenography, what is taught and how

In order to translate concepts and content into a space, one needs suitable means of communication as well as tools. As Aleksandar Denić stated in his lecture at the conference *The Art of Scenography* in Munich (2016): 'You can have 100 ideas per minute. But to communicate them and to bring them to life is hard work!'[3]

All of the different programmes concur in that they provide the students with a fundamental level of practical education, such as working with scale models, drawing plans and basic knowledge about technical as well as material questions of stage, costume and lighting. Students usually have the opportunity to develop presentation techniques fitting to their needs – be it scale models, designing with photo collages, moodboards, 3D programmes or just three strokes on a napkin. This development is necessarily influenced by the profile of the university, the programme and the professor(s), while the individual approach or preference of the student remains its driving force. The extent, drill, and content of the basic education level can differ due to the structural and 'ideological' direction of each school or university. For example, the class at Salzburg's Mozarteum, headed by Henrik Ahr and rather descriptively entitled 'Bühnen- und Kostümgestaltung, Film- und Ausstellungsarchitektur' (Stage and Costume Design, Film and Exhibition Architecture), features the motto 'stage design is conceptual art'; yet the first one-and-a-half years are focused on technical basics, drawing, nude drawing and geometry. Content and topics are predefined – the proper approach is of greater importance. There are no teacher-centred lectures for the main artistic subjects; instead, direct feedback and criticism prevails, the professor deals with each individual student in person. The students present their work as a scale model, iteratively showing different stages of their project. They learn to find out what it means to work with large spaces within the model, even though most of these designs are never going to be realized. Following this basic level, there is a practical phase: this includes cooperation with theatres, with the actors from the theatre department of the Mozarteum, as well as the stage directors' department. This latter aspect is specifically essential for independent work, as directors are still the most important clients for stage designers.

The course aims at promoting dramaturgical and scenographic thinking; topics and concepts are elaborated independently in order to support self-confidence and professionalism at the start of the career. This educational profile is certainly sound and may at first not appear all too surprising – however, things may also work out in a radically different manner. For example, in Hamburg or in Katrin Brack's classes at the Munich Academy, students, if they prefer, can undertake their studies almost entirely, and later on even graduate, without having built a single scale model. But just as at the more 'conventional' schools, the goal here lies in the development of artistic autonomy.

The specific form of communication and openness that is present at the Academy of Fine Arts Munich in the stage design programme run by Katrin Brack draws a parallel to contemporary theatre, which in recent years went through a significant opening towards postdramatic aesthetics, including more open formats, interaction with the audience, diluting the boundaries to performance and fine arts as well as those of the working structures and hierarchies still in place. These changes affect the way in which stage design is conceived, taught and studied, and many programmes are trying to take this into account. For Katrin Brack, one of the main obstacles for students is to 'think simple' and learning to focus on topics. This is why the tasks given to the class may consist of just a single word or a concept, rather than a play – tasks that are more likely to stimulate an experimental approach than an interpretation of an all too well-known subject or play. The aim is not to push the students to produce (fine) arts; rather, any and everything that tells a story in a certain space is considered to be stage design respectively scenography. This notion is reflected in forgoing a fixed study structure, course sequence or class hierarchy. Grades or credit points do not play a (significant) role. Is this a fair deal of freedom? Possibly – except for the first two semesters of probation, after which the decision is made whether or not the student can continue on with their studies. Of course, the overall aim is still to become stage designers, and so, for the students to be able to graduate, they still have to be able to build a scale model of a stage and draw plans. There are several lecturers who offer seminars on particular topics, and theatre professionals are invited to the class to talk about their work life and experience. Last but not least, there are joint projects with young directors and actors from the Theaterakademie August Everding, the Otto Falckenberg School and the Munich Film School so that students are able to gain practical experience and try out alternative approaches. New teams and networks can be formed that may continue to work in the theatre and beyond – this being an aspect of great significance when it comes to one's professional life as a freelancer.

The Munich class that we have described serves as a positive example of a programme that is dealing with aesthetic tendencies as well as structural changes quite openly. In addition, at the Hochschule für Bildende Künste

(University of Fine Arts) in Hamburg, in the class of Raimund Bauer, and at the HfBK Dresden, one can observe a focus towards freer working concepts and partially, at least, on a performative and more experimental approach to art in space. In Hamburg, after one year of basic training, there are no guidelines except for the one that – no matter what you're working on – you have to present your project every week. In Dresden, Barbara Ehnes and Kattrin Michel pointed out in their interview with Nicole Gronemeyer:

> We have noticed that our students are increasingly self-organizing and even perform themselves or try out formats that create a theatre even without actors. Very diverse and eclectic works have emerged from this. We are not providing many guidelines. We believe that our students must be able to build their own path from what we offer. We are trying to support the development that takes place within these five years, without building up the expectation that we are working towards a very certain direction of theatre. Instead, new ways of thinking and working are to be developed, that reflect and influence the change of the theatre landscape. I am in favour of the approach that the structures should remain flexible, because we see that theatre is changing, which means we have to confront the students with reality. The earlier they realize, the better. (Gronemeyer 2017: 48)

Here, too, we see the clear aspiration to go along with the changes happening in the world of theatre during the students' course of studies.

From the profiles of most stage design programmes, we do see something like a minimum consensus about the fields that need to be covered. Technical aspects include modelling, technical drawing and knowledge about the materials being used. Content-related aspects include conceptual and dramatic work, the creation of a story, environment, space or costumes that tell stories or induce a certain physicality. However, the emphasis on this differs strongly between the programmes. All of these aspects apply to the fields of stage design, set design and costume design, but also exhibition design, video production, performance, light, spatial installation and conceptual or object art, drawing and photography – branches that find their place or at least niches in most of today's studies.

In Berlin, both Hartmut Meyer at the University of the Arts (UdK) and Peter Schubert at the Kunsthochschule Weißensee (Weißensee Academy of Art) provide a solid basic education including all of the mentioned technical aspects. However, while the UdK already points out the diversifying aesthetics and work areas of a stage designer on its website, and many of their students are encouraged to develop their own authorship through various technical means and artistic expressions, the KHB Weißensee stands for a much more consequent analysis of text and dramaturgy. There, each semester ends with the presentation of a fully comprehensive visual concept including stage model, drawings and costumes. The emphasis and analysis of content and narration build the starting point for the development of an individual artistic approach as well as language. Until few years ago, the dramaturge and theatre theorist Hans-Joachim Ruckhäberle, who died in 2017, taught at Weißensee. Along with Peter Schubert, he played a decisive role when it came to implementing this approach. Somewhat 'newer' theatre aesthetics such as performative formats, or even film, are just now slowly finding their place within the course. There are no steady cooperation partners. It is left to the students to exchange ideas and gain practical experience outside of the university, which of course requires a substantial individual effort.

In this regard, the UdK of course has a structural advantage due to the sheer size of the university and its various branches. There are plenty of collaborations with the musicians as well as with the actors within the university and the UniT (the stage in one of the university's locations). In addition, Hartmut Meyer has created a funding institution (called K.O. existenz Stiftung) that aims to support cooperation projects between stage designers and other artists, recognizing the importance of developing such professional networks. After retiring in 2019, Hartmut Meyer was followed by Janina Audick at UdK, who continues with a strong interdisciplinary approach.

Also located in Berlin is the programme 'Bühnenbild und szenischer Raum' (stage design and scenic space) at the TU Berlin. This programme is run by Kerstin Laube. Being a two-year master's course, having evolved in 2000 at the Department of Architecture, it only has a limited time to teach stage design principles, theatre history and aesthetics in detail. Such basic knowledge is taught in block seminars, whereas the main focus is to actively guide the students, who come from diverse professional backgrounds, towards becoming scenographers, starting during the first semester, through group or individual work that focuses on practical projects. This integration into the future work environment intends to promote the earliest possible professionalization. There are numerous collaborations with theatre houses, museums, exhibition rooms and agencies. In addition, there is a strong link between artistic and scientific research, which finds space within the 'Interdisziplinäres Raumlabor' (Interdisciplinary Space Laboratory), led by Albert Lang. This interdisciplinary branch also cooperates with other courses at the TU Berlin and with external partners, such as architects, computer scientists or urban researchers.

Fruitful interplay? On the relationship between theoretical discourse and scenography practice

All courses and study programmes that we have discussed offer dramaturgy classes, or seminars for reading theatre texts, and implement a credit system for attending various basic classes such as art history or theatre studies. These are required to be able to take the final exams and obtain the diploma. Still, for the students, acquiring a profound knowledge of theatre, art and architecture throughout their course of studies is, to a large extent, based upon their individual effort. In contrast to other fields of theatrical and art education (drama, dance, media art, etc.), stage design respectively scenography seems to be less connected to theoretical discourse and academic research. One can see this by having a look at the curricula and cooperating institutions. Hartmut Meyer, professor at the University of the Arts in Berlin (until 2019), called it a 'marginalization' and a 'creeping theory isolation' of the stage design/scenography courses in an interview with the *Bühnentechnische Rundschau* (Winkelesser 2013: 25).

During the course of our own studies and later on as well, we got the impression that there is, in general, hardly any communication or a discursive culture concerning the artistic practice and the 'design knowledge' of stage designers that goes beyond a rather restricted canon of professional (stage design) literature – as, for example, opposed to the abundance of literature on drama practice and theatre theory. We assume that each individual scenographer has a 'tacit knowledge' about his or her work, and keeps developing, expressing and expanding this knowledge on a continuous basis. Yet apart from our blog and a monograph series by *Theater der Zeit*, which portrays a selected choice of renowned stage design colleagues, there is hardly any attempt or even medial interest in making these individual working methods and knowledge visible and accessible. This would be an undertaking that would help future students as well as giving directors, actors and so on a better understanding of how scenographers work. Reasons for this could be of a historical nature: stage design and scenography is, traditionally, a rather marginal research subject within theatre and art sciences. Within most academic publications dealing with theatre, it receives little attention, just as in theatre reviews. Considering the ongoing change within the field of scenography, there also seems to be a certain indifference towards the theoretical input, which often comes in its own, scientifically coded, language. After graduating from university, the quite time-consuming practice leaves little time for reflecting on one's own work in a historical contextualization. In our experience, this will most likely happen through exchanging ideas with the artistic team (director, dramaturges) of a given project. Stage and costume designers are, according to our experience, a rather interested and educated bunch of people, with a sometimes very specific 'particular knowledge'. However, the knowledge of what is happening in their own field of work is largely derived from what they have seen and experienced in the theatre: a rather 'regional' or ephemeral knowledge, accompanied by the non-curated multitude of internet and social media iconoclasm. Being theoretically trained at university may be an important skill to have in the face of the current trend that is moving towards dissolving semiotic interrelations.

As far as we know, the only scenography courses which employ theatre science scholars who are dedicated to scenography as lecturers are those in Dresden, as well as the masters' courses 'Bühnenbild' (stage design) at the Zurich University of the Arts and the TU Berlin. The course 'Ausstellungsdesign und Szenographie' (Exhibition Design and Scenography) at the HfG Karlsruhe, which even has its own professorial chair for curatorial theory and dramaturgical practice, is also theoretically founded. The HfG Karlsruhe, in cooperation with the ZKM | Center for Arts and Media, which was conceived as a 'digital Bauhaus' in the 1990s in Karlsruhe, has its focus on media art and exhibition design where theatre-related projects can also be realized. As its website clearly states: 'The critical contemplation and the performative approach to the perception and representation of our environment make it possible to develop exhibition design and scenography as forms of a critical practice.'[4]

By acknowledging our environment as designed, scenography becomes the art of designing our reality. This wide-ranging approach with a strong focus on theory (the students usually have to write two or three seminar papers per semester) is a lot different from most other stage design courses at art colleges. Here, all artists are also art scientists. There is a students' journal, which is co-designed and edited by the students, as well as an annual symposium on immersive work as exhibition rooms, organized by them.

But how do artistic research and the focus on theory, as practised in Karlsruhe, influence the artistic work of the students and future scenographers? 'Every stage designer or scenographer has to present his or her work. Presenting helps to formulate what is at stake. Especially when one is working experimentally, one must also know about the historical context', Anja Dorn of HfG Karlsruhe told us,[5] adding: 'It's the same in exhibition design; one should know how the point of view is guided, or why certain structures and institutions have led to the museum being a didactic and authoritarian space. You have to develop an intuition for things in order to tackle them differently' (Hoffmann-Axthelm 2017). The curriculum is founded on the basic assumption that scenography and exhibition design without theoretical backup simply does not work: 'Everything that surrounds us is design. And sometimes it is art, sometimes it is not. But one has to start with techniques and design processes and to look at how they represent society as well as political conditions of everyday life' (Hoffmann-Axthelm 2017). It is the attempt to look at historical and culture specific processes and to create a transhistoric concept of scenography: to support scenography not only as a staging, but also as being a decisive part of each artistic production and to treat it as such. This effort and process is rarely acknowledged or honoured by public perception. From Brecht, Neher and Erwin Piscator to today, the documentation of theatre (mainly through photography) focuses on stage play and actors. Yet, experimental stage productions of influential theatre makers like Peter Zadek, Wilfried Minks, Peter Stein, Christoph Marthaler, Frank Castorf and so on, would not be recognizable as such without their avant-garde stage design. The programme at HfG Karlsruhe was created as an attempt to counteract this perception, by giving the students a proper contextual and artistic knowledge, as well as artistic and intellectual self-confidence – as nowadays the fields covered range from such the theatre, film, exhibitions, public and virtual space all the way to installations, temporary architectures, choreographies and performances.

Work hard, play hard: On the importance of early practice

In many courses, practical training while at the same time studying is seen as some kind of getaway or early career fixation. We do not share this view. Many programmes, including the two in Vienna at the Academy of Fine Arts and at the University of Applied Arts, are rather reluctant when it comes to involving theatre practice in the early stages of studying. In Hamburg even assisting is not appreciated. The motives for some professors' reluctance may seem somewhat old-fashioned, but are not without reason: they want the students to focus on their own development, before adapting to a practical world of labour and (narrow) structures. Furthermore, one has to recognize that studying scenography/stage design and so on, like most art study programs, is a very exclusive thing to do. Most programs take an average of seven new students each year, with the number of applicants ranging from 100 to 350 or more. By 'taking leave' from one's study programme for the first theatre job available, a state-funded position that other not-so-lucky applicants were very keen on is left behind. Of course, there are widely varying opinions of and approaches by the different professors when it comes to gaining early practical experience. Some classes, for example, serve as a pool for assistants for their respective professors, as seen at the Kunstakademie Düsseldorf with Johannes Schütz. Others keep the practice within the curriculum, exploiting their close connection to the theatres or theatre directing courses, such as in Dresden, the TU Berlin or at the ZHdK in Zurich.

In the facilities of the ZHdK, for example, students have the opportunity to use rehearsal stages, workshops and dedicated small budgets to develop their own projects. The MA course 'Bühnenbild' (stage design) is headed by the stage designer and theatre director Michael Simon; in addition, there is also a BA programme that used to have the name 'Scenography'. This has, however, been removed and has now formally been included in the BA courses 'Bühnenbild (Theater)' and 'Production Design (Film)'; with these generic classifications, the transdisciplinary direction of the programme, which was signalized beforehand, is taken back.[6] The MA programme 'Stage Design' in turn defines the terms 'stage design' and 'scenic design' quite experimentally and very broadly, with the theatre as the starting point. In addition, the university provides a wide range of theoretical and practical possibilities, giving the students a real chance to specialize in a certain aspect or emphasize their personal artistic development. Another main motivation for applicants to study here is the good connection to and cooperation with master students from directing, dramaturgy and acting classes. Collaborations such as joint projects for final presentations and exams are encouraged, and teams with other young theatre or film artists can be formed – which may be helpful in dipping their toes into the practical world. Apart from that, most of those who come to the ZHdK have already gained experience in theatre through internships and/or assistance jobs beforehand, and know what to expect from their future profession rather well. Some have been disappointed, of course, when realizing that they are stuck in hierarchies, unable to develop themselves further within the structure of 'classic' theatre institutions. Choosing the master's programme in Zurich allows them to work more independently, or artistically, for a certain amount of time anyway. Those studying here are encouraged to think of the stage as a whole. The stage is seen as an independent art form that cannot be thought of or played without a holistic concept – in the theatre or anywhere else for that matter. The students work independently on a master's thesis, which can be either theatre-specific, interdisciplinary or a collaboration with other students working in that field (as mentioned above) – but in any case, the theoretical research also needs to be realized practically.

Learning from one another

The programme of the ZHdK intends to encourage the students to share topics and content among their peers, to learn from each other, and to train to work in teams, while simultaneously developing themselves as independent artists. As Laura Groendahl (who is a lecturer at the University of Helsinki) pointed out at the conference *The Art of Scenography* in Munich, she learns together with her students and she learns about what they are actually wanting to learn (Groendahl 2016). Teachers who adopt this approach function – in accordance with Jacques Rancière – as somewhat 'ignorant school masters' (Rancière 1991); they 'teach what they do not know' (by teaching that there is *not only one* valid definition of scenography) and inspire students to gain a certain independence and self-reflectiveness and, thus, invite them to discover for themselves what contemporary scenography and stage design can be.[7] Study programs should always encourage such processes – that is, promoting 'intellectual emancipation' and 'collective learning', and not only keeping students within the artistic 'safe space', but also supporting them with their first jobs 'outside' the academic institution. Many students who miss out on gaining practical experience during their studies have a tough time with their first assignments, and are pretty much left on their own when dealing with, for example, contracts and working conditions; discussing these challenges with fellow students and professors during one's studies and profiting from their experience form an opportunity that should not be missed. Apart from developing individual skills, such shared knowledge creates a sense of solidarity that reaches beyond the university walls: it helps to reflect on the working conditions within the shifting field of scenographical engagement, strengthening those fighting against wage dumping and the (self-)exploitation that takes place within the industry, and breaking the isolation of scenographers from their fellow colleagues. We need a sense of unity when it comes to recognizing and improving our working circumstances and conditions! This is an endeavour that does not only involve us (*ueberbuehne*). There are many interested groups, such as Bund der Szenografen, the ensemble-netzwerk, and art but fair, and numerous individuals who feel strongly committed to this cause.

Preliminary conclusion

At this point, it should have become clear that anyone who considers studying stage design or scenography in the German-speaking (theatre) world should definitely have a long, close look at the different courses on offer, paying attention to things such as: how does the team structure work, how do the professors conduct their classes, how is one actually supported? – or even more fundamentally: do I feel acknowledged and understood, and does the course's approach and programme align well with the experiences I have already gained and with my artistic vision? It is highly advisable to research these matters first, making up one's mind before commencing with one's studies – which, of course, requires a certain level of basic maturity and independence. It is good to see that classes, which have been rearranged in recent years, are looking for ways and concepts to actively position themselves in the fast and constantly changing theatre, art and performance world. There is a real attempt at keeping the courses vivid and up to date with the latest developments. This can happen in many different ways, such as in Dresden with its emphasis on theoretical reflection, in Salzburg, where conceptual thinking is at the forefront, in Munich, where the students are selected very carefully and challenged as artists, or at the TU Berlin, which promotes early cooperation in the practical world between young teams, while offering an open-minded and interdisciplinary research program. It is desirable – and of great benefit for the future generations of scenographers – that these different avenues remain open and are continuously being enhanced. Scenography is and will always be a discipline that has a very wide scope and within which very independent artists develop concepts that involve all sorts of media techniques, even quite far-fetched ones. Students should therefore have as much access as possible to educational and theoretical content, and the broadest possible support for their artistic development – be this through study projects or first-hand practical experience.

Notes

1 See for example the workshop programme of the artistic group raumlaborberlin, http://raumlabor.net/open-raumlabor-university-2/ (accessed 10 June 2018)
2 For more details on the history of the academy see www.hfbk-dresden.de/en/about-us/profile/introduction/the-academys-history/ (accessed 10 June 2018)
3 Aleksandar Denić in his artist's talk at the conference *The Art of Scenography: Epistemes and Aesthetics*, Munich, 18 November 2016.
4 HfG Karlsruhe, Exhibition Design and Scenography, Course Website, https://adsz.hfg-karlsruhe.de/information-en (accessed 10 June 2018)
5 In a conversation with Thea Hoffmann-Axthelm on 3 September 2017. Anja Dorn has since left the Academy of Design Karlsruhe to become Director of the Leopold-Hoesch-Museum in Düren.
6 According to Michael Simon, the quite minimal genre or job-specific classification that the term 'scenography' signals led to the case that there was a temporary decline in the number of applicants for the university places; after the programme had been split and a nominal adjustment had been made towards theatre and film the numbers increased again.
7 A similar, strongly research-oriented approach is pursued at the Scenography Dept. of Norwegian Theatre Academy (artistic director: Serge von Arx) at Østfold University College, NO; von Arx also teaches and gives lectures in the German-speaking context. See Eeg-Tverbakk and Ely 2015: 34–8 and 101.

Staging the unknown
Scenography and its future potentials – preliminary résumé

Birgit E. Wiens and Serge von Arx

There is a broad consensus within the artistic discourse and in more recent theoretical discussions that scenography has to be analysed as an art and design practice that does not simply 'portray' a space but, much more, *produces* space by generating constellations of actions and observations, as well as triggering events and performative processes and, thus, putting these into motion. Today scenography can be seen in the most varied of art fields and cultural contexts; to describe these, generic terms such as 'extended scenography' or 'expanded scenography' have become common in the anglophone world.[1] As the various case studies and the analyses within this book have documented, a corresponding differentiation of the scenographic can also be observed in the German-speaking countries. These developments (which we have explored by mainly looking at Germany, with a few glimpses at Switzerland and Austria as well) must be seen within the history of (European) scenography; in its course McKinney and Palmer have identified three major shifts and 'restructurings' of scenographic design practices and discourse which have laid the foundations for its expansion (2017: 4). The first, as they argue, is the shift to be observed in the twentieth century, when artists did away with the illusion and 'optical deception' (Appia cited in Beacham 2006: 92) of the traditional proscenium stage, to reorganize the scenic space and to allow for new forms scenographic expression. The second shift that they describe under the umbrella term 'postdramatic theatre' (a term coined by Hans-Thies Lehmann in 1999) marked a detachment of theatre scenography from the predominance of literature, and the third, most recent shift to be observed around the millennium brought the 'proliferation of new spatial forms for theatre and performance' (McKinney and Palmer 2017: 4) as well as manifold cross-border expansions of scenographic practices and discourse into other arts and cultural fields. This perspective on recent (European) scenography history, including the suggested periodization, may seem to be a more schematic even if very apt description of these developments that we are seeing, especially within the German-speaking countries. A lot of it – just think of Appia, the Bauhaus school or the Brecht stage, or even the Gießener school which is directly connected to the discourse on postdramatic theatre and the artists Robert Wilson, Heiner Goebbels or Rimini Protokoll – did actually take place in Germany or started out there. In addition, nowadays one can observe a proliferating extension and expansion of the scenographic, above and beyond theatre, into the most varied of fields and a substantial differentiation of scenographic forms, aesthetics and practices. At the same time, as already stated in the introduction to this book, within the German-speaking countries – especially compared with the discourse that is taking place mainly in the Anglo-American and Scandinavian countries – there is a certain need to catch up when it comes to theory development, the academic discourse as such and the meta-reflections on scenography that we are, to a certain extent, confronting with our contributions.

As noted in the introduction, as well as in several of the chapters within this book, the term 'scenography' has only slowly asserted itself within the German-speaking countries. When it has, it is only partially and with regard to certain areas (e.g. in the fields of exhibitions and museums);[2] terms such as 'set design', 'scenic design' or 'stage design' (those that, in the sense of 'contemporary stage design' or 'experimental stage design', are being extended content-wise or filled with new meaning), 'temporary architecture' or 'scenography' (also filled with different definition approaches) are partially used in parallel. This means that the discussion on this has, to date, been mostly focused on genre and classification (theatre, exhibition/museum, architecture, spatial design),[3] which to a certain extent runs counter to the hybridity, plurimediality and increasing inter- and transdisciplinary differentiation of scenography that we can observe in practice. Hereby scenography, contemporary stage design and performative architecture (or under which term or label whatsoever the praxis described as 'scenographic' decides to appear) show up in numerous contexts, are institutionally situated in manifold ways, are integrated into organizational, financial and other conditions or even set free from them within an 'intermediate space' between various genres and institutions. In principle, as one can recognize when it comes to the variety and vibrancy of scenographic practice, there is a fertile breeding ground for scenography in the German-speaking countries. On the one hand this is anchored in tradition, a well-equipped and funded university landscape as well as a rich knowledge culture, and, on the other hand, in institutions (such as theatres and museums) that receive state funding; the same is true, to a certain degree, for an experimental art practice, that, above and beyond the classic institutions, also can get funding through project support; for example, through funding programmes of the Kulturstiftung des Bundes (the Federal Cultural Foundation), the Goethe Institute or, in Berlin, the Hauptstadtkulturfonds (Capital City Cultural Fund). In addition to scenographic works in these various art contexts, commercially oriented projects such as those realized by design ateliers such as Atelier Brückner are also taking place in which scenography, more or less noticeably, is leaving the realm of the predefined field of art. That, for example, the main trading hall of the German Stock Exchange in Frankfurt, as everybody knows it from the usual press photos and daily newscasts, was redesigned in 2008 by a scenography atelier and trained stage designers – and with a focus on television to 'illustrate the location and networking of Frankfurt within the global financial market'[4] – leads us to conclude that scenography, above and beyond the arts, also has taken over an influential role in everyday life and life's reality. Thus, it does not only have an aesthetic dimension but also social, political and ethical ones as well which we need to explore and bear in mind. Following sociologist Andreas Reckwitz's observations in his recent study *The Invention of Creativity* (2017), it can be assumed as stated, that scenography has become an aspect of a widening, extending 'creative *dispositif*' and a part of the processes of a 'social aestheticization' (Reckwitz 2017: 9) that nowadays is a mark of (mainly Western) societies; it puts its stamp on these in an all-encompassing manner, however, at the same time, in a quite ambivalent way. Understood in this way scenography not only has aesthetic dimensions, but also social, political and ethical impacts that have to be observed and analysed. Scenography – ever since it has gained in cultural and social relevance – therefore needs critical analysis and meta-reflection, as is suggested by this book and, as is also pointed out, ongoing research needs to be undertaken.

To draw a preliminary conclusion within this summarizing chapter on the state of the debate and what has been achieved until this point in time, the editor asked Swiss-born Serge von Arx, international architect and scenographer, Professor for Scenography at the Norwegian Theatre Academy/Østfold University College and a member of the curatorial board for the Prague Quadrennial (PQ), to join her for a discussion on the subject.

If one takes a look 'from the outside' on the practice and theory of scenography as well as contemporary stage design in the German-language countries, what is your impression?

I understood that during the preparatory stages for this book there were discussions about what one is actually describing when using the term 'contemporary German scenography': Does such a term even make sense, and what comes about within our globalized cultural exchange if one explicitly focuses on such a specific cultural area – that is, the German-speaking countries? In my opinion, such a focus does indeed make sense, as an observation rather than a postulate, in terms of cultural-comparative perspectives on the other European countries or even taking the whole matter to a global scale. Let us, for example, look at theatre – as an institution and the conditions which art is produced on, made and received: Obviously, we find a very special situation within Germany, Austria and Switzerland. All three – across their borders – share a similar way of making theatre; their catchment area is quite big and differs from, for example, the situation in France or Italy. However, the most important factor is the theatre tradition as well as the institutional structures that these three countries, Germany, Austria and Switzerland, have in common. The generous state funding that theatres receive also benefits stage designers and scenographers. Moreover, Germany represents a special case in that funding for the many city and state theatres from Munich, in the south of Germany, all the way to Kiel and Hamburg in the north, takes place in an explicitly decentralized manner. Due to the federal structure of the country, there is, in fact, no one national theatre as such (Michalzik 2017). These circumstances characterize the fertile ground that has allowed a manifold variety of theatrical expressions to spring to life. Institutional conditions have a strong impact on artistic production, on aesthetics as a whole. Extensive public funding is rooted in a cultural as well as a social agreement that the state is charged with financing the arts. This, of course, is quite different in other parts of the world. For example, Robert Wilson's Watermill Center on Long Island never received any funding from the state of New York; instead, it is financed by fundraising drives and events such as the annual Watermill Benefit. Obviously, these are quite different conditions, in the case above, corresponding to the self-conception and cultural identity in the United States. Consequences and the influence on art practice and on artistic projects are apparent: guaranteed, ongoing state funding providing a carte blanche is a very different agency than the repeated effort to ask for money from private partners, corporations and businesses. The results inevitably relate to a more commercial approach, not necessarily as a mere consumerist focus, but in distinct awareness of a theatre audience. Merging the artistically fruitful from both worlds, Wilson for example has, since the 1970s and over many decades until today, realized the majority of his projects in Europe, foremost in Germany and France.

Wilson was extremely influential here in Germany as one of the main proponents of the 'postdramatic theatre' (Lehmann 2006 [1999]) and had a view to reconsidering and reappraising scenography as art and as an autonomous artistic practice. Today, using 'scenography' we describe a further changed inter-respectively transdisciplinary field which is wide open. This is what we are trying to describe for the German context within this book, in comparison to other countries. But what does such a comparative cultural perspective result in? Does using such an approach today even make sense? On the other hand, this is actually being done officially every four years when the Prague Quadrennial (PQ) opens its gates. The PQ was founded in 1967 as an exhibition platform for stage and set design and by now has become the internationally most renowned platform for scenography. Traditionally, the core focus of its programme is the 'Exhibition of Countries and Regions', which is undertaken as a competition and a presentation judged by a jury that awards prizes; today the focus is more on the cultural dialogue. Last time, around sixty countries participated. Theatre makers, exhibition scenographers and architects – as can be observed at PQ – work globally nowadays, be it in an artistic context or for commercial projects. Obviously, there is – on the international level – an exchange of artistic ideas and an intercultural transfer of scenographic design practices and tools taking place as well as a wide distribution and circulation of scenographic knowledge. Convergences emerge on the aesthetic level, and also on the content level, for example, when scenographers deal with global phenomena topics such as migration, tourism, transportation, international trade, connectivity and the impact of communication technologies. All this generates a type of 'global feeling',[5] while at the same time, as I would argue, the cultural context is still, explicitly or implicitly, relevant most of the time. One could ask in which ways artistic traditions, production conditions, cultural perspective and context remain noticeable in scenographic works.

The spectrum of stage design and scenography that we can view in the German-language countries since the millennium is, in fact, very wide – if one just thinks about the works of and the approaches taken by artists such as Bert Neumann, Anna Viebrock, Katrin Brack, Aleksandar Denić, as well as Barbara Ehnes, Janina Audick, Herbert Fritsch or Ulrich Rasche, just to name a few. In addition, we have witnessed the temporary structures by Vegard Vinge/Ida Müller, the 'narrative spaces' and immersive constellations by Mona el Gammal and the documentary spatial explorations by Rimini Protokoll and Dominic Huber/Blendwerk. And then, there are the spatial designs, exhibition scenographies and commercially oriented projects by globally working design ateliers such as Atelier Brückner, Tamschick Media+Space or TRIAD Berlin, among others. On the other hand you have – and again with a clearly different approach and social agenda – the urban scenographies, interventions and participatory projects of artist groups such as raumlaborberlin. Given this wide and very rich spectrum, one would expect a quite remarkable contribution at the Prague Quadrennial. Instead, though, I have noticed that Germany's contribution was not very visibly distinct at the country pavilions, whereas other nations spent a lot of effort and money to stage current designs and project examples, to identify scenographic movements and to enter into a discussion with others. Maybe this indicates a certain saturation: the German theatre and museum landscape and all in all the entire field of art is very large; it is recognized and acknowledged internationally. Due to the complexity in expressions within the German-speaking context and the attention that these works have already received, a strong urge to present oneself at the PQ may not be a priority. There are of course relevant individual representatives that appear in the discursive events of the PQ, having their own branding. But above and beyond this, the understanding of scenography on a 'meta level' as well as creating a wider framework do not seem to have been strongly promoted in the German-language countries so far.

Indeed, there seems to be a noticeable theory deficit, which has only been alleviated by individual initiatives at certain selective points.[6] This has grown historically and is partly structurally contingent as we can see when looking at the academic landscape in the German-language countries.[7] At the universities – in the arts and art-related sciences that have established themselves over many years – stage design and scenography traditionally fall into a 'gap' between different disciplines (i.e. theatre studies, art studies, architecture); there – and with the label assigned to them as being 'applied art' (versus the so-called 'free arts') – it has remained a topic more or less on the margins when it comes to academia and the theoretical discourse. This even includes the recent debate on 'artistic research' within the interplay of universities, universities of art and art academies. Here, at least, dealing with and confronting modern day scenography occurs on a selective basis, but all in all it also does remain a marginal phenomenon.[8] If a publication is focused on 'scenography' or if a course of studies is named as such, then it still seems to be necessary to first of all agree on a definition[9] for said subject which at the moment is making its first tentative steps to actually be accepted and used in the German-language countries. Christopher Balme, in the foreword of this book, demonstrated this empirically with the aid of the online search engine Google Books Ngram.

This, though, is also still true above and beyond the German-language countries, even if the term is more in use or the discourse on scenography is more established in other areas of the world. Even Arnold Aronson starts his edited *Routledge Companion to Scenography*, published in 2018, with a definition of the term (from the Greek etymological origin to the use of the term within European theatre tradition all the way to today's inter-/transdisciplinary operating, expanded scenography that includes the global discourse on the horizon). At the Prague Quadrennial in 2015, when curating the architecture section 'Performing Space or Ephemeral Section of Architecture', I engaged scenography not as juxtaposition but as amalgamation of architecture and theatre, inquiring its essence by dilating the term even more. During the presentations, Hadi Damien, the Lebanese curator, shared his concern with me that he felt scenography should first of all be defined before we used it in a global cross-cultural context, where almost each country or nation had a somewhat differing understanding of what was actually meant. This relates to the fact that scenography as an art practice and discourse always is part of a larger disposition, that is, of the theatre, the museum, the respective audience and the social circumstances. At the PQ, often curious and at the same time fruitful situations emerge with contributors using the same term but partially meaning something very different.

How would you describe your perspective on the subject and your approach to it, as an artist and a scenographer, as a professor of scenography at a Norwegian theatre academy, and as a curator?

My own perspective is that of a trained architect: in the late 1990s I began working with Robert Wilson on stage, exhibition and installation design projects; our collaboration started in Hamburg, at the Thalia Theater, and since then I have collaborated with him, realizing more than fifty projects all over the world. Since 2003, I have also worked as a regular mentor and architectural consultant at the Watermill Center on Long Island, New York. My working and theoretical thinking has certainly been to a large degree influenced by Wilson. However, particularly in my own projects and teaching, I work somewhat differently, take different trajectories when creating a space. I would consider myself as a protagonist in that wide, somewhat confusing field of 'expanded scenography' (McKinney and Palmer 2017). I cannot give a concluding definition of what scenography is (and it seems nobody really can), but I can describe my approach: When designing a space for the street, the stage, or for an exhibition the most important thing, in my opinion, is to listen with all your senses. This should always be the first step, to sense what is there and what has been there. The goal of these processes – that have been described elsewhere as processes of 'responsive listening' (von Arx 2015; Eeg-Tverbakk and Ely 2015) – is, of course, not to 'decorate' a stage, but to create a spatial and sensory potential for events to unfold. Even if a production takes place in a 'black box' or in a 'white cube', the artistic creation process never starts at zero. There is no 'point zero' to start from because at any point there has always been something beforehand, there is always a spatial and temporal context; in architecture this relates to the *genius loci*. Each place – even a 'black box' or a 'white cube' – is loaded with its own history; the space has a certain dimension, there are walls which are made out of a certain material, there's paint, there are traces from previous productions, there are specific curtains, it all blends together to a certain acoustic, and even smell, and then, most often, there is also technical equipment that can be worked with – so there's a lot of given conditions. Whatever a scenographer intends to do and whatever a planned project is about, one always should start by listening with all of one's senses to the respective context. If an aspect is ignored, that lack of awareness or negligence will become a part of the theatre performance, the exhibition or whatever the event is that is supposed to take place. If a theatre or dance project is presented at the Lincoln Center in New York, or at the Schauspielhaus Zurich, or if it takes place somewhere in an abandoned factory building: the audience will, of course, always have a different perception of it, even with identical performances, based on the sensation before, during and after the performance; all of this becomes part of the performative event. In terms of production aesthetics, scenography, as I would define it, is always connected to something (even at various levels): it refers to a certain concept or topic (a play, an exhibition project, etc.) while at the same time, as just explained, it also inevitably relates to its actual given context. Put simply, 'doing scenography' means to deconstruct reality, to analyse and to recompose existing elements – to artistically cast a new light on the cultural means through which we create, build and perceive space. Thus, 'doing scenography' – which always implies both theory and practice – also has a social and ethical dimension. In terms of perception and reception, like all theatre, scenography necessarily implies audience involvement; it triggers experience and spatial perception and, by addressing all human senses, provokes activity, movement, reflection and an active response from the audience. To sum it up: contemporary scenography is an inherently interdisciplinary, complex art and design practice, which is not about 'building' or visualizing spaces; instead 'doing scenography' is about compositional processes, or as I have put it elsewhere:

> Scenography as such does not exist. It is agency, consisting of the invisible relationship between spatially and temporally active constituents. It is a catalyst, rendering the hidden visible, or obscuring what we believe to see and know. A space is only the starting point. ... What exists inside things, behind things, and in-between things is more relevant than the immediate appearance of a space beset with objects. Scenography is ephemeral. ... Scenography's main concern is potentiality; relationships are set as frames around an unknown, to be filled with the spectators' imaginations. (von Arx 2015: 34)

In this sense, I tend to use the often confusing and culturally varying term 'scenography' in its literal meaning of 'writing space' (from the Greek: *skene*, backdrop, front of the stage building, and *graphein*, to write). Robert Wilson's stage works and artistic procedures have been described as 'scenic writing'[10] within the frame of the proscenium stage, using visual elements (scenographic objects, costumes, makeup, colour, light). In my approach, I am focusing more beyond linearity, into open gravitational fields of narratives, in the realms of exhibition design, art in the public environment, and even on stage. Speaking of Wilson: in this context, one of the most important projects I worked on with him is the *Tapio Wirkkala Park* in the Arabianranta district of Helsinki (2011/12). The aim here was not to create an exhibition design or a theatre performance, but a public park – and for me it became a key example of how to bring performing art, architecture and, in addition, even urban planning together. The first step, again, was to listen, to observe and to get to know the context; we then decided to insert a square-shaped structure into the park and divide it into nine rooms. Each room has its individual variety of surface textures and featured artistic elements typical of private homes: a bench, stools, a fireplace, two toy horses. They were like spatial chapters that could be experienced in various sequences, evoking a narrative. That toy horse I built at the house we rented in Oslo; in the cellar, I found a very old window frame and some old nails, which I used to build a little wooden horse. Then, we cast the wooden toy horse in bronze and made a copy of the small horse, scaled to the size of a real horse, also in bronze. In a quarry near Helsinki we hunted the perfect granite blocks, which filled two of the rooms to make them like labyrinths. The park was opened in October 2012. The design is obviously theatrical; there's a non-linear spatial structure and those rooms tell a story, which is open. The audience has almost total freedom when deciding how to move through the park and bring the scenographic potential to life.

Wilson was definitely among the artists who prepared the ground for what we now describe as 'expanded scenography'. Scenography, understood in this sense, stages on the most varied of fields constellations of space, actors and things that set processes and events into motion. As the example of Tapio Wirkkala Park *clearly demonstrates, scenographies do actually transport meaning (in this case, an open story) and for their audiences they do – even though there is a lot of freedom given – in certain terms define ways of moving and perceiving things so that they integrate and physically involve the visitors. Here, potentially, scenography can act as a guiding system that, on the one hand, creates the action- and perception-related options and, on the other hand, steers them. In this sense the art academic Pamela Scorzin suggested – interdisciplinarily – some time ago that scenography should be defined as a 'more or less observable structuring, programming, organization and steering of interactive situations, i.e. as an audience-addressed configuration ... of a setting or a platform that promotes mutual knowledge production and creativity processes' (Scorzin 2009: 313). Such a comprehension of scenography goes above and beyond the aesthetic and obviously also involves a social as well as a political dimension. Accordingly, scenography would not just be the focal object of theatre and art studies but it rather should also be explored from an analytical, cultural and technical, epistemological, sociological and practice-oriented perspective. Especially for the production side of things, the design phase (which is especially focused on in this book), this has consequences: the design goals, the tools, the drafting processes and the design knowledge that one needs are all changing. Design research defines such a turn as 'redesigning design'.*[11]

Art for me is about framing an unknown, finding the perfect balance between establishing a clear frame and keeping the limits as open as possible. Be it a theatre piece, a sculpture, a poem or a film, or even a town square, it is the unknown, the uncontrollable which is filled by our imagination, or by human interaction, and hence this is what makes the reading of any art work personal, or a public square to shape a communal identity, allowing us to relate to. In performance design, the most interesting part is what rigidly rejects control. In the drafting phase we can often see an emphasis on control, that is, attempting to control the design processes themselves, while at the same time having to deal with what is always there as well, the uncontrollable. Give it its space! For example, the design and rehearsal phases of Wilson's theatre projects usually proceed the same way. There is a 'table workshop' in Watermill with the entire artistic team; emanating from the discussions, Wilson sketches a storyboard and the whole project is thought through to the end. In the theatre (or the venue where we realize the project), the scenic design is then mocked up in a very simplified manner, remaining versatile on the rehearsal stage (using cheap materials such as cardboard, pieces of wood and old fabrics). This is called 'Stage A'. Everything can and does still change at this stage – the whole piece is sculpted with all its components, set, movement, music and costumes. Based on this workshop, the scenography is being developed and detailed and subsequently exemplified and tested in a 'Bauprobe', a real scale mock-up with material samples. Eventually the final rehearsal period, 'Stage B', will begin on stage in the final set. And from there it's a rigorous, tedious work that goes all the way chronologically through the piece. With some of my own projects, I have tried to subvert these standardized procedures, for instance, by using an approach that I (ironically) call 'non-scenographies'; as an example, when creating the scenic design for the staging of *Death of a Salesman* at the Trøndelag Theatre in Norway in 2013. During the model presentation, I had nothing physical to show, because my idea was that the salesman's house already existed, somewhere in reality, and we only had to find it and put it on stage! We actually found a house that was abandoned twenty to thirty years ago. A big real estate company planning a large housing area did not have any need for the house and allowed us to use it in whatever way. We took it, removed three of the four walls, and put it on a turntable on the stage, where it was slowly rotating; the house made one full round as the story of the salesman evolved in the house, the actors went from room to room, in between all the true traces and leftovers of that house. As a scenographer, you have a certain bandwidth of artistic and technical tools at your disposal, starting with models that one constructs or generates with a computer, going to storyboards and all the way to the most differentiated of notations and scenographic scores. Standardized methods or design processes should always be avoided; the tool or the approach that one chooses should fit to the project and, to break a certain routine, one should – or rather one must – vary this.

As a tendency one can say that with these turns, the performatization and the mediatization as well as scenography appearing in the most varied of artistic and cultural fields, have markedly changed the cultural techniques and processes of scenographic staging itself. In addition to the well-known processes such as sketching, drafting, drawing and model building (or even as a replacement of these), compository processes have now come to the fore with which scenography – on the work's level or on the level of appearing – has, in a certain sense, become 'invisible'. The conceptual ideas that through it spaces becoming aesthetic, that the narratives, atmospheres and (material, visual, acoustic) effects so to speak are triggered and 'steered' by it has moved on to an operative level. This level articulates itself through notation, for example drafts, sketches, storyboards, performance scripts and scenographic scores. In this sense as well scenography, as you have mentioned, has become, in a stricter sense, 'invisible' but always having an agency, being ephemeral at the same time.

Scenography is art, it is design and it stimulates a discourse above and beyond the individual works of art which includes the theoretical reflection on spaces. To be a scenographer today, one actually needs to have a basic understanding of architecture as well as theatre, urban development, the fine and visual arts, music – and one has to be able to bring all of this together. There is a need to undertake more research to understand these phenomena better and to be able to categorize them. On the other hand, you will barely ever see a job offer posted with the words: 'Looking for a scenographer.' Within the German-language countries, the specializations are clearly defined; study courses that are laid out in an interdisciplinary manner have been partially relabelled and redefined according to genres once again as, for example, 'Stage Design' and 'Production Design for Film' at the Zurich University of the Arts, which formerly was known as 'Scenography'. This was connected with the hope that the career opportunities for the students would improve; the indefinable, the openness is in stark contradiction to our understanding that focuses on specialization, efficiency and also commercial interest. When one on the other hand states that scenography is art and examines things in an artistic way, reflecting on how spaces change socially, through migration, tourism, gentrification or even connectivity and ubiquitous media, then one should definitely strengthen the openness. For the universities, this means that one is attempting to train artists that are able to think independently. We at the Norwegian Theatre Academy encourage the students to explore the widest possible variety of scenographic approaches to be able to create stage designs, exhibitions, film sets, memorials and other works within the public space. Through these experiences, the students gain a freedom when working with space. The field of scenography is open; it is in motion and in constant flux. The continuing discussion on how 'scenography' should be defined is the very symptom for this. Maybe one should – instead of trying to define it – maintain its precarious quality of being an open field that is consciously being reconceived as both open and indefinable. This also means that there is a need for an ongoing discussion: rethinking and understanding scenography as a research-oriented practice and, in addition to this, as an interdisciplinary, socially relevant discourse is at the core.

Notes

1 On this debate, focusing on the Anglo-American context, see Joslin McKinney and Scott Palmer, 'Introducing "Expanded" Scenography', in McKinney and Palmer 2017: 1–19.
2 Exceptions are the scenography colloquia of the DASA Dortmund, which have been taking place annually since 2000 (focus is on exhibition design), and the International Scenography Biennial, Ludwigsburg (2013), which has, since 2015, continued on a biannual basis as the congress 'Raumwelten' ('Spatial Worlds: Platform for Scenography, Architecture and Media'), Ludwigsburg. Also, the publication series on 'Scenography & Scenology', edited by Heiner Wilharm and Ralf Bohn, FH Dortmund (in collaboration with Transcript publishers), can be mentioned here.
3 On these issues also see the introduction of this book.
4 Brückner 2016: 230; see also the project description on Atelier Brückner's website, http://www.atelier-brueckner.com/en/projects/deutsche-boerse-main-trading-hall (accessed 30 June 2018).
5 See Jon McKenzie's reflections on scenography as a globally operating art form; McKenzie 2008.
6 See note 2 above.
7 See the contribution by Hoffmann-Axthelm and Kraatz in this book.
8 See as an example the research project 'Das Wissen der Künste' (Knowledge in the Arts), UdK Berlin.

9 See for example Oliver Langbein, 'What is "Scenography"?', website of the University of Applied Sciences and Arts, Dortmund, www.fh-dortmund.de/de/fb/2/studium/studiengaenge/szeno_ma/Szenografie.php (accessed 30 June 2018).

10 This term (*'szenische "Graphie"'* in the original) was coined by Hans-Thies Lehmann when discussing Wilson's scenography and aesthetics; Lehmann 2005 [1999]: 159.

11 Quoted from Susanne Hauser, 'Spaces in Process: Designs', paper presentation at *The Art of Scenography: Epistemes and Aesthetics*, International Conference, Munich, 17–18 November 2016.

References

Abulafia, Y. (2016), *The Art of Light on Stage: Lighting in Contemporary Theatre*, London: Routledge.

Anders, G. (2002 [1956]), *Die Antiquiertheit des Menschen, Bd. 1: Über die Seele im Zeitalter der zweiten industriellen Revolution* [The Outdatedness of Human Beings, Vol. 1: On the Soul in the Era of the Second Industrial Revolution], Munich: Beck.

Anon (2008), 'Technisches Wunderwerk belebt "Stifters Dinge". Eine Theateraufführung ohne Akteure von Heiner Goebbels' ['Technical miracle brings "Stifters Dinge" to life'], *Bühnentechnische Rundschau*, 1, available online: www.heinergoebbels.com/en/archive/texts/articles/read/523 (accessed 9 March 2018).

Appia, A. (1993), 'Actor, Space, Light, Painting (1919)', in R. Beacham (ed.), *Texts on Theatre*, 114–15, London, NY: Routledge.

Armstrong, T. (2007), 'Player Piano: Poetry and Sonic Modernity', *Modernism/Modernity*, 14 (1): 1–19.

Arnott, J. F., ed. (1977), *Theatre Space: An Examination of the Interaction between Space, Technology, Performance and Society; 8th World Congress, Munich, 18–25 Sept. 1977*, Munich: Prestel.

Aronson, A. (2018), *The Routledge Companion to Scenography*, London, New York: Routledge.

Aronson, A. (2018 [1981]), *The History and Theory of Environmental Scenography* (2nd revised edition), London, New York: Bloomsbury.

von Arx, S. (2015), 'On Scenography', in C. Eeg-Tverbakk and K. Ely (eds), *Responsive Listening: Theater Training for Contemporary Spaces*, 34–8, New York: Brooklyn Art Press.

Atelier Brückner, ed. (2016 [2011]), *Scenography / Szenografie – Making Spaces Talk / Narrative Räume: Projects / Projekte 2002–2010* (bilingual publication), Ludwigsburg: av edition.

Atelier Brückner, ed. (2019), *Scenography / Szenografie 2: Staging the Space / Der inszenierte Raum* (bilingual publication), Basel: Birkhäuser.

Audick, J., V. Bärenklau and M. Dresenkamp, eds (2018), *Talent*, Zurich: Edition Frey.

Austin, J. L. (1975 [1963]), *How to Do Things with Words*, Oxford: Clarendon Press.

Bachmann-Medick, D. (2009 [2006]), *Cultural Turns* [Cultural Turns. Re-orientations in the Cultural Sciences], Reinbek: Rowohlt.

Bachelard, G. (2002 [1938]), *The Formation of the Scientific Mind* (La Formation de l'Esprit scientifique), trans. Mary McAllister Jones, Manchester: Clinamen Press.

Badura, J., S. Dubach, A. Haarmann, D. Mersch, A. Rey, C. Schenker and G. Toro Pérez, eds (2015), *Künstlerische Forschung. Ein Handbuch* [Artistic Research. A Handbook], Berlin, Zurich: Diaphanes.

Bakhtin, M. (1981), *The Dialogic Imagination: Four Essays*, ed. Michael Holquist; trans. C. Emerson and M. Holquist, Austin: Texas University Press.

Barad, K. (2003), 'Posthuman Performativity: Toward an Understanding of How Matter Comes to Matter', *Signs: Journal of Women in Culture and Society*, 28 (3): 801–31.

Barbieri, D. (2017), *Costume in Performance: Materiality, Culture, and the Body*, London, New York: Bloomsbury.

Barthes, R. (1966), 'Die strukturalistische Tätigkeit' (The Structuralist Activity), *Kursbuch*, 5: 190–6.

Bateson, G. (2013), *Steps to an Ecology of Mind: Collected Essays in Anthropology, Psychiatry, Evolution, and Epistemology*, Chicago: Chicago University Press.

Baugh, C. (2013 [2005]), *Theatre, Performance and Technology: The Development and Transformation of Scenography*, Basingstoke: Palgrave Macmillan.

Beacham, R. (2006 [1994]), *Adolphe Appia. Künstler und Visionär des Modernen Theaters* [Adolphe Appia. Artist and Visionary of the Modern Theatre], Berlin: Alexander Verlag.

Beer, T. (2016), 'Ecomaterialism in Scenography', *Theatre and Performance Design*, 2 (1–2): 161–72.

Behr, B. (2013), *Bühnenbildnerinnen: Eine Geschlechterperspektive auf Geschichte und Praxis der Bühnenbildkunst* [Female Stage Designers: A Gender Perspective on the History and Practice of Stage Design], Bielefeld: Transcript.

Benjamin, W. (1974 [1916]), 'Über Sprache überhaupt und über die Sprache des Menschen' ['On Language as Such and on the Language of Man'], in R. Tiedemann and H. Schweppenhäuser (eds), *Walter Benjamin. Gesammelte Schriften II.1* [Walter Benjamin. Collected Works II.I], 140–57, Frankfurt a. Main: Suhrkamp.

Bell, G. (2010), 'Driving Deeper into That Thing: The Humanity of Heiner Goebbels's Stifters Dinge', *TDR: The Drama Review*, 54 (3): 150–8.

Bennett, J. (2010a), 'A Materialist Stopover on the Way to a New Materialism', in D. Coole and S. Frost (eds), *New Materialisms: Ontology, Agency, and Politics*, 47–69, London: Duke Univerity Press.

Bennett, J. (2010b), *Vibrant Matter: A Political Ecology of Things*, Durham, London: Duke University Press.

Berka, R. (2011), *Schlingensiefs Animatograph. Zum Raum wird hier die Zeit* [Schlingensief's Animatograph. Here Time becomes Space], Vienna, New York: Springer.

Beyes, T., A. Deuflhard and S.-T. Krempl, eds (2009), *Parcitypate: Art and Urban Space*, Zurich: Niggli Verlag.

Beyst, S. (2005), 'John Cage's *Europeras*: A Light- and Soundscape as a Musical Manifesto', available online: http://d-sites.net/english/cage.html (accessed 30 May 2018).

Biesenbach, K., A.-C. Gebbers, A. Laberenz and S. Pfeffer, eds (2014), *Christoph Schlingensief* (Exhibition catalogue, Berlin-KW and MoMA PS1, New York), Cologne: W. König.

Biggs, M., and H. Karlsson, eds (2011), *The Routledge Companion to Research in the Arts*, London, New York: Routledge, Taylor & Francis.

Bishop, C. (2004), 'Antagonism and Relational Aesthetics', *October – MIT Press Journals*, 110: 51–79.

Blank, C., ed. (2018), *Faust-Welten. Goethes Drama auf der Bühne* [Worlds of Faust. Goethe's Drama on the Stage], Leipzig: Seemann Henschel.

Bleeker, M. (2017), 'Thinking That Matters: Towards a Post-Anthropocentric Approach to Performance Design', in J. McKinney and S. Palmer (eds), *Scenography Expanded: An Introduction to Contemporary Performance Design*, 125–35, London, New York: Bloomsbury.

Blievernicht, L., J. Fehrmann and B. Neumann (2004), *LSD Berlin* [LSD Berlin. Graphic Design and Photography], Berlin: Synwohlt.

Boenisch, P. M. (2010), 'Frank Castorf and the Berlin Volksbuehne: "The Humiliated and Insulted"', in S. Bay-Cheng, C. Kattenbelt, A. Lavender and R. Nelson (eds), *Mapping Intermediality and Performance*, 198–203, Amsterdam: Amsterdam University Press.

Boeser, K., and R. Vatkova, eds (1986), *Erwin Piscator: Eine Arbeitsbiographie in 2 Bänden* [Erwin Piscator: A Work Biography in 2 Volumes], Vol. 1: Berlin 1916–31, Berlin: Fröhlich & Kaufmann.

Böhme, G. (1993), 'Atmosphere as the Fundamental Concept of a New Aesthetics', *Thesis Eleven*, 36: 113–26.

Böhme, G. (2013), 'The Art of the Stage Set as a Paradigm for an Aesthetics of Atmospheres', *Ambiances*, http://ambiances.revues.org/315 (accessed 8 March 2018).

Bohn, R., and H. Wilharm, eds (2009), *Inszenierung und Ereignis: Beiträge zur Theorie und Praxis der Szenografie* [Staging and Event: Contributions to the Debate about the Theory and Practice of Scenography], Bielefeld: Transcript.

Borgdorff, H. (2012), 'Künstlerische Forschung und Akademische Forschung' ('Artistic Research and Academic Research'), in M. Tröndle and J. Warmers (eds), *Beiträge zur transdisziplinären Hybridisierung von Wissenschaft und Kunst* [Contributions to the transdisciplinary Hybridisation of the Sciences and Arts], 69–89, Bielefeld: Transcript.

Bourriaud, N. (2001), *Relational Aesthetics*, Dijon: Les Presses du réel.

Brandstetter, G., and B. Wiens, eds (2010), *Theater ohne Fluchtpunkt. Das Erbe Adolphe Appias* [Theatre without Vanishing Points. The Legacy of Adolphe Appia: Scenography and Choreography in Contemporary Theatre], Berlin: Alexander Verlag.

Brandstetter, G., F. Hofmann and K. Maar, eds (2010), *Notationen und choreographisches Denken* [Notations and Choreographic Thinking], Freiburg i. Br.: Rombach.

Brejzek, T., ed. (2011), *Expanding Scenography: On the Authoring of Space*, Prague: Arts and Theatre Institute.

Brejzek, T., and L. Wallen (2018), *The Model as Performance: Staging Space in Theatre and Architecture*, London, New York: Bloomsbury.

Brejzek, T., W. Greisenegger and L. Wallen, eds (2009), 'Introduction', in *Space and Truth: Monitoring Scenography* 02, 5–8, Zurich, CH: ZHdK University of the Arts.

Brejzek, T., G. Mueller von der Hegen and L. Wallen (2009), 'Szenografie', in S. Günzel (ed.), *Raumwissenschaften* [Spatial science], 370–85, Frankfurt M.: Suhrkamp.

Brückner, U. R. (2007), 'Corporate Scenography – vom intravenösen Zugang zur Marke' ['Corporate Scenography – On the Intravenous Access to the Brand'], in M. Beyrow, P. Kiedaisch and N. Daldrop (eds), *Corporate Identity und Corporate Design*, 126–37, Ludwigsburg: avedition.

Brückner, U. R., and L. Greci, eds (2016), *EMEE Toolkit 4: Synaesthetic Translation of Perspectives. Scenography – a Sketchbook*, Vienna: edition mono.

Brown, B. (2016), *Other Things*, Chicago, London: Chicago University Press.

Brown, R. (2009), *Sound: A Reader in Theatre Practice*, Basingstoke: Palgrave Macmillan.

Bryant, L., G. Harman and N. Srnicek, eds (2011), *The Speculative Turn: Continental Materialism and Realism*, Melbourne: re.press.

Buchmann, S. (2015), 'Rules of the (Im-)Possible. On Artistic Practice in the Late 1980s and Early 1990s', in M. Michalka (ed.), *To Expose, To Show, To Demonstrate, To Inform, To Offer: Artistic Practices around 1990*, 22–34, Vienna: mumok.

Buchmann, S., I. Lafer and C. Ruhm, eds (2010), *Putting Rehearsals to the Test: Practices of Rehearsal in Fine Arts, Film, Theatre, Theory, and Politics*, Berlin: Sternberg Press.

Butler, J. (1990), 'Performative Acts and Gender Constitution: An Essay in Phenomenology and Feminist Theory', in S.-E. Case (ed.), *Performing Feminism: Feminist Critical Theory and Theater*, 270–82, Baltimore: Johns Hopkins University Press.

Butte, M., K. Maar, F. McGovern, M.-F. Rafael and J. Schafaff, eds (2014), *Assign & Arrange: Methodologies of Presentation in Art and Dance*, Berlin, New York: Sternberg Press.

Carlson, M. (1993 [1987]), *Places of Performance: The Semiotics of Theatre Architecture* [Reprint], Ithaca, NY: Cornell University Press.

Carp, S., ed. (2015), *Barbara Ehnes. Alles auf Anfang / Starting Over. Bühnenbilder, Konzepte / Stages, Concepts* (bilingual publication), Berlin: Theater der Zeit.

Coole, D. (2010), 'The Inertia of Matter and the Generativity of Flesh', in D. Coole and S. Frost (eds), *New Materialisms: Ontology, Agency, and Politics*, 92–115, London: Duke University Press.

Coole, D., and S. Frost, eds (2010), *New Materialisms: Ontology, Agency, and Politics*, London: Duke University Press.

Cornish, M. (2018), 'Worlds of German Design in the Twenty-First Century', in A. Aronson, *The Routledge Companion to Scenography*, 465–77, London, New York: Routledge.

Crang, M., and N. Thrift, eds (2000), *Thinking Space*, London, New York: Routledge.

Daniels, D. (2002), *Kunst als Sendung. Von der Telegrafie zum Internet* [Art and Transmission. From Telegraphy to the Internet], Munich: C.H.Beck.

Danielson, P. (1998), *Modelling Rationality, Morality, and Evolution*, Oxford: Oxford University Press.

Danvers, J. (2005), 'In Beauty I Walk. Beauty, Nature and the Visual Arts', in D. Meyer-Dinkgräfe (ed.), *The Future of Beauty in Theatre, Literature and the Arts*, 1–11, Newcastle: Cambridge Scholars Publishing.

Debord, G. (1967), *La Societé du Spectacle*, Paris: Buchet-Chastel.
Dege, S. (2016), 'Architect Francis Kéré to build huge mobile theatre at Berlin's Tempelhof airport ramp', www.dw.com/en/architect-francis-kéré-to-build-huge-mobile-theater-at-berlins-tempelhof-airport-ramp/a-36415167 (accessed 1 May 2018).
Deleuze, G. (2001), *Difference and Repetition*, trans. P. Patton, London, New York: Continuum.
Dolphijn, R., and I. van der Tuin (2012), *New Materialism: Interviews and Cartographies*, Ann Arbor: Open Humanities Press.
Donald, M. (2014), 'Entided, Enwatered, Enwinded: Human/More-than-Human Agencies in Site-Specific Performance', in M. Schweitzer and J. Zerdy (eds), *Performing Objects and Theatrical Things*, 118–31, Basingstoke: Palgrave Macmillan.
Donald, M. (2016), 'The Performance "Apparatus": Performance and its Documentation as Ecological Practice', *Green Letters*, 20 (3): 251–69.
de Ponte, S., and the German Theatre Museum Munich (2006), *Caspar Neher – Bertolt Brecht: Eine Bühne für das epische Theater* [Caspar Neher – Bertolt Brecht: A Stage for the Epic Theatre], Leipzig: Henschel.
Dreissigacker, T. (2015), 'Modellieren' ['Modelling'], in J. Badura, S. Dubach, A. Haarmann, D. Mersch, A. Rey, C. Schenker and G. Toro Pérez (eds), *Künstlerische Forschung. Ein Handbuch* [Artistic Research. A Handbook], 181–4, Berlin, Zurich: Diaphanes.
Dyrssen, C. (2011), 'Navigating in Heterogeneity: Architectural Thinking and Art-based Research', in M. Biggs and H. Karlsson (eds), *The Routledge Companion to Research in the Arts*, 223–39, London, New York: Routledge.
Eberspächer, M., G. M. König and B. Tschofen, eds (2007), *Gottfried Korff. Museumsdinge. deponieren – exponieren* [Gottfried Korff. Things in the Museum: Storing – Exposing], Köln, Weimar, Wien: Böhlau.
Eckert, N. (2006 [1998]), *Das Bühnenbild im 20. Jahrhundert.* [Stage Design in the 20th Century], Berlin: Henschel.
Eeg-Tverbakk, C., and K. Ely, eds (2015), *Responsive Listening: Theater Training for Contemporary Spaces*, New York: Brooklyn Art Press.
Eiermann, A. (2009), *Postspektakuläres Theater* [Post-spectacular Theatre. On the Otherness of the Staging and the Dissolution of Artistic Limits], Bielefeld: Transcript.
Féral, J. (2008), 'Introduction: Towards a Genetic Study of Performance – Take 2', *Theatre Research International*, 33 (3): 223–33.
Ferraris, M. (2014), 'Was ist der Neue Realismus?' ['What is New Realism?'], in M. Gabriel (ed.), *Der Neue Realismus* [The New Realism], 52–75, Frankfurt a. Main: Suhrkamp.
Fetterman, W. (1996), *John Cage's Theatre Pieces: Notations and Performances*, Amsterdam: Harwood Academic Publishers.
Fischer-Lichte, E. (2008 [2004]), *The Transformative Power of Performance: A New Aesthetics*, trans. S. I. Jain, London, New York: Routledge .
Fischer-Lichte, E., D. Kolesch and M. Warstat, eds (2014 [2005]), *Metzler Lexikon Theatertheorie*, Stuttgart, Weimar: J.B. Metzler.
Flügel, K. (2005), *Einführung in die Museologie* [Introduction into Museology], Darmstadt: WBG.

Foerster-Baldenius, B., and J. Liesegang (2013), 'Architektur als Werkzeug' ['Architecture as a Tool'], *Kunstforum International, Special Issue: Urban Performance I*, ed. H. Schütz, 233: 164–72.

Forsythe, W. (2008), 'Choreographic Objects', in Ursula Blickle Foundation and M. Weisbeck (ed.), *Suspense*, 8–11, Zurich: Ringier.

Forti, S. (1974), *Handbook in Motion: An Account of an Ongoing Personal Discourse and its Manifestations in Dance* (1st edition), ed. K. Königand and E. Williams, Halifax, NS: The Press of the Nova Scotia College of Art and Design.

Foster, H. (2011), *The Art-Architecture-Complex*, New York: Verso.

Foster, S. L. (2011), *Choreographing Empathy: Kinesthesia in Performance*, New York, London: Routledge.

Freud, S. (1912), 'Recommendations to Physicians Practicing Psychoanalysis', in J. Strachey (ed.), *The Standard Edition of the Complete Psychological Works of Sigmund Freud*, Vol. 12, 109–20, London: Hogarth Press.

Fried, M. (1995 [1967]), 'Art and Objecthood', in G. Battcock (ed.), *Minimal Art: A Critical Anthology*, 116–47, Berkeley: California University Press.

Frietsch, U., ed. (2012), *Praxeologische Begriffe. Handwörterbuch der Historischen Kulturwissenschaften* [Praxeological Terms. Concise Dictionary of Historic Cultural Studies], Bielefeld: Transcript.

Gaensheimer, S., and M. Kramer, eds (2016), *William Forsythe: The Fact of Matter.* (Exhibition Catalogue), Bielefeld, Berlin: Kerber.

Gethmann, D., and S. Hauser, eds (2009), *Kulturtechnik Entwerfen. Praktiken, Konzepte und Medien in Architektur und Science Design* [Designing as a Cultural Technique. Practices, Concepts and Media in Architecture and Science Design], Bielefeld: Transcript.

Gibson, J. J. (1968), *The Senses Considered as Perceptual Systems*, London: Allen & Unwin.

Goebbels, H. (2003), '"Den immer anderen Bauplan der Maschine lessen". Widerstände zwischen Theorie und Praxis' ['Reading the ever-changing Construction Plan of the Machine. Resistances between Theory and Practice'], in H. Kurzenberger and A. Matzke (eds), *TheorieTheaterPraxis* [TheatreTheoryPractice], 17–26, Berlin: Theater der Zeit.

Goebbels, H. (2012), '"It's all part of one concern": A "Keynote" to Composition as Staging', in M. Rebstock and D. Roesner (eds), *Composed Theatre. Aesthetics, Practices, Processes*, 111–20, Bristol: Intellect.

Goebbels, H. (2015), *Aesthetics of Absence: Texts on Theatre*, trans. D. Roesner and C. M. Lagao, Berlin: Theater der Zeit.

Goodman, N. (1968), *Languages of Art: An Approach to the Theory of Symbols*, Indianapolis: Hackett Publishing.

Gordon, C., ed. (1980), *Michel Foucault: Power/Knowledge Selected Interviews and Other Writings 1972–1977*, New York: Pantheon Books.

Greci, L. (2012), *Museale Markenpräsentation. Vergleichende Museumsanalyse* [Brand Presentation and the Museum. A Comparative Analysis], MA Thesis (unpublished), Universität Tübingen.

Grenzmann, T. (2018), 'Minimalismus in ganz großen Mengen. Die Bühnenkunst von Katrin Brack' ['Minimalism in large amounts. Katrin Brack and her stage art'], *Frankfurter Allgemeine Zeitung*, www.faz.net/aktuell/feuilleton/buehne-und-konzert/ein-portraet-der-buehnenbildnerin-katrin-brack-15490507.html (accessed 30 June 2018)

Griffero, T. (2017), *Quasi-Things: The Paradigm of Atmospheres*, trans. S. de Sanctis, Albany: State University of New York Press.

Groendahl, L. (2012), 'Redefining Scenographic Strategies', Conference Paper Presentation at: *Interdisciplinary.net*, 3rd Global Conference, Salzburg, Austria, 13–15 November, available online: www.inter-disciplinary.net/critical-issues/wp-content/uploads/2012/10/lauraperpaper.pdf (accessed 10 June 2018)

Groendahl, L. (2016), 'How to Be(come) a Scenographer? Design Education as a Site for Researching the Scenographic Practices and Discourses in Motion', Conference Paper Presentation at: *The Art of Scenography: Epistemes and Aesthetics*, Munich, 17/18 November (unpublished manuscript).

Gronemeyer, N. (2017), 'Handwerk und Kritik' ['Craft and Critique. A Conversation with Barbara Ehnes and Kattrin Michel on the Stage and Costume Design Program at the HfBK Dresden'], *Theater der Zeit*, 48–9.

Gropius, W. / Staatliches Bauhaus, Weimar (1923) *Staatliches Bauhaus in Weimar 1919–1923* [The State Bauhaus in Weimar 1919-1923], Weimar, Munich: Bauhaus Edition.

Halprin, L. (1970), *The RSVP Cycles: Creative Processes in the Human Environment*, New York: G.Braziller Inc.

Hann, R. (2019), *Beyond Scenography*, Abingdon and New York: Routledge.

Hannah, D. (2011), 'Event-Space: Performance Space and Spatial Performativity', in J. Pitches and S. Popat (eds), *Performance Perspectives: A Critical Introduction*, 54–61, Basingstoke: Palgrave Macmillan.

Hannah, D. (2017), 'Scenographic Screen Space: Bearing Witness and Performing Resistance', in J. McKinney and S. Palmer (eds), *Scenography Expanded: An Introduction to Contemporary Performance Design*, 39–60, London, New York: Bloomsbury.

Hannah, D., and O. Harsløf, eds (2008), *Performance Design*, Copenhagen: Museum Tusculanum Press.

Harman, G. (2011), *The Quadrupel Object*, Alresford, Hants: Zero Books.

Hass, U. (2005), *Das Drama des Sehens. Auge, Blick und Bühnenform* [The Drama of Seeing. The Eye, the Gaze and the Stage Form], Munich: Fink.

Hauser, S. (2016), 'Spaces in Motion: Designs', Conference Paper Presentation at: *The Art of Scenography: Epistemes and Aesthetics*, Munich, 17/18 November (unpublished manuscript).

Hegemann, C., T. Aurin and R. Witt, eds (2017), *Volksbühne am Rosa-Luxemburg-Platz 1992-2017. Ein Fotoalbum* [Volksbühne at the Rosa-Luxemburg-Platz 1992-2017. A Photo Album], Berlin: Alexander Verlag.

Heidegger, M. (1978 [1957]), *Der Satz vom Grund* [The Principle of Reason] (3rd edition), Pfullingen: Günther Neske.

Hemken, K.-U., C. Pias and S. Schimpf (2012), *Annett Zinsmeister – Searching for Identity*. Berlin: Jovis.

Howell, A. (1999), *The Analysis of Performance Art*, Amsterdam: Harwood Academic Publishers.

Huber, D./Blendwerk and Rimini Apparat (2013), 'SR_TechRider_130926' ['Situation Rooms', technical rider: internal document].

Humphrey, D. (1991 [1958]), *The Art of Making Dances*, ed. B. Pollack, Princeton, NJ: Princeton Book Company.

Hurtzig, H., ed. (2001), *'Imitation of Life'. Bert Neumann – Bühnenbilder*. ['Imitation of Life'. Bert Neumann – Stage Designs], Berlin: Theater der Zeit.

Ingold, T. (2010), 'The Textility of Making', *Cambridge Journal of Economics*, 34: 91–102.

Ingold, T. (2011), *Being Alive: Essays on Movement, Knowledge and Description*, New York: Routledge.

Initiative StadtBauKultur NRW, ed. (2005), *Temporäre Architektur an besonderen Orten* [Temporary Architecture at Special Locations], 26–31, Düsseldorf: In-house publishing.

Irmer, T. (2013), 'Neither', *Journal of Beckett Studies*, 22 (1): 127–9.

Irmer, T. (2017), 'Die Ibsen-Explosion: Vegard Vinge und Ida Müller' ['The Ibsen Explosion: Vegard Vinge and Ida Müller'], *Theater der Zeit*, 9: 34–6.

Irmer, T. (n.d.), *Portrait of Katrin Brack*, www.goethe.de/kue/the/bbr/bbr/ag/bra/por/enindex.htm (accessed 8 March 2018).

Irwin, K. (2017), 'Scenographic Agency: A Showing-Doing and a Responsibility for Showing-Doing', in J. McKinney and S. Palmer (eds), *Scenography Expanded: An Introduction to Contemporary Performance Design*, 111–24, London, New York: Bloomsbury.

Kahn, D. (1999), *Noise, Water, Meat: A History of Sound in the Arts*, Cambridge, MA, London: MIT Press.

Kaye, N. (2000), *Site-Specific Art: Performance, Place and Documentation*, London: Routledge.

Kedves, A. (2014), 'Zürich – ein Sprudelbad ohne Sprudel' ('Zurich – a Bubble Bath without Bubbles' – Interview with Dominic Huber), *Tages-Anzeiger*, www.tagesanzeiger.ch/kultur/theater/Zuerich-ein-Sprudelbad-ohne-Sprudel/story/15758996?track (accessed 30 January 2018).

Kemp, W. (1974), 'Disegno – Zur Geschichte des Begriffs zwischen 1547 und 1607' ['Disegno – On the History of the Term Between 1547 and 1607'], *Marburger Jahrbuch für Kunstwissenschaft* [Marburg Art Studies Annual], 19: 219–40.

Kendrick, L., and D. Roesner, eds (2011), *Theatre Noise: The Sound of Performance*, Newcastle upon Tyne: Cambridge Scholars Publishing.

Kettle, M. (2013), 'Castorf has become the Villain of the Bayreuth *Ring* Cycle', *Guardian*, 2 August, www.theguardian.com/music/musicblog/2013/aug/02/frank-castorf-bayreuth-ring-cycle (accessed 1 May 2018).

Kiedaisch, P., S. Marinescu and J. Poesch, eds (2019), *Szenografie. Das Kompendium zur vernetzten Gestaltungsdisziplin* [Scenography. The Compendium to a Networked Design Discipline], Stuttgart: av edition.

Kiedaisch, P. and S. Marinescu, eds (2020), *Szenografie. Das Kompendium zur vernetzten Gestaltungsdisziplin* [Scenography. Compendium of a cross-linked design discipline], Stuttgart: av edition.

Klein, G., ed. (2005), *Stadt. Szenen. Künstlerische Praktiken und ästhetische Positionen* [City. Scenes. Artistic Practices and Aesthetic Positions], Vienna: Passagen.

Korff, G. (2007), '13 Anmerkungen zur aktuellen Situation des Museums als Einleitung zur 2. Auflage' [13 Remarks on the current Situation of the Museum. Introduction to the 2nd edition], in M. Eberspächer, G. König and B. Tschofen (eds), *Gottfried Korff. Museumsdinge. Deponieren – exponieren* [Gottfried Korff. Things in the Museum: Storing – Exposing], IX–XXIV, Cologne, Weimar, Vienna: Böhlau.

Kotz, L. (2007), *Words to Be Looked At: Language in 1960s Art*, Cambridge, MA: MIT Press.

Krauss, R. (1990), 'The Logic of the Late Capitalist Museum', *October – MIT Press Journals*, 54: 3–17.

Kümmel, P. (2010), 'Das Notglück. Ein Gespräch mit dem Bühnenbildner Bert Neumann' ['Happiness in a World of Misery. An Interview with the Stage Designer Bert Neumann'], *Die Zeit*, 18, Feuilleton: no page.

Lachenmann, H. (2001), 'Das Mädchen mit den Schwefelhölzern' ['The Girl with the Matches']. *Programmheft zur Inszenierung von Peter Mussbach* [Programme Booklet], Staatsoper Stuttgart.

Latour, B. (1994), 'On Technical Mediation – Philosophy, Sociology, Genealogy', *Common Knowledge*, 4 (2): 29–64.

Latour, B. (1996), 'On Actor/Network Theory: A Few Clarifications Plus More than a Few Complications', *Soziale Welt*, 47: 369–81.

Latour, B. (2005), 'On the Difficulty of Being an ANT: An Interlude in the Form of a Dialog', in B. Latour (ed.), *Reassembling the Social: An Introduction into Actor-Network Theory*, 141–58, Oxford: Oxford University Press.

Latour, B. (2013 [2011]), 'Some Experiments in Art and Politics', in L. Feireiss (ed.), *Space Matters: Exploring Spatial Theory and Practice Today*, 84–95, Vienna: AMBRA | V.

Laudenbach, P. (2002), 'Ich schau dir in die Augen, Baumarkt' ['Here's Looking at You, DIY Store'. Interview with Bert Neumann], *Theater Heute*, Yearbook: 110–25.

Lavender, A. (2014), 'Modal Transpositions towards Theatres of Encounter, or: in Praise of "Media Intermultimodality"', *Theatre Journal*, 66 (4): 499–518.

Lefebvre, H. (1991 [1974]), *The Production of Space*, trans. D. Nicholson-Smith, Oxford: Wiley-Blackwell.

Léger, F. (1971 [1924]), *Mensch. Maschine. Malerei. Aufsätze und Schriften zur Kunst* [Human Being. Machine. Painting. Essays and Writings on Art], Bern: Benteli.

Lehmann, H.-T. (1999), *Postdramatisches Theater* [Postdramatic Theatre], Berlin: Verlag der Autoren.

Lehmann, H.-T. (2006), *Postdramatic Theatre*, trans. K. Jurs-Munby, London, New York: Routledge.

Lepecki, A. (2013), 'Choreopolice and Choreopolitics: Or, the Task of the Dancer', *TDR: The Drama Review* (T220), 57 (4): 13–27.

Lotker, S., and R. Gough (2013), 'On Scenography: Editorial', *Performance Research*, 18 (3): 3–6.

Maack, U., and W. Minks (2011), *Wilfried Minks – Bühnenbauer* [Wilfried Minks – Stage Builder], Frankfurt a. M.: Suhrkamp.

Maar, K. (2015), 'Le Musée de la danse – or: What a Body Can Do: Reconsidering the Role of the Moving Body in Exhibition Contexts', in *Stedelijk Studies*, Amsterdam, www.stedelijkstudies.com/journal/what-a-body-can-do/ (accessed 10 November 2018).

Machon, J. (2009), *(Syn)aesthetics: Redefining Visceral Performance*, Basingstoke: Palgrave Macmillan.

Maclaurin, A., and A. Monks (2015), *Costume: Readings in Theatre Practice*, Basingstoke: Palgrave Macmillan.

Margolies, E. (2014), 'Return to the Mound: Animating Infinite Potential in Clay, Food, and Compost', in D. N. Posner, C. Orenstein and J. Bell (eds), *The Routledge Companion to Puppetry and Material Performance*, 322–35, London, New York: Routledge.

Matzke, A. (2015): 'Proben' ['Rehearsing'], in J. Badura, S. Dubach, A. Haarmann, D. Mersch, A. Rey, C. Schenker and G. Toro Pérez (eds), *Künstlerische Forschung. Ein Handbuch* [Artistic Research. A Handbook], 189–92, Berlin, Zurich: Diaphanes.

McAuley, G. (1999), *Space in Performance: Making Meaning the Theatre*, Ann Arbor: Michigan University Press.

McAuley, G. (2012), *Not Magic But Work: An Ethnographic Account of a Rehearsal Process*, Manchester, UK: Manchester University Press.

McGovern, F. (2016), *Die Kunst zu zeigen* [The Art of Showing. Artistic Exhibition Displays by Joseph Beuys, Martin Kippenberger, Mike Kelly and Manfred Pernice], Bielefeld: Transcript.

McKenzie, J. (2008), '"Global Feeling": (Almost) all you need is Love', in D. Hannah and O. Harsløf (eds), *Performance Design*, 127–42, Copenhagen: Museum Tusculanum Press.

McKinney, J. (2012), 'Empathy and Exchange: Audience Experience of Scenography', in D. Reynolds and M. Reason (eds), *Kinesthetic Empathy in Creative and Cultural Practices*, 221–35, Bristol: Intellect.

McKinney, J. (2015), 'Vibrant Materials: The Agency of Things in the Context of Scenography', in M. Bleeker, J. F. Sherman and E. Nedelkopoulou (eds), *Performance and Phenomenology: Traditions and Transformations*, 121–39, London, New York: Routledge.

McKinney, J., and P. Butterworth (2009), *The Cambridge Introduction to Scenography*, Cambridge: Cambridge University Press.

McKinney, J., and H. Iball (2011), 'Researching Scenography', in B. Kershaw and H. Nicholson (eds), *Research Methods in Theatre and Performance*, 111–36, Edinburgh: Edinburgh University Press.

McKinney, J., and K. McKechnie (2016), 'Interview with Katrin Brack', *Theatre and Performance Design*, 2 (1–2): 127–35.

McKinney, J., and S. Palmer, eds (2017), *Scenography Expanded: An Introduction to Contemporary Performance Design*, London, New York: Bloomsbury.

Mersch, D. (2002), *Ereignis und Aura. Untersuchungen zur einer Ästhetik des Performativen* [Event and Aura. Investigations for an Aesthetics of the Performative], Frankfurt a. Main: Suhrkamp.

Mersch, D. (2002), *Was sich zeigt. Materialität, Präsenz, Ereignis* [What is Shown. Materiality, Presence, Happening], Munich: Fink.

Mersch, D. (2004), 'Performativity and Event. Considerations on the Revision of the Performance Concept of Language', in J. Fohrmann (ed.), *Rhetoric. Figuration and Performance* [Series Germanistische Symposia], 25: 502–35.

Mersch, D. (2008), 'Tertium datur. Einleitung in eine negative Medientheorie' ['Tertium Datur. Introduction to a Negative Media Theory'], in S. Münker and A. Roesler (eds), *Was ist ein Medium* [What is a Medium?], 304–21, Frankfurt a. Main: Suhrkamp.

Mersch, D. (2009), 'Chiasmus. On the Indeterminate Space', in I. U. Dalferth, P. Stoellger and A. Hunziker (eds), *Unmöglichkeiten. Zur Phänomenologie und Hermeneutik eines modalen Grenzbegriffs* [Impossibilities. The Phenomenology and Hermeneutics of a Modal Boundary Concept], 21–37, Tübingen: Mohr Siebeck.

Mersch, D. (2015), *Epistemologies of Aesthetics*, trans. L. Radosh, Zurich, Berlin: diaphanes.

Mersch, D. (2018), 'Dés-oeuvrément. Entwerkung von Kunst' ['Dés-oeuvrément. Desubjectification of Art'], in J. P. Hiekel and D. Roesner (eds), *Gegenwart und Zukunft des Musiktheaters. Theorien, Analysen, Positionen* [Presence and Future of the Music Theatre. Theories, Analysis, Positions], 47–70, Bielefeld: Transcript.

Mersch, D. (2018), 'Heiner Goebbels' "Musik/Theater" als "Ästhetik der Abwesenheit"' ['Heiner Goebbels' "Music/Theatre" as "Aesthetics of the Absence"'], in U. Tadday (ed.), *Musik-Konzepte*, 179: 40–55.

Michalka, M., ed. (2015), *To Expose, To Show, To Demonstrate, To Inform, To Offer. Artistic Practices around 1990*, Vienna: mumok.

Michalzik, P. (2017), 'From Court Theatre to the Federal System. The German Stage is known for its Diversity. But why is there no National Theatre in Germany?', www.goethe.de/en/kul/tut/gen/tup/20941533.html (accessed 10 June 2018).

Michel, J.-B., Y. Shen, A. Aiden, A. Veres, M.K. Gray, J.P. Pickett, D. Hoiberg, D. Clancy, P. Norvig, J. Orwant, S. Pinker, M. Nowak and E. Lieberman Aiden (2011), 'Quantitative Analysis of Culture Using Millions of Digitized Books', *Science*, 331 (6014): 176–82.

Michels, U. (2001), *dtv-Atlas Musik. Systematischer Teil. Musikgeschichte von den Anfängen bis zur Gegenwart* [dtv Atlas Music. The History of Music from the Beginnings to the Present], Kassel, Basel, London, New York, Prag: dtv.

Morton, T. (2016), *Dark Ecology: For a Logic of Future Coexistence*, New York: Columbia University Press.

Müller-Tischler, U. (2010), 'Setting of a Drama. Der Raum muss ein Geheimnis haben' ['Setting of a Drama. A Theatre Space Should Have Some Sort of Secret'], *Theater der Zeit*, 11: 7–11.

Müller-Tischler, U. and M. Ubenauf, eds (2011), *Anna Viebrock. Das Vorgefundene erfinden* [Anna Viebrock. Inventing What is Found], Berlin: Theater der Zeit.

Nancy, J.-L. (1991 [1983]), *The Inoperative Community*, Minneapolis: University Press.

Nancy, J.-L. (2000 [1996]), *Being Singular Plural*, trans. A. O'Byrne and R. Richardson, Stanford: Stanford University Press.

Neumann, B. and B. Wiens (2013), 'Kunstproduktion ist permanenter Ausnahmezustand: Die Theaterbühne als "Gegenort"' ['Art Production is a Permanent State of Emergency: The Theatre Stage as a "Counter Space"'], public talk, moderation: B. Wiens, LMU Munich, Studio Stage, 28 October (unpublished manuscript).

Neumann, B. (2016 [2015]), 'Das Projekt Volksbühne' ['Project Volksbühne'], in F. Raddatz (ed.), *Republik Castorf. Die Berliner Volksbühne am Rosa-Luxemburg-Platz seit 1992* [Republic Castorf. The Berlin Volksbühne at Rosa-Luxemburg-Platz since 1992], 19–41, Berlin: Alexander Verlag.

Nioduschewski, A., ed. (2010), *Katrin Brack: Bühnenbild / Stages* (bilingual publication), Berlin: Theater der Zeit.

Nonnenmann, R. (2005), 'Music with Images – The Development of Helmut Lachemann's Sound Compositions between Concretion and Transcendence', *Contemporary Music Review*, 24 (1/February): 1–29.

Oberender, T., and J. Petkiewicz, eds (2017), *Limits of Knowing: Immersive Art*. (Berliner Festspiele/ Martin-Gropius Bau, festival booklet), Bielefeld: Kerber.

Palmer, S. (2014), *Light: Readings in Theatre Practice*, Basingstoke: Palgrave Macmillan.
Pavis, P. (2007), 'Szenographie', in M. Brauneck and G. Schneilin (eds), *Theaterlexikon, Bd. 1: Begriffe, Epochen, Bühnen und Ensembles* [Theatre Dictionary, Vol. 1: Concepts, Periods, Stages and Ensembles], 969–71, Reinbek b. Hamburg: Rowohlt.
Pavis, P. (2013), *Contemporary Mise en Scène. Staging Theatre Today*, trans. J. Anderson, London, New York: Routledge.
Pavis, P. (2015 [1996]), 'Scénographie', in P. Pavis, *Dictionnaire du Théâtre* [Dictionary of the Theatre], 314–17, Paris: Armand Colin.
Phelan, P. (1993), *Unmarked: The Politics of Performance*, London, New York: Routledge.
Pollesch, R. (2015), 'Jeder Raum, den du gebaut hast, erzählt diese Autonomie, lieber Bert. Und lässt einen an der eigenen Autonomie bauen' ['Each room that you have built speaks of this autonomy, dear Bert. And lets one build one's own autonomy'], Laudation on the occasion of the award ceremony for the Hein-Heckroth prize 2015 (Brochure of the Hein-Heckroth Society for Stage Design, Gießen, no page).
Pomian, K. (2013), *Der Ursprung des Museums – Vom Sammeln* [The Origin of the Museum – On collecting], Berlin: Wagenbach.
Raddatz, F., ed. (2016), *Republik Castorf. Die Berliner Volksbühne am Rosa-Luxemburg-Platz seit 1992* [Republic Castorf. The Berlin Volksbühne at Rosa-Luxemburg-Platz since 1992], Berlin: Alexander Verlag.
Rae, P. (2015), 'Workshop of Filthy Creation: The Theatre Assembled', *TDR: The Drama Review*, 59 (4): 117–32.
Rancière, J. (1991 [1987]), *The Ignorant Schoolmaster: Five Lessons in Intellectual Emancipation*, trans. K. Ross, Palo Alto, CA: Stanford University Press.
Rancière, J. (2013 [2006]), *The Politics of Aesthetics. The Partition of the Sensible*, trans. G. Rockhill, London, New York: Bloomsbury.
Raumlaborberlin and Theater der Welt 2014 – A Festival by the International Theatre Institute (ITI), eds (2014), *HOTEL shabbyshabby* (bilingual publication), Leipzig: Spector Books.
Rebstock, M. (2004), '"Die Resultate widersprachen meinem Instinkt: gerade das wollte ich...": Zum Kompositionsprozess im Instrumentalen Theater von Mauricio Kagel' ['"The Results did not Match my Instincts: but That's what I Wanted". Composition Processes in the Instrumental Theatre of Mauricio Kagel'], *Edition text+kritik. Musik Konzepte*, IV (124): 25–49.
Rebstock, M. (2012), 'Composed Theatre: Mapping the Field', in M. Rebstock and D. Roesner, *Composed Theatre. Aesthetics, Practices, Processes*, 17–51, Bristol: Intellect.
Rebstock, M., and D. Roesner (2012), *Composed Theatre: Aesthetics, Practices, Processes*, Bristol: Intellect.
Reckwitz, A. (2017), *The Invention of Creativity: Modern Society and the Culture of the New*, trans. S. Black, Cambridge, UK: Polity Press.
Reichle, I., S. Siegel and A. Spelten, eds (2008), *Visuelle Modelle* (Visual Models), Munich: Fink.
Rheinberger, H.-J. (2001), *Experimentalsysteme und epistemische Dinge* (Experimental Systems and Epistemic Things), Göttingen: Wallstein.

Rimini Protokoll (2013), *Situation Rooms* [Programme Booklet], Münchner Kammerspiele/SpielArt.
Roesner, D. (2010), 'Musicking as *Mise En Scéne*', *Studies in Musical Theatre*, Special Issue: *Music on Stage* 4 (1): 89–102.
Rosenthal, S., ed. (2012), *Move: Choreographing You: Art and Dance since the 1960s*, Cambridge, MA: MIT Press.
Sabisch, P. (2005), 'A Little Inventory of Scores. Self-Conversation by Petra Sabisch', *Maska, Performing Arts Journal*, Issue: *Open Work*, 20: 30–5.
Sauter, J. (2011), 'Die Renaissance des Physischen. Kinetische Installationen in Museen, Ausstellungen und Transiträumen' ['The renaissance of physical life. Kinetic installations in museums, exhibits and transit areas'], in G. Kilger (ed.), *Szenografie in Austellungen und Museen* [Scenography in Exhibitions and Museums], 224–9, Essen: Klartext.
Sauter, W. (2014 [2000]), *The Theatrical Event: Dynamics of Performance and Perception*, Iowa City, IL: Iowa University Press.
Schechner, R. (2003), *Performance Theory*, New York: Routledge.
Schnebel, D. (1970), *Mauricio Kagel: Musik, Theater, Film* [Mauricio Kagel: Music, Theatre, Film], Cologne: DuMont Schauberg.
Schneider, R. (2015), 'New Materialisms and Performance Studies', *TDR: The Drama Review*, 59 (4): 7–17.
Scholze, J. (2004), *Medium Ausstellung. Lektüren musealer Gestaltung* [Exhibition as Medium. Readings of Museum Design], Oxford, Leipzig, Amsterdam, Berlin, Bielefeld: Transcript.
Schuppelius, H. (2014), 'The Set Design Mock-up', in raumlaborberlin and Theater der Welt (eds), *HOTEL shabbyshabby*, 110–11, Leipzig: Spector Books.
Schwanecke, C. (2017), 'Mobile People, Weapons, and Data Streams; Mobile Audiences and Theatre Spaces: Rimini Protokoll's "Situation Rooms" as a Globalised Theatre Experience', *Journal of Contemporary Drama in English*, 5 (2): 358–71.
Scorzin, P. C. (2009), 'Metaszenografie. "The Paradise Institute" von Janett Cardiff & Georges Bures Miller' ('Metascenography. On "The Paradise Institute" by Janett Cardiff & Georges Bures Miller'), in R. Bohn and H. Wilharm (eds), *Inszenierung und Ereignis. Beiträge zur Theorie und Praxis der Szenografie* [Staging and Event: Contributions to the Debate about the Theory and Practice of Scenography], 301–14, Bielefeld: Transcript.
Scorzin, P. C. (2011), 'Metascenography: On the Metareferential Turn in Scenography', in W. Wolf (ed.), *The Metareferential Turn in Contemporary Art and Media: Forms, Functions, Attempts at Explanation*, 259–77, Amsterdam, New York: Rodopi.
Searle, J. R. (1996 [1995]), *The Construction of Social Reality: On the Ontology of Social Facts*, London: Penguin Books.
Siegert, B. (2015), *Cultural Techniques: Grids, Filters, Doors, and Other Articulations of the Real*, trans. G. Winthrop-Young, New York: Fordham University Press.
Siepmann, E. (2001), 'Ein Raumverhältnis, das sich durch Bewegung herstellt. Die performative Wende erreicht das Museum' ['Spatial Relations, Created Through Movement. The Performative Turn reaches the Museum'], *Museums Journal*, 3: 7–10.

Sievernich, G., B.-M. Baumunk, P. Bexte and M. Kampmeyer-Käding, eds (2000), *Sieben Hügel. Bilder und Zeichen des 21. Jahrhunderts* [Seven Hills. Images and Signs of the 21st Century], Berlin: Henschel.

Simhandl, P. (1993), *Bildertheater. Bildende Künstler des 20. Jahrhunderts als Theaterreformer* [Theatre of Images. Visual Artists of the 20th Century as Theatre Innovators], Berlin: Gadegast.

Skramstad, P.-E. (2013), 'There Will be Blood. Frank Castorf has Entered the Ring', available online: www.wagneropera.net/articles/articles-bayreuth-2013-castorf-ring-skramstad.htm (accessed 1 May 2018).

Small, C. (1998), *Musicking. The Meanings of Performing and Listening*, Hanover: University Press of New England.

Sullivan, L. H. (1896), 'The Tall Office Building Artistically Considered', *Lippincott's Magazine*, 57: 403–9.

Swiss Architecture Museum (SAM), ed. (2011), *In Space and Marked by Time – Stage Design as Architecture | Anna Viebrock: Im Raum und aus der Zeit – Bühnenbild als Architektur* (Exhibition catalogue, bilingual), Zurich: C.Merian.

Tamschick, C., and M. Tamschick, eds (2015), *Tamschick Media+Space: Immersive Narrative Installations*, Ludwigsburg: avedition.

Thiemeyer, T. (2012), 'Inszenierung und Szenografie' ['Staging and Scenography. Tracing a Basic Understanding of the Museum and its Challenges'], *Zeitschrift für Volkskunde* [Journal for Ethnology], 108 (2): 199–214.

Trueby, S. (2010), 'Die gesprengte Skene', *archithese*, 4: 36–41.

Union des Théâtres de l'Europe, ed. (1997), *Wilfried Minks, Bühnenbildner* [Wilfried Minks, Stage Designer] (Exhibition Catalogue), Berlin: Parthas Publishers.

University of Applied Sciences Bielefeld, ed. (2012), *Leonardo da Vinci – Bewegende Erfindungen* [Leonardo da Vinci – Moving Inventions] (Exhibition Catalogue, 3rd edition), Bielefeld: In-house publishing.

Vilain, R., ed. (2011), *Rainer Maria Rilke. Selected Poems with Parallel German Text*, trans. S. Ranson and M. Sutherland (Oxford World's Classics), Oxford: Oxford University Press.

Virilio, P. (1995), *The Art of the Motor*, trans. J. Rose, Minneapolis: Minnesota University Press.

von Amelunxen, H., D. Appelt and P. Weibel, eds (2008), *Notation: Form und Kalkül in den Künsten* [Notation: Form and Calculation in the Arts], Berlin, Karlsruhe: Akademie der Künste.

von Arx, S. (2016), 'Unfolding the Public Space: Performing Space or Ephemeral Section of Architecture, PQ 2015', *Theatre and Performance Design*, 2 (1–2): 82–94.

Vujanovic, A. (2016), *Transindividuality in Dance and Performance* (HZT open lecture), available online: www.anavujanovic.net/2017/04/transindividuality-in-dance-and-performance-berlin-2016/ (accessed 10 November 2017).

Wagner, R. (1850), *Das Kunstwerk der Zukunft*, Leipzig: O.Wigand.

Warstat, M. (2014 [2005]), 'Theatralität' ['Theatricality'], in E. Fischer-Lichte, D. Kolesch and M. Warstat (eds), *Metzler Lexikon Theatertheorie*, 382–8, Stuttgart, Weimar: J.B. Metzler.

Wehrli, P., and D. Schneider, eds (2010), *raum partituren. 'Ich wohne in der Möglichkeit'* [spatial scores. 'Inhabiting Potentialities'], Bern, Zurich: Benteli.

Wendel-Poray, D. (2018), *Painting the Stage. Artists as Stage Designers*, Milan: Skira.

Wiens, B. (2014a), *Intermediale Szenographie: Raum-Ästhetiken des Theaters am Beginn des 21. Jahrhunderts* [Intermedial Scenography. Spatial Aesthetics of the Theatre at the Beginning of the 21st Century], Paderborn: Fink.

Wiens, B. (2014b), '"Mich interessieren offene Systeme ..."' Bert Neumanns transgressive Szenographien' ['"I am interested in Open Systems ..."' Bert Neumann's Transgressive Scenographies'], in B. Büscher and B. von Pilgrim (eds), *Raumverschiebung: Black Box – White Cube* [Shifting Spaces: Black Box – White Cube], Hildesheim, 93–110, Zurich, New York: Olms.

Wiens, B. (2016), 'Szenografie als Dispositiv' ['Scenography as Dispositif. Sketching out a Research Approach'], in G. Isenbort (ed.), *Topologie des Immateriellen. Formen der Wahrnehmung* [Topology of the Immaterial. Forms of Perception] (Series Szenografie in Ausstellungen und Museen, VII), 222–7, Essen: Klartext.

Wiens, B. (2018), 'Re-thinking Bertolt Brecht's Model Productions: Notes on René Pollesch's Project "Bühne frei für Mick Levčik!" ("Clear the Stage for Mick Levčik!"), Zurich 2016', *Theatre and Performance Design*, 4 (1–2): 119–33.

Wildermann, P. (2017), '"Borderline Prozession": Nichts so richtig und alles zugleich' ('"Borderline Procession": Not really something but all at the same time'), www.tagesspiegel.de/kultur/theatertreffen-borderline-prozession-nichts-so-richtig-und-alles-zugleich/19756990.html (accessed 30 July 2018).

Winkelesser, K. (2013), '"... Sezier dich nicht." Koproduktionsprojekt der Hochschule für Musik und der UdK Berlin' ['"...Don't Dissect Yourself." Report on Co-Productions between the Academy of Music and the University of the Arts, Berlin'], *BTR – Bühnentechnische Rundschau*, 6: 24–7.

Wihstutz, B. (2015), 'Unbekannte Räume, Grenzen und Schwellen. Beobachtungen zur Topologie experimenteller Theaterformen' ['Unknown Spaces, Borders and Thresholds. Observations on the Topology of Experimental Theatre Forms'], in J. Schafaff and B. Wihstutz (eds), *Sowohl als auch dazwischen: Erfahrungsräume der Kunst* [Both as well as in Between: Realms of Artistic Experience], 147–64, Munich: Fink.

Wittgenstein, L. (1958), *Philosophical Investigations*, trans. G. E. Anscombe (2nd edition), Oxford: Basil Blackwell.

Wolfrum, S., and N. von Brandis, eds (2015), *Performative Urbanism: Generating and Designing Urban Space*, Berlin: Jovis.

Young, L. M. (1963), *An Anthology of Chance Operations*, available online: www.ubu.com/historical/young/AnAnthologyOfChanceOperations.pdf (accessed 10 November 2017).

Ziegenrücker, W. (1997), *ABC Musik. Allgemeine Musiklehre* [ABC of Music. A General Teaching in Music], Wiesbaden, Leipzig, Paris: Breitkopf & Härtel.

Zillner, G., P. Bogner and D. Bogner, eds (2017), *Friedrich Kiesler. Architekt, Künstler, Visionär* [Friedrich Kiesler. Architect, Artist, Visionary], Vienna: Prestel.

Zinsmeister, A. (2003), 'Virtual Constructions – the Standards of Utopia', in *Medium Architektur – Zur Krise der Vermittlung* [Architecture as Medium. On the Crisis of Mediating], 9th International Bauhaus Colloquium, Thesis 3/4, 2, 108–15.

Zinsmeister, A. (2005), 'Analogien im Digitalen. Architektur zwischen Messen und Zählen' ['Analogies in the Digital. Architecture between Measuring and

Counting'], in M. Warnke, W. Coy and G. C. Tholen (eds), *HyperKult II – Zur Ortsbestimmung analoger und digitaler Medien* [HyperCult II – Locating Analogue and Digital Media], 95–109, Bielefeld: Transcript.

Zinsmeister, A., ed. (2010), *Update! 90 Jahre Bauhaus – und nun? / Update! 90 Years of Bauhaus – What Now?* (bilingual publication), Berlin: Jovis.

Zinsmeister, A., ed. (2013), *Kunst und / oder Design? Ein Grenzgang. Art and / or Design? Crossing Borders* (bilingual publication), Berlin: Jovis.

Index

actor–network theory (ANT)   17, 171, 183, 187, 217. *See also* Latour, Bruno
aesthetics
    aesthetic experience   69, 110–12, 115, 170, 186
    aesthetics of production   25, 65, 120, 128, 220
    aesthetics of reception   25, 65, 71, 128, 183, 189, 220
    aesthetic strategy   66
agency   59, 63, 65, 68, 71, 113–14, 171, 182–4, 190–1, 193–4, 216, 220, 223
Ahr, Henrik   203
Altmann, Olaf   10
Animatograph   15, 16. *See also* Schlingensief, Christoph
von Appen, Karl   2, 4
Appia, Adolphe   xvi, 4, 7, 74–5, 87, 119, 143, 184, 213–14
Archigram   154
architecture
    performative architecture   19, 140, 214
    provisional architecture   xvii, 47, 95, 165
    theatre architecture   xvii, 93
Aronson, Arnold   xx, 2, 16, 58, 93, 119, 139, 165 n.4, 218
art, art and technology   143, 170, 188
    art and/or design   6, 24, 140
    art as research   25, 27, 200
    free vs. applied arts   140
ART+COM Berlin   10, 22, 23
artistic activism   10
artistic knowledge   141, 176–7, 209. *See also* scenographic knowledge
artistic research   6, 24, 28, 33, 100, 199, 201, 208, 218
assemblage. *See* Bennett, Jane
Atelier Brückner   10, 22, 27, 44 n.1, 119–38, 198, 215, 217, 224 n.4
    Expedition Titanic (1997)   121, 132
    Experiencing Frontiers (2002)   132–3
    GS Caltex Pavilion (2012)   121, 133–4
    State and Textile Museum Augsburg (2010)   121, 134–5
    That's Opera (2008)   135–7
atmosphere, atmospheres   11–12, 16, 35, 41, 60, 62–3, 67, 75, 95–6, 163, 170, 174, 181, 189, 191, 223
Audick, Janina   10, 56 n.12, 206, 217. *See also* Pollesch, René
    Heidi Hoh arbeitet hier nicht mehr (Heidi Hoh Doesn't Work Here Any More; 2000)   51
    World Wide Web Slums 1-10 (2000)   51
audience
    audience involvement   18, 100, 220
augmented theatre   96
aura   126, 132. *See also* Benjamin, Walter
autopoiesis. *See* Fischer-Lichte, Erika
    autopoietic feedback loop   4, 68

Bachelard, Gaston   28. *See also* phenomeno-technique
Balme, Christopher   3–4, 218
Barad, Karen   13, 58–9, 68–9, 72 n.5. *See also* intra-action
Bauckholt, Carola   80
Bauer, Raimund   202, 205

Bauhaus school 87, 143–4. *See also* Gropius, Walter; Moholy-Nagy, Laszlo; Schlemmer, Oskar
Baumgarten, Sebastian 91 n.3
Bauprobe (build-up rehearsal) 42, 158, 222
Beacham, Richard 74, 184
Beckett, Samuel 94, 96, 98, 101
Benjamin, Walter 88, 126, 175. *See also* thing languages
Bennett, Jane 13
 assemblage 59, 63, 65–6, 68, 71, 91, 113–15, 117, 174–5, 179
 materiality 13, 58–9, 61, 63, 65–6, 68–9
 'thing power' 59, 61, 63, 65, 68
Berghaus, Ruth 75
Beuys, Joseph 16, 177
Beyer, Sven Sören 94, 96–8
 Neither (2012) 94, 97, 101
Bleeker, Maaike 59, 69, 71
Böhme, Gernot 62–3, 67. *See also* 'ecstasy of things'
Bondy, Luc 50
Bourriaud, Nicolas 113. *See also* relational aesthetics
Brack, Katrin xx, 10, 12–13, 15, 44 n.1, 48, 57–72, 198, 202, 204, 217
 Anatol (2008) 60
 Das grosse Fressen (*Blow-Out*; 2006) 60, 64
 Friedrich von Homburg (*The Prince of Homburg*; 2006/7) 12, 60, 67
 Hermannsschlacht (*The Battle of Hermann*; 2010) 60
 Iwanow (*Ivanov*; 2005) 60
 John Gabriel Borkmann (2015) 60, 67
 Kampf des Negers und der Hunde (*Black Battles with Dogs*; 2003) 60–2
 Molière (2007) 60
 Radetzkymarsch (*Radetzky March*; 2017) 60, 67
 Tartuffe (2006) 60
 Ubukönig (*Ubu Roi*; 2008) 60, 66
Brecht, Bertolt 4, 9, 12, 34, 45 nn.7, 10, 53–5, 199, 209, 214. *See also* Neher, Caspar
Brejzek, Thea 2, 6, 41, 58
Brunelleschi, Filippo 142
Bund der Szenografen, Berlin 211
Buñuel, Luis 51

Cage, John 21, 80–3, 110, 195
 Europeras I–V (*see* Goebbels, Heiner; Grünberg, Klaus)
Cardiff, Janet 101
Castorf, Frank 5, 11, 14, 19, 34–7, 39–43, 45–7, 49–51, 55, 56 n.2, 94–6, 209 *See also* Denić, Aleksandar; Neumann, Bert
Chéreau, Patrice xvi
Chezweitz Berlin 22
choreography 21, 105, 107–9, 111, 113, 115–16, 124–5, 129, 134, 144, 170, 192
 choreographic installations 107, 113
 choreographic object 21, 107, 112–13. *See also* Forsythe, William
 choreographic thinking 112
 choreo-politics 113
collaboration 24, 34, 37, 48, 65, 76–7
 collaborative design practice 153–65
composition
 composed theatre 79–81
 compositional process ('doing scenography') 19, 79, 220
 compositional techniques 21, 79
 compositional thinking 79, 91
control, uncontrollability 12–13, 25, 40, 66, 84, 86, 88, 169, 171, 176, 180–1, 222
Cornish, Matt 9, 18, 34–5
Craig, Edward Gordon xvi, 4
cultural production of space 155. *See also* Lefebvre, Henri
cultural technique 4, 24, 28, 145, 148, 157, 223

INDEX

Debord, Guy 115
Denić, Aleksandar 10–12, 15, 27, 33–45, 48, 203, 212 n.3, 217.
See also Castorf, Frank
  Der Ring des Nibelungen (The Ring of the Nibelung; 2013) 36–9, 44, 45 n.7
  Goethe, Faust (2014) 39
  Goethe, Faust (2017) 11, 41–4, 45 n.11
  Gounod, Faust (2016) 36
  Journey to the End of the Night (2013) 35, 44
design. See also collaborative design practice; exhibition design; re-designing design
  art and/or design 6, 140
  design method 22, 27
  design parameters 5, 121
  design tools (see scenographic tools)
dispositif 7, 26, 106, 112, 215. See also Foucault, Michel
Dorn, Anja 208, 212
Duchamp, Marcel 141, 177

'ecstasy of things' 62. See also Böhme, Gernot
Ehnes, Barbara 10, 198, 202, 205, 217
Eliasson, Olafur 115
environmental scenography 3, 93, 140, 155, 199
exhibition design 12, 119–37, 140, 202, 205, 208, 221
expanded scenography 2, 6, 20, 23–5, 201, 213, 218–19, 221
EXPO 2000 5, 19, 22, 95, 123

figuration/figuration of the non-figurative 173, 175–7
Fischer-Lichte, Erika 3, 4, 67–8, 160
Forsythe, William 21, 72 n.10, 105–9, 112–14
  City of Abstracts (2000) 106–7, 112
  Instructions 2015 (2015) 107–8, 112
  Nowhere and Everywhere at the Same Time (2015) 112
Foucault, Michel 7, 26, 47

Freyer, Achim 9, 98
Fritsch, Herbert 10, 47, 49, 217

el Gammal, Mona 10, 217
Gerstner, Muriel 10
Gesamtkunstwerk 37, 127, 136, 143, 170
Goebbels, Heiner 5, 65–6, 72 n.10, 74, 77, 80–1, 84–90, 91 n.3, 92 n.17, 170, 214
Gotscheff, Dimiter 12, 61. See also Brack, Katrin
Groendahl, Laura xx, 200, 210
Gropius, Walter 143
Grünberg, Klaus 5, 10, 27, 73–92. See also Goebbels, Heiner
  De Materie (2014) 77–9
  Europeras I–V (2012) 79–83
  Stifters Dinge (Stifter's Things, 2007) 84–8, 90, 170

Hageneier, Stefan 10
Hannah, Dorita 2, 58
Haussmann, Leander 56 n.2
Heidegger, Martin 177–8, 190
Herrmann, Karl-Ernst xvi
Huber, Dominic/Blendwerk 10, 184, 189, 191–2. See also Rimini Protokoll
hybridization 2, 188

immersion 18, 20, 89
  immersion experience 98
  immersive theatre 58
improvisation 48, 64, 155
interaction 7, 20, 24, 40, 51, 60, 68, 76, 87, 121, 134, 183–4, 191, 204, 222
  social interaction 153, 155
intermediality xvii
  intermedial scenography 94
International Federation for Theatre Research (FIRT/IFTR) xv
intervention 5, 10, 16, 23–4, 36, 153, 156, 161, 217
  scenographic intervention 14, 25, 140, 149, 163
intra-action 68–9, 71. See also Barad, Karen

INDEX

Kéré, Francis xviii
Kiesler, Friedrich 4, 14
Kokkos, Yannis xvi
Konwitschny, Peter 56 n.2
Kosky, Barrie 91 n.3
Kurz, Annette 10
Kušej, Martin 39, 40
Kusturica, Emir 40

Lapa, Vanessa 47
Latour, Bruno 13, 25, 162–3, 183–4, 187, 190–1, 194–6
Laube, Kerstin 206
Lefebvre, Henri 154. *See also* cultural production of space
Léger, Ferdinand 144
Lehmann, Hans-Thies 4, 12, 34, 213, 216. *See also* postdramatic theatre
linguistic/non-linguistic expression 67

Marthaler, Christoph 5, 47, 80, 209
materiality 12, 20, 25, 37, 53, 58–61, 64–6, 69, 71, 88, 170
McAuley, Gay 64, 73. *See also* rehearsal, rehearsal studies/ rehearsal ethnography
McKenzie, Jon 3, 138 n.9, 224
Meese, Jonathan 15, 48
Mersch, Dieter 19, 25, 28, 172, 173, 180
Meyer, Hartmut 15, 48, 202, 205–7
Michel, Kattrin 205
Minks, Wilfried xvi, 9, 26, 44 n.1, 209
mise-en-performance 124. *See also* Pavis, Patrice
mise-en-scène xvi, 6, 81, 116, 122–4
model 27, 34, 38–43, 49, 54–5, 76, 79, 120, 146, 158, 201–6, 222–3
 computer model 39
 model making 38, 40
 model productions (Brecht/ Neher) 43, 199
Moholy-Nagy, László 144

narrative space 19, 121, 123, 127, 129, 133–4, 217
Neher, Caspar 4, 7, 12, 34, 53–5, 199, 209

Nel, Christoph 91 n.3
Neumann, Bert xvii–xviii, 22, 32, 36–8, 41, 44 n.1, 46–56, 94–6, 99–102, 217.
 Amphitheatre project (2009) 47
 'Black Space' (2015–17) 19, 95
 Bühne frei für Mick Levčik (*Clear the Stage for Mick Levčik*, 2016) 54
 Der Idiot (*The Idiot*, 2002) 15, 29 n.11, 49
 Der Spieler (*The Player*, 2011) 29 n.11
 Die Brüder Karamasow (*The Brothers Karamazov*, 2015) 29 n.11, 53
 Die Zofen (*The Maids*, 2008) 50
 Diktatorinnengattinnen (*Wives of Dictators*, 2007) 49, 51
 Diskurs über die Serie, Volksbühnen-Diskurs, Teil 1 und 2 (*Discourse on the Series, Volksbühne Discourse, Part 1 and 2*, 2016) 95–6
 Ein Chor irrt sich gewaltig (*A Choir is Totally Wrong*, 2009) 50–1
 Erniedrigte und Beleidigte (*The Humiliated and Insulted*, 2001) 29 n.11
 New Globe (1999) 47
 Neustadt (2002/3) 15, 47, 49, 101 n.2
 Rolling Road Show (2000–7) 95, 101 n.2
 Ruhrtrilogie (*Ruhr Trilogy*, 2008–10) 102
new materialism 13, 25, 57, 59, 68–9
new realism 171
Newton, Lena 10
notation 21, 27, 55, 80, 107–9, 111–12, 118, 173, 223
 notational systems 109
Nottrodt, Katrin 10

ontology 191
 object-oriented ontology 171
Otto, Teo 2, 4

Paik, Nam June 110
Pappelbaum, Jan 10

INDEX

participation 7, 25, 100, 112–13, 133, 153. *See also* audience involvement; collaborative design practice
parCITYpation 153–66
Pavis, Patrice xvi, 28 n.1, 119, 124, 184
Peduzzi, Richard xvi
Perceval, Luc 12, 61
Petras, Armin 12, 61
Phelan, Peggy 111
phenomeno-technique 28. *See also* Bachelard, Gaston
Picabia, Francis 177
Piscator, Erwin 4, 12, 14, 44, 45 n.10, 47, 209
Platel, Alain 56 n.2
politics of the in/visible 117
Pollesch, René 12, 48–55, 56 n.2, 12, 95–6, 101, 102 n.2. *See also* Audick, Janina; Neumann, Bert; Rois, Sophie
postdramatic theatre 4, 6, 34, 213–14, 216. *See also* Lehmann, Hans-Thies
Prague Quadrennial of Performance Design and Space (PQ) 215, 217–19
presence/absence 87–8, 113
Price, Cedric 154
provisional architecture (*Architektur auf Zeit*) xvii, 47, 95

Quesne, Philippe 72 n.10, 162

Ranciére, Jacques 111–13, 116, 210
Rasche, Ulrich 10, 13–14, 29 n.8, 217
raumlaborberlin 10, 24, 153–66, 198, 212 n.1, 217
  Eichbaumoper / Eichbaum Countdown (2009–11) 153, 156
  Forms of Turmoil (2017) 153, 163
  Hotel Shabbyshabby (2014)
  Le Théâtre des Negotiations (2015) 153, 162
  Rush Hour Rest Stop (2014) 153, 160
  Shabbyshabby Apartments (2015) 153–60

re-designing design 23, 121, 222
Regietheater (director's theatre) xvi
rehearsal, rehearsal studies 14, 33–4, 37, 40, 42, 48–52, 54, 73, 77, 86, 158, 193, 209, 222
  rehearsal practices 73
  rehearsal studies/rehearsal ethnography 73 (*see also* McAuley, Gay)
relational aesthetics 25, 1130
revolving stage 4, 11–13, 16, 35–6, 38, 44, 45 n.10, 143
Rheinberger, Hans-Jörg 28
Rimini Protokoll xviii, 10, 18, 20, 25, 101
  Call Cutta (2005) xviii
  Cargo Sofia – X (2006–8) xviii
  Situation Rooms (2013) xviii, 18, 25, 183–96, 197 n.1
Rois, Sophie 27, 46–56

scenography
  'doing scenography' 5, 47, 220
  education and training 25, 109, 123, 155, 198–212
  environmental scenography 3, 93, 140, 155, 165 n.4, 199 (*see also* Aronson, Arnold)
  expanded scenography 2, 6, 20, 23–5, 201, 213, 218–19, 221, 224 n.1
  intermedial scenography 94, 197 n.1 (*see also* Wiens, Birgit)
  meta-scenography 27, 94 (*see also* Scorzin, Pamela C.)
  non-scenography 220
  scenographic intervention 14, 140, 163
  scenographic knowledge 3, 7, 19, 198–200, 217 (*see also* artistic knowledge)
  scenographic objects 13, 72, 183, 221
  scenographic score 28, 179, 223
  scenographic tools 126
  scenographic turn 2, 19 119

INDEX

Schleef, Einar   14, 52, 74
Schlemmer, Oskar   4, 143–4, 199
Schlingensief, Christoph   xviii, 15–16, 47, 49
Schubert, Peter   205–6
Schuppelius, Heike   158
Schütz, Johannes   10, 202, 209
Scorzin, Pamela C.   xx, 27, 29 n.18, 94, 221
Sieberock-Serafimowitsch, Michael   17
Simon, Michael   10, 198, 209, 212 n.6
Simons, Johan   12, 56 n.2, 81
space
   spatial choreography   124–5, 129
   spatio-temporal practice   108
spectator
   moving spectator   93
stage technology   89–90
Stein, Peter   xvi, 209
Steiner, Barbara   56 n.12

Tamschick Media+Space   10, 22, 217
temporality   7, 12–13, 20–1, 71, 83, 85, 100, 113, 170, 191, 219–20
theatre architecture   xvii, 93
theatre as a machine   89
things   13, 183, 221. *See also* scenography, scenographic objects
   'ecstasy of things'   67 (*see also* Böhme, Gernot)
   thing languages   175 (*see also* Benjamin, Walter)
   'thing power'   59, 61, 63, 65, 68. (*see also* Bennett, Jane)
Thor, Harald B.   10
Tiravanija, Rirkrit   113, 115
TRIAD Berlin   10, 22, 29 n.16, 217
Tsangaris, Manos   80
Tykwer, Tom   47

Verdonck, Kris   10, 72 n.10, 202
video   xvii, 14–16, 18, 25, 44, 79, 81, 86, 99, 106, 150, 183, 185–8, 191, 205
   live video   15, 36, 98
Viebrock, Anna   5, 10, 15, 48, 198, 202, 217
da Vinci, Leonardo   142, 144
Vinge, Vegard and Ida Müller   10, 15, 18, 48, 94, 99, 101, 217
   Nationaltheater Reinickendorf. Container 1-9 (2017)   18, 94, 99
Vitez, Antoine   xvi
Voges, Kay   17
Volksbühne at the Rosa-Luxemburg-Platz, Berlin/Volksbühne Berlin   xvii–viii, 5, 11, 14–16, 19, 34, 42, 44, 46–53, 55, 65, 94–6. *See also* Castorf, Frank; Denić, Aleksandar; Kéré, Francis; Neumann, Bert; Pollesch, René; Vinge, Vegard and Ida Müller

Wagner, Richard   11, 15–16, 18, 36–7, 98, 121, 127, 136, 170, 184
Wehrli, Penelope   10, 15, 48
Wieler, Jossi   56 n.2
Wiens, Birgit   xv, xvii, xviii, 7, 94, 184
Wilson, Robert   5, 9, 26, 74, 214, 216, 219–22
   Wirkkala Park, 2011/12   221
Wonder, Erich   75

Zadek, Peter   xvi, 9, 209
Zehetgruber, Martin   10, 202
Zinsmeister, Annett
   Memodul (2002)   151
   outside_in / virtual interior (2009)   148, 151
   Virtual Interior (2007/15)   151
ZKM | Center for Arts and Media Karlsruhe   208

www.ingramcontent.com/pod-product-compliance
Lightning Source LLC
Chambersburg PA
CBHW060947230426
43665CB00015B/2091